T0381007

Praise for *Enlivening Consciousness: Deepening Your Journey through Vision, Movement, Nutrition, Nature, and Spirit*

"Calling for a reawakened understanding of eyesight, vision, nutrition, and health, *Enlivening Consciousness* provides a delightful blending of spirituality, science, and the author's personal experiences as an optometrist and as an adventurous soul. Elisa weaves together a remarkable array of insights and practical tips that all illuminate an empowering holistic approach to wellness. She dances through the pages, tossing out poetic embellishments and reminding us of the many truths we have forgotten in our world today: how our body and mind are one and how movement, nature, and our spirituality rescue us from the reductionistic materialism that erodes our health. This is an inspiring book that helps us reconnect with our inner wisdom and remember the deeper truths about our shared life on this beautiful and fragile Earth."

—Will Tuttle, PhD, visionary author of the best-selling book *The World Peace Diet*, recipient of the Courage of Conscience Award and the Empty Cages Prize, former Zen monk and dharma master in the Zen tradition.

"Life-changing! A must-read for anyone who wants to have a life of wholeness. Dr. Elisa Beck weaves her lifelong journey of learning to guide people to use thought, emotion, breathing, posture, movement, and nutrition to improve their vision. She exquisitely describes how our eyes are an extension of our brain, and they are only one part of the entire visual process. She understands that each person has unique experiences that create their vision. Dr. Beck shows us how to work from within by using our vision to be whole and well. Her calm, quiet approach comes through in her writing, and it is obvious she cares deeply for those she has helped in the past and those she will help in the future. I know Dr. Beck will continue to shine bright and use her vast knowledge to guide others to develop their light."

—Brenda Montecalvo, OD, FCOVD, FAAO, FCSO

"*Enlivening Consciousness* is an experiential book, written in an engaging conversational style by Dr. Elisa Beth Haransky-Beck. It is full of questions to consider (self-inquiry), suggested movements (experiential exploration), and includes periodic break times built into the reading process. It is not simply words on a page, but an opportunity to explore the self in ways most of us haven't yet considered. I look forward to using it as a tool to more fully integrate my own body-soma."

—Denise Allen, host, *Healing Our Sight* podcast

"Part autobiography and part to-do book, this comprehensive, remarkable work details how vision, nutrition, movement, and nature are intimately connected. Whether you throw away your glasses, adopt a plant-based diet, embrace yoga, or begin listening to the trees, your thinking will be changed forever. As you become embodied, you will never take a walk with the same eyes, gait, and spirit again."

—Patricia S. Lemer, MEd, LPC, author of *Outsmarting Autism*

"Elisa condenses a wealth of life knowledge into a handful of categories. As a fellow optometrist, I can only focus on her insights into the vision section. She discusses the retina as brain tissue, offering a 21st Century perspective on diagnosis and treatment of eye conditions. Her book does an admirable job of exploring the vast network of profound connections that retinal processing has with other physical and mental systems. Its many analogies and simple explanations allow a layperson to comprehend the crucial impact that eyeglasses and contact lenses can have on brain activity."

—Deborah Zelinsky, OD, FCOVD, founder of
the Mind-Eye Institute, MindEye.com

"An enlightened perspective of eyesight with many important considerations for expanding overall insight, wellness, balance, and vitality!"

—Carryn Fletcher, PsyD

"There have been a number of books written about veganism, but Elisa Beck, OD, has made an important contribution to the genre by bringing our vision literally to the fore of our consciousness. All readers will learn a great deal from Elisa about the connection between our vision, our diets, and our overall well-being."

—Jeffrey Spitz Cohan, writer for *The Alignment* on Substack

"In my work with babies for over thirty years, I've explored eye tracking with parents and babies in the first six months. In floor time, visual explorations are an essential part of each of the developmental movement patterns. Elisa's work reinforces this foundational relationship between movement and vision for all ages in her belly-on-the-floor activities, interweaving eyesight and movement. Through Elisa's guided explorations, you will find new ways to enhance your visual clarity and embody developmental movement patterns that will increase your daily vitality and benefit your overall health and wellness."

—Beverly Stokes, CMA, MPA, RSME, author of *Amazing Babies Moving: Essential Movement to Enhance Your Baby's Development in the First Year* and *Your Self-Motivated Baby: Enhance Your Baby's Social and Cognitive Development in the First Six Months through Movement*

"Elisa Beck, OD, has put together an intriguing combination of vectors that give us [a] unique perspective in understanding our consciousness development and applying it to life in the world."

—Gabriel Cousens, MD, author of *Into the Nothing, Spiritual Nutrition, There Is a Cure for Diabetes*, and ten other books on spirituality and nutrition

"Elisa infuses us with vital and interesting insights in a caring, knowledgeable, and encouraging manner. Her professional understanding and approach to visual health and sight are deeply rooted in the development of movement as a foundation for integrated coordination of the eyes. She speaks to us personally and directly, encouraging us to become aware of our own inner life and choices."

—Bonnie Bainbridge Cohen, author of *Basic Neurocellular Patterns: Exploring Developmental Movement*

"I went to the eye doc, and my eyesight has improved since my last pair of glasses two or three years ago. I give my work with you credit!"

—Robin Quinn, *Quinn's Word for Word*

"Having been born legally blind, I was deeply intrigued by the idea of an optometrist's view on how diet and lifestyle affect vision. I got so much more from this book than I thought I would. Elisa's writing style makes the information extremely accessible, and she presents Truth. The vision that is interpreted through our eyes is just the surface. There are many different ways to *see*, and Elisa navigates them with grace and deep insight. I'm sure this book will change many lives. Me first!"

—Cyndi Dodick Schwimmer, OTR, MS, MA, SNC, LMLDT

"[The author] brings together, through her vast knowledge, professional expertise, personal and spiritual experiences, insights, and practices, the guide we need as individual beings and as a collective to bring forth a future that heals the vast damages inflicted on the planet we live on, to the multiple forms of life that share this planet, and to the hearts and souls of the humyn collectively. ... As a holistic eye care professional, integrative optometrist Elisa Beth ... shares her personal experiences and the broad range of healing modalities and practices she embraces and has incorporated into her commitment to the health and well-being of those she has the opportunity to serve. Wherever you are on your journey, this book will enlighten, embolden, and invigorate you on that path."

—Carlotta Geesen, humyn

"Dr. Haransky-Beck shares her personal exploration of life and the impacts on ourselves spiritually, physically, and our connection to the earth. Her exploration of life shares the importance of what goes in your body is what you may get out of your body. Her words show how this exploration of life has impacted not just her personal *wellbeing* but even her professional *wellbeing* while sharing various techniques, recipes, and insights to improve your life."

—Jeffrey L. Kraskin, OD

"As a human who lives her soul song, I always find it a pleasure to read another's life story, especially that of one who has the vision to connect the dots of her journey in a way that provides steps and inspires other humans to do the same. Elisa Beth's book provides a lot of food for new thought during this time in human history when we are at a crossroads. Her book contains a wealth of techniques and references to examine our visions and ourselves and provides an integrative approach to reset ourselves, the planet, and the cosmos—the bridge we need to cross—to successfully arrive at the next phase of our human and collective story. Her book also provides a wealth of references and resources for those who wish to dig deeper—new terminologies and new movements for our new regenerative lifestyles.

As the author reminds us, the time is Now for the human collective to pull back the veil and shift our perspective to embody our greatness. It's not too late to return to our crystalline vision and the upward spiral! The author has done a great job in lifting the veil for those of us who have been living unaware and in bringing us back on track for living more connected and mindful lives."

—Carol L. Arnett, Port Angeles, Washington

"'Where there is no vision, the people perish' (Proverbs 29:8). Optometrist Elisa Beth Haransky-Beck's wonderful, potentially game-changing book not only provides a vision of a compassionate, just, peaceful, environmentally sustainable world but also the tools to help create it."

—Richard H. Schwartz, PhD, professor emeritus at College of Staten Island; president of Society of Ethical and Religious Vegetarians; and author of five books and numerous articles on vegetarianism and Judaism

"There comes a time when we must lift each other up as optometric colleagues, women, and inhabitants of this cosmos. That is the case for Dr. Elisa Beth Haransky-Beck. She has done a phenomenal job of tying together a lifetime of her understandings and teachings. She ties together many concepts which have remained unrelated until now. She intertwines topics which include, first and foremost, vision, then movement, nutrition, nature, and one's spiritual beliefs. If you are seeking a holistic treatment plan of care, then Dr. Haransky-Beck is at your service and will be a great partner in your health journey. Dr. Haransky-Beck, may your light continue to shine as you help those who are fortunate enough to have you as their holistic mentor and neuro-behavioral-developmental optometrist."

—Carla Adams, OD, FCOVD, Mind-Eye Institute

"This is a brilliant and totally transformational take on the concept of healing. These methods for improving vision can easily be applied to any area of the body."

—Reverend Dr. Bonnie M. Russell, AllOne Healing Academy

"*Choosing to Make a Better World:* We are living in a time when the limits of the world's natural resources are colliding with the needs of its life-forms. Unless we make important shifts in our attitudes, appetites, assumptions, and habits, we will suffer the fate of the dinosaurs. Unless we learn to see, act, and live in new ways, life will get much harder, more people will suffer, more conflict, more failure, more illness, more death, and no more dreams. We must learn to see farther and wider and to act more responsibly. Elisa has written a holistic guidebook with recipes for better health, better climate, better heart, and better vision. Like Noah, Elisa is an example of one person's deep commitment to bringing positive change for a better future. People must become smarter, healthier, more capable, more cooperative, and more committed to helping to make a better world. My heart is moved by your expression of pure heart energy that flows from every page. It's time to join the Enlivening Consciousness movement."

—Dr. Raymond Gottlieb, OD, PhD, dean of the College of Syntonic Optometry

"Dr. Elisa Beth Haransky-Beck writes with a heartfelt and gracious style that readers will appreciate. She shares vast insights about how to not just improve but, more to the point, thrive in our personal and collective journeys through day-to-day living. I suggest reading this book with a curiosity and openness to what Haransky-Beck has to offer. She shares numerous ways to put recommendations into daily practice and, as a bonus, includes myriad recipes for whole-food, plant-based eating. This book offers unique, valuable approaches to nurture body, mind, and spirit—something we all surely can use."

—Sally Lipsky, PhD, author of *Beyond Cancer: The Powerful Effect of Plant-Based Eating*

"This book is a wonderful invitation to experience our lives with greater intention, self-observation, and spiritual awareness. Dr. Haransky-Beck inspires us to expand our concept of wellness in a truly holistic way, where the state of our health goes beyond the physical to considerations of how elevated levels of life energy and consciousness can enhance our daily lives. Readers will come away with not only practical tools but inner wisdom to help guide them on their life journeys."

—Dr. Joanne Kong, editor of *Vegan Voices: Essays by Inspiring Changemakers*

"It is said that what we need will enter our lives at the right place and time. I do believe that about this book. It told me many things I have been discovering and relearning in the past several years. So often, I found myself pausing to reread a paragraph or mull over some phrasing, almost as if the words were being savoured or absorbed in a special new way. Dr. Elisa conveys some complex concepts about mass consciousness using such simple language and such a gentle approach, yet I found it surprising that she never comes across as condescending to the reader. She acknowledges how current prevailing lifestyles introduce challenges we may not see as causing undue stress on our physical, mental, emotional, and spiritual states and helps us to begin growing awareness of our state so we can level up our lives in gentle but impactful ways. A way-shower who is not afraid to challenge mainstream approaches and integrate holistic approaches *like* somatics (movement), inner work, and diet, with traditional optometric (allopathic) approaches, she reminds us of the terrain we are navigating; gives tips about how best to enjoy the trek; reveals how we tend to think, feel, and act if we are even slightly out of homeostasis (balance); and nods to the routes that would benefit us. A deeply beneficial focus of the book is integration of our intuitive insight and physical eyesight. Dr. Elisa provides many general teachings to improve both and complements these with specific exercises to help the reader enhance their holistic well-being, including the actual improvement of their physical eyesight."

—Marcia Nathai-Balkissoon, PhD, author of *Lighting the Path*

"Dr. Elisa Haransky-Beck has created a guide for us all as we enter this tumultuous and entrancing time of transformation in which we are currently living. In this important book, she weaves together her deep knowledge of holistic vision improvement with her extensive work in the healing power of nutrition, body movement, nature, and spirituality and shows how they are all interconnected. As we look around us, there can be no doubt we are living in a time of seismic spiritual transformation. We are all being called to grow in love and compassion for ourselves, each other, and all of life. Dr. Elisa's heart speaks from this book to us all and shows us there is a way through to the ecstatic joy that awaits us."

—Judy McCoy Carman, MA, author of *Peace to All Beings and Homo Ahimsa: Who We Really Are and How We're Going to Save the World*, peacetoallbeings.com

"With *Enlivening Consciousness*, Elisa Beth Haransky-Beck serves up a recipe for a vibrant life. Drawing on her lifelong learning, work, study, and insight, she demonstrates that vision, movement, diet, spirituality, body, and mind are truly one. With a poetic spirit and a scientific mind, Elisa provides a prescription for a mindful life connected with nature that is healthy, energetic, and fulfilling."

—Darrell E. Frey, Three Sisters Permaculture, author of *Bioshelter Market Garden: A Permaculture Farm* and coauthor of *Food Forest Handbook*

Enlivening Consciousness

*Deepening Your Journey
through Vision, Movement,
Nutrition, Nature, and Spirit*

Elisa Beth Haransky-Beck, OD

BALBOA.PRESS
A DIVISION OF HAY HOUSE

Balboa Press books may be ordered through booksellers or by contacting:

Balboa Press
A Division of Hay House
1663 Liberty Drive
Bloomington, IN 47403
www.balboapress.com
844-682-1282

Because of the dynamic nature of the Internet, any web addresses or links contained in this book may have changed since publication and may no longer be valid. The views expressed in this work are solely those of the author and do not necessarily reflect the views of the publisher, and the publisher hereby disclaims any responsibility for them.

The application of protocols and information in this book is the choice of each reader, who assumes full responsibility for their understandings, interpretations, and results. The information in this book is meant for educational purposes only and is not a substitute for advice from your own health care professional. The author assumes no responsibility for the actions or choices of the reader.

Book cover and interior book drawings by artist Eli Helman; front book cover design by Mary Long and Balboa Press.

This book has been printed on recycled paper.

Print information available on the last page.

ISBN: 979-8-7652-4722-8 (sc)
ISBN: 979-8-7652-4723-5 (hc)
ISBN: 979-8-7652-4724-2 (e)

Library of Congress Control Number: 2023922057

Balboa Press rev. date: 02/27/2024

With much gratitude, I dedicate this book to those who have been here with me throughout my time in this physical form on planet Earth—my parents; my husband; our children; my sisters and brother; my brothers-in-law and sisters-in-law; my in-laws; our nieces, nephews, great-nieces, great-nephews, and cousins; all my relatives near and far; and my friends and colleagues—for their love, support, and never-ending encouragement to dream on and to manifest my dreams into reality, whether or not they yet understand or believe any of it!

CONTENTS

NATURE

SPIRIT

FOREWORD

"Everything is connected."
"We're all one."
"There is a quantum reality that underlies all we see."

Since you've picked up this book, it's safe to say that concepts such as these are not new to you. You probably read them just now and thought, *Sure, doesn't everybody know that?* Well, no, not everybody, but since you do, it's safe to say you've already glimpsed the Big Picture. You've sensed that your miraculous body houses an ineffable spirit, and you've known, the way you know you're breathing, that life has a purpose that could not be fulfilled without you. You're ready then for your next deep dive into "Aha! I knew it!" and "Yes, this author just put into words what I've always felt."

Like you, I came to *Enlivening Consciousness* from India and Western mysticism. At their core, the two seem to be one and the same. Along with a lifetime of soulful pursuits, I've long been interested in holistic well-being, believing that somehow the Divine will ought to "be done on earth" (in the body) as surely "as it is in heaven" (in the mind of God). To that end, I was a longtime vegan and practitioner of yoga when I started to read this book in manuscript form, thinking, *This will be nice, a good review.* I wasn't ten pages in before I realized, *Whoa! This is no brush-up course; this is a game changer.*

Dr. Elisa Beth Haransky-Beck brings her decades of experience as a functional optometrist to bear on our eyesight and insight. With all my vagabonding through books in both the spirituality and wellness realms, I'd never come upon one that uses physical vision as a practical metaphor for how we see life and purpose and all those around us, our soul kin, having earthly experiences at the time we are. To call this eye-opening is both an irresistible pun and a serious understatement. After reading this volume, you will, if you're at all like me, never regard the capacity to see in the same way again.

And then Haransky-Beck weaves in movement, our relationship with nature, our spiritual development, and food choices, which both imbue this planet with lovingkindness and nourish our cells with an abundance of just-about-magical phytochemicals and a nonstop supply of life-force energy––the prana of yoga, the *ch'i* of martial arts.

A bit of forewarning: there's a lot here. You may find yourself thinking, *"Wait a minute. I was just absorbing one concept, and here's another one."* But that's just it: these various areas of subject matter are the antithesis of divergent and disconnected. You might be improving physical vision or inner sight by moving the body. Perhaps you're re-creating your physical form with lots of fresh, raw foods from the plant kingdom, imbued with life and color. Or you could be practicing gratitude, making peace within your family, or moving through duality into recognition of Oneness. In all these ways and so many others that Dr. Haransky-Beck lays out in these pages, you'll come to realize more fully who you truly are: Divine love housed in star-stuff, having a grand adventure.

Victoria Moran, author of *Creating a Charmed Life*,
The Love-Powered Diet, and *Main Street Vegan*

ACKNOWLEDGMENTS

Thank you. Thanks so much to my dear, incredible, loving, kind mom for holding me so close. I love you. I honor you in each moment for birthing me and being there for me for so many precious moments in my life in physical form until you passed when I was thirty-six years old. Thanks, Dad, for modeling everything in moderation—when really, what you were modeling was everything in its own time in just the right dosage. Thank you for showing us how to live until almost 104 years young with dignity and respect. I love you both so much, even though you left us years ago. In every precious moment I am alive, I feel held by you. It is an honor and an incredible blessing to be surrounded by many relatives and dear ones, whether they're physically present or not. We were and still are one love! Huge extra heartfelt thanks and deep gratitude and love to my husband, Stan, and our daughters, Laura and Rachel. I would not be who I am without living the loving lessons we've grown into together.

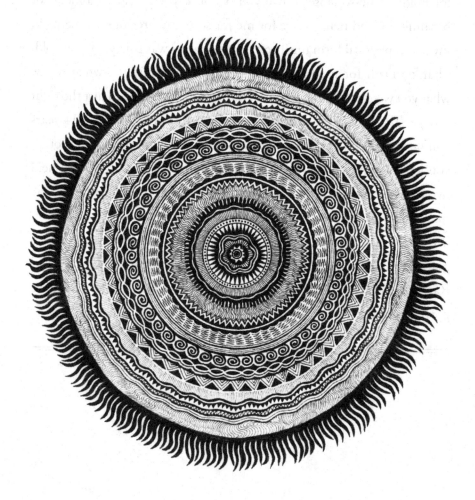

Chapter 1

AN INTRODUCTION TO ENLIVENING CONSCIOUSNESS

Open Sesame!

How do we step into our fullness? How do we rise into our incredible potential from love? This book is an introductory deep dive for some, and for others, the subject matter will be familiar and comforting.

Why care about improving our eyesight and insight? Why study movement? Why care about the food, drink, and other substances we put inside our bodies (ingest)? Why do so many have so-called medicine cabinets? Do we really need supplements? What do preserving and creating living soil have to do with anything, and how does the soil relate to the water and air being pure, fresh, and good for us? Why connect with nature daily, our inner and outer nature? How does our inner nature, our multiple microbiomes, relate to the natural world, earth, sky, and cosmos? What am I doing here? What are we doing here? What is this humyn experience? What do meditation, mindfulness, prayer, and present-moment awareness have to do with enlivening our consciousness and allowing G-d, or Spirit, to work through us?

These are some of the questions we will ponder in this book. We'll weave in and out, back and forth, up and down, and all around between different subjects and different ways of BEing.

Recovery 101

Our Mother Earth is in deep recovery from many counterintuitive paradigms that have been thrust on us for perhaps five thousand to ten thousand years or more. The development of the strong patriarchal industrial revolution dominating our society came on gradually in some regards. In many ways, we are habituated to the slave mentality. We've become an extreme Western culture of disconnect from our inner-balance divine feminine and divine masculine guidance. And we have not been able to break free of this paradigm—until now!

All people, depending upon who they are and what they were meant to be and do in this lifetime, will create their own ways of being. I've realized my life is very much that of an artist in these elder years. I do not stay in set routines, as others might—at least not in the same way. How about you? Do you have a flexible schedule? Do you thrive on routine? What are your behavioral habit patterns? Would you like to explore other ways of BEing, but you don't yet know how? Are some ideas about creative ways to shift your habits bubbling up in you?

Important and Meaningful Perspectives

Our perception creates our reality. When we look at things from different angles, these things appear differently. Color, shape, texture, and meaning can vary depending on your view or perspective. Once, when preparing to wallpaper our bathroom, my husband and I were perusing a giant wallpaper sample book while sitting across from each other. We had a lively discussion about the colors of one particular sample. We could not agree on the colors and patterns we were seeing—that was, until we realized the colors appeared differently depending on the viewing angle. When we switched places and saw the sample from the other's perspective (which now had become our own), we agreed 100% with each other on the shade we had been wondering about.

How are we living our lives? How much loving are we engaged in? From what perspective are you living your life? When each of us brings our own heart and nervous system and all our other systems—both physical and etheric—to the table, we can play, play, play! We can really have fun! With clear intention, choosing meditation and mindful action, and with the clear interaction of our hearts, minds, and spirits, we can choose to play with all of our experiences. In joy Enjoy. With gratitude. In harmony and symbiosis.

Let's begin!

What Does *Enlivening Consciousness* Mean?

Breathe into that thought. Then let the thought go and feel into the phrase. Feel it in your body. How do you feel in these moments? How are you BEing? How often do you notice that you and the things around you change on the somatic (physical), mental, emotional, and spiritual plane? What is different? What is the same? In this moment, I am listening to soul-soothing music as I edit this introduction. It is break time during the virtual 2022 Somatic Movement Summit. I am feeling myself relaxing into my body, my breath. I am aware of my breathing and my legs and noticing the support of Mother Earth coming up to meet me through the soles of my feet. I'm feeling good and feeling a sense of urgency to stay the course of this editing journey. And as I breathe, blink, and move around in my chair, I'm feeling grateful for these present moments. I'm feeling grateful for you, dear reader, for sharing this space. I invite you to move around a bit in a way you might not be used to—yes, while reading or listening to this! Then, if you feel comfortable doing so, ask yourself the questions posed at the top of this paragraph.

There are many definitions of *consciousness* and many levels and layers of the experience of enlivening one's consciousness, so the definition will be left to all of us collectively, dear one. Let's see where we wind up as this journey unfolds. We are all in this together, forming the reawakening moment by moment. And all our experiences are unique and valid.

It turns out much of our existence occurs subconsciously in our dreams or in other states of consciousness that we've forgotten we experience, cannot yet access easily, or do not fully understand. I was so charged up with thoughts and ideas flowing through my mind this morning while showering that I couldn't wait to get out of the shower to put pen to paper, or words on the computer, lest I might forget. Eldora of the quantum healing couple Eldora and Siman reminded us once to be sure to write it all down when life comes streaming through. I've taken that advice to heart! How was it that my thoughts were so clear this morning? Were they—are they—my thoughts? Or is Spirit Source G-d Energy flowing through me onto the page? What layers of consciousness are involved when we are freely flowing in life and not thinking it through?

We'll go through some details that involve these layers, thinking, feeling, and acting from our integrated brains. In the nature section, we'll dive into the biological roots of our inner ecosystem, the inner terrains of our bodies, and the paradigm shifting that has been going on over the past few years. We'll begin to understand how we can settle into, care for, and be comfortable with our most authentic selves. In the nutrition section, we'll move through an understanding of why the raw living-foods lifestyle could be the best top-of-your-list immune-boosting choice (beginning anywhere on the eating and drinking spectrum) in this era of inflammation on all levels of consciousness.

Along the way, we'll explore our own consciousness and some possible ways to focus, coordinate, expand, and widen our vision to open and enliven our consciousness to include the wisdom of the ages. As we continuously integrate our vision, we realize we are, as individuals, part of a community—a community based in cooperation, loving wonder, service, and gratitude. We are an amazing species on this planet right here right now. We'll begin to see more fully with an open heart!

It is my hope that with this book, you will reconnect with nature, your inner and outer nature, and move beyond 3D addiction and beyond artificial intelligence (AI) into embracing your innate intelligence with self-responsibility. Minimally, my wish is that you will awaken to the understanding that there's a hugely addicted population in our midst worldwide. And the addiction goes way beyond addiction to opiates and other drugs. AI is an addiction on many levels—an addiction of dissociation from self-love and self-care as health care. Could the lenses, prisms, colored filters, and surgeries we've had to improve our eyesight be part of the addictive paradigm? Or can these be helpful tools at times? The mindset, or hypnotic set, that external tools or crutches can permanently heal us rather than serve as guides for improving our body, mind, spirit, and soul is a myth. The spell is about to be broken—if you choose to read on!

There are some critically important movement patterns we've developed from even before we were born. These reflex and developmental movement patterns underlie humans' and other species' overall development. Most fascinating to me is that these patterns include visual development as well. In the movement section, we'll experience and understand why it is important to integrate or reintegrate our primitive reflexes through movement practices as we improve our eyesight and insight naturally and glide into many layers of proprioceptive awareness and consciousness.

Throughout, we'll explore some of the nuances of the natural world that are invisible to the naked eye and see why it is important to consider the microscopic and intuitively felt sense of life in our transformational journeys into our true, authentic selves. In the spirit section, we'll weave together body, mind, spirit, and soul within the context of some ancient teachings from the Five Books of Moses, from the Tanach (other Jewish teachings), and from other spiritual traditions. The experience will continue to become an inner exploration and shift into your true essence of insightful intuition and beginner's mind as you choose to participate on any level!

Heart Consciousness

Reading Susan Aposhyan's book *Heart Open, Body Awake: Four Steps to Embodied Spirituality* reminded me that I've been most comfortable writing, practicing, and living from my heart and soma (body) awareness for most of my life. I learned about the science of heart math[1] (brain and heart coherence) from Gregg Braden[2] in New Mexico and independently at the College of Syntonic Optometry (CSO)[3] conference years ago. Perhaps that's why, in my life, I've resonated most strongly with others who integrate their brains, hearts, and bodies and not resonated as much with those who live mostly in their heads, especially in the field of optometry, my area of expertise (whatever that means!). That said, it is nice to sometimes put words to our observations and actions. It can be important to read trustworthy scientific studies to reinforce (or not) what you think you know on a conscious level. This allows (on a cognitive, or mind, or thinking level) for clearer communication. It is

---

[1] HeartMath.org, accessed July 17, 2023.
[2] https://greggbraden.com, accessed July 19, 2023.
[3] https://csovision.org, accessed July 19, 2023.

also important to realize that science and our understanding of so many disciplines are constantly changing.

The heart. Our hearts. Our heart space and the electric and electromagnetic energy of our hearts reign supreme. And what of the connection between our brains and nervous systems and our hearts and entire somas (bodies)? Is consciousness all about the smooth interweaving of all our blessed systems, both physical and ethereal? I believe so. That is my premise for this book!

In January 2022, I listened to author and speaker Charles Eisenstein caution about the dangers of attempting to define consciousness. We are just beginning to define consciousness. I resonate with open-ended interpretations. How about you? Does open-endedness resonate or cause you discomfort? For me, at this moment, the untethered, open interplay of our hearts and minds fits beautifully within the context of enlivening consciousness.

Recent studies have been incredibly supportive of these awarenesses and what my field of developmental optometry, functional optometry, behavioral optometry, and neurodevelopmental optometry practice has been about for my entire professional career. The studies are affirming the importance of keeping our minds, bodies, spirits, and souls active and vibrant in all stages of life to stoke our physiology, including our neurology, so the spiralic energy of our hearts remains flexible, active, and growing and to keep our immune systems strong. Being fully present for our babies and small children is crucial for our human development. When we tone our awareness and physical bodies, we maintain our connection with ourselves, our cells, Pachamama (Mother Earth), Father Sky, and the cosmos. Presence with our core families and community, whether they are blood relatives or not, and connection to nature and the earth with direct loving attention on all levels are what life in this humyn form is really all about!

Through our hearts, we reveal our souls in this physical form we call a body. The electrical energy by which we interact and interrelate on a microscopic, subatomic level to one another, to all that exists that surrounds us, and to the cosmos is incredible energy. This is the electric nature of our bodies, our BEings. And because we are electrical beings, we can and do heal through electricity, through electromagnetics, and through consciously and subconsciously changing the electrical patterning of our nervous systems through clarifying the conductivity and clear communication of our muscles and bones.

There are recent studies and testimonials in the fields of physics and spirituality (the quantum field), nutrition, and health and wellness, including somatics, affirming the truth of the connections between deep heart knowingness and energy healing modalities. The works of Jill Bolte Taylor, Rebecca Campbell, Caroline Myss, Eleanor Criswell Hanna, Richard Gerber (author of *Vibrational Medicine*), Deepak Chopra, Christiane Northrup, Howard Gardner, Joe Dispenza, Bruce Lipton, and many others affirm these notions.

What I Know

What I do Know
Is that life is a Flow
And when you admit you don't know
It's often a go go go
When we mentate and gyrate with our conscious mind
All the time
Without letting go of having to know
Then oh no
Where do we go?
Down the rabbit hole!!!

8

Shifting Awareness

The period of the past three years, 2020–2022, has been one of monumental shifting for the human collective and surely for all living beings, planet Earth, and the universe at large. In part, my writing and publishing this book have to do with my experiences of those years, in combination with my wanting to share some gleanings of a life that has been and continues to be well lived.

I've changed my tune and my approach over the past number of months. I took time off and then became miraculously inspired during this turning of the ages to simply put what I've got on paper. Mostly, the book is without direct references, yet I will reference some of the people, books, articles, and electronic sources that have influenced me over the years. Influenced my flow. Influenced the thoughts and inspirations moving from my heart and soul. I encourage you, dear reader, to do the same.

What are your daily routines? Consider writing them down and then reading them over or dancing around the room with them and deciding both consciously and unconsciously if you'd like to shift anything about who you are currently BEing. Then begin somewhere—anywhere. Just BEgin!

What experiences have you had or are you having in which you can awaken your eyesight, vision, and consciousness? These can be activities of daily living, such as teeth brushing or tongue scraping, sports, or anything. Let's explore these ideas together and continue on the journey of enlivening our consciousness!

The Five Sections in *Enlivening Consciousness*

This book is written in five main sections, with two or more chapters in each section. For some readers, the sections may appear as unrelated topics. From my embodied brain and body perspective, nothing could be further from the truth. Each of the sections is part of the whole story of all our Beings, all related, all connected, as the spiral nature of life is. Interwoven and webbed. This is an introduction to ways of BEing you might not yet have considered.

Read this book in whatever way you see fit, in whichever way you are moved. Perhaps you'd love to simply open to a certain page and read from there, allowing the words to wash over you. Or look at the table of contents and see what calls you. You may not get to certain sections. And that's just fine! The book is eclectic. Like me. Perhaps like you. However it flows for you is just right!

The book covers some tangible actions we can take with CURIOSITY, INTEGRITY, and COURAGE! It describes how to step into ACTION as a Humyn BEing. BEing While DOing into BEing!

Step into your highest expression gracefully through:

❖ Vision/Eyesight/Insight
❖ Movement/Somatics
❖ Nutrition
❖ Nature
❖ Spirit/Source Connection

The basics run deep. It's time to lean into the collective intelligence for sure! It certainly helped me write the forthcoming pages.

VISION

- ❖ Insight and eyesight = vision
- ❖ Typical eye care
- ❖ Holistic vision care
- ❖ Optometric vision therapy
- ❖ Vision tips for inquiring minds!
- ❖ Vision and nutrition

Chapter 2

EXPLORING VISION, EYESIGHT, AND BEYOND

Opening into Your Self

> The moment in-between what you once
> were and who you are becoming
> is where the dance of life really takes place.
>
> —Agnes De Angelis

*T*HESE ARE IN-BETWEEN TIMES. IF you're here reading this book, you understand that either you're stepping into this liminal (in-between) space, or you know that like me, you've been dancing for your entire lifetime! Do you feel a need to sharpen and deepen your consciousness, however you define *consciousness*? Or not? In any case, you've come to the right place. In *Wherever You Go, There You Are*, Jon Kabat Zinn, PhD, reminds us that wherever we are in the present moment is the perfect place to be. Wherever we are in the present moment is the place to begin opening to the possibility of shifting awareness.

A passion of mine during my adult professional life and even when I was younger has been to develop myself to my highest potential—to feel well and vibrant and, in turn, to help and facilitate the same in others. As a woman raised in the 1960s and 1970s, looking after myself was often perceived as selfish. Moving into the understanding that

13

mindfully caring for oneself is of utmost importance was a big step *pour moi* and one I continue to work with daily. One thing I know for sure is that I've been doing a lot of dancing for my entire life!

My understanding has become that by my diving deep within and balancing my own body, mind, and soul, my new vibration is healing not only myself but also you and the entire Earth community. As we work with ourselves and collectively on self-improvement, these shifts ripple out into the universe. We are healing ourselves, each other, Mother Gaia, Father Sky, and the entire cosmos.

Are you a self-help and self-improvement guru like I am? Were you put here on this planet in these precious moments to enliven your consciousness and the consciousness of others through continuously diving deep within yourself? Do you love meditating and coming back to beginner's mind? Or is this a new thought or understanding for you? Are you dipping your toe in?

In any case, yay for you. Yay for all of us! Get ready for a combination of a linear, circuitous, and spiralic journey—and an eclectic mix of subject matter, modalities, writing forms, illustrations, experiences, tips, tools, and surprises. Let's play!

The Important Question

Individually and collectively, we are answering the question

"What are we all doing here now in these moments?"

An Overview of a Journey through Enlivening Consciousness

I have been a licensed eye care professional for much of my adult life. Some might say I'm on the edge, edgy, on the perimeter of the mainstream of my field of developmental, functional, behavioral, or neurorehabilitation vision therapy optometry. Why on the edge? I've given those I work with, if they choose, the ability to look through different lenses—both literally and figuratively—in the discipline and creative process of natural eyesight improvement through optometric vision and movement therapy, nutrition, nature, and spirit. My practice, and the practice I offer those I work with, is an integrative process from the mind, body, heart, soul, and source. From the inside out and outside in.

We'll begin this book with a journey into yourself—your soul self; consider identity and thought forms; and look at our vision journeys. Then we'll step into a variety of eye doctors' offices and consider how to prepare for your vision exam. Along the way, we'll experience different aspects of insight and eyesight through the lens of an eye doctor whose roots are in nutrition, dance, movement, nature, playfulness, and spirit.

Beginner's Mind

Beginning Again and Again
Based on What Came Before Us
What We Are Experiencing Now and
What We Will Be Experiencing
As One

Thought Forms and Identities

Who Am I? Who Are You? Jot down some of your identities. Some of your titles. (See some of mine below.) Which identities and titles are you comfortable with? Which would you love to let go of? What meaning do these roles in the physical plane have for how you consciously or unconsciously define your Self? What is a self? A strong and influential mentor of mine, Rabbi Gabriel Cousens, MD, often pontificates that "personality is a case of mistaken identity!" I have participated in Dr. Cousens's Zero Point[4] course on more than a few occasions to learn how to move through zero point and dissolve the thought patterns of my identities and to let go of my identification with ego. We are our pure soul selves.

That said, some of my current identities include:

- a dedicated and loving mother, wife, sister, sister-in-law, aunt, great-aunt, great-great-aunt, and cousin
- a free-spirited woman
- a clinician of life
- a developmental, behavioral, functional neuro-optometrist
- an EmbodyVision natural eyesight improvement and integrative movement practitioner
- a yoga teacher in EmbodiYoga™ (500 hours) and Hanna somatic yoga
- a somatic movement educator and therapist
- a permaculturist
- a spiritual nutrition counselor

Why bother listing my identities when I'm also busy zero pointing them away and burning them up? It's just a list of my ego identities and my Herstory. It's because I believe you'll see some of your story in my story. We all have stories as unique individuals.

---

[4] https://www.drcousens.com/zeropoint.

A Deep Dive into Beginner's Mind, the Mind of the Inner Ecosystem of Ourselves!

Let's go back to where we began. We can release our old stories together and move on! And we'll have the opportunity to rise together as one in these precious moments on this planet. After all, there is a reason you are reading these words, and there is a reason we are crossing paths right now. Identities are simply labels and thought forms. These labels and thought forms serve a purpose on some level and are meaningless on other levels. We can always zero point these thought forms away. (Zero point info is in the resource section.) Really, it's a way of letting these limiting thought forms go and stepping into new or newly remembered territory! "We are born originals, but most of us die copies. Zero point gives the opportunity to become an original again. It helps one to become free to find and follow one's soul design," notes Gabriel Cousens.

You are a creator, and you, like all of us humyn beings, are here to rise to your highest potential. You may not have thought your eyes, your visual system, and the ease, or dis-ease, by which you "see" has much to do with your Being. Well, I'm here to let you know a reality I've been living as it allows us to understand that the way we SEE has everything to do with how we BE! I welcome you to reach out and let me know your Vision stories. You'll find information

Discover Ho'oponopono

The Ho'oponopono technique is also a form of releasing thought patterns. This ancient Hawaiian healing technique taught by Dr. Hew Len, Joe Vitale, and others involves repeating the four statements below. The statements can be said in any order and can be expanded or condensed, depending upon the situation you're working with.

I'm sorry.

Please forgive me.

Thank you.

I love you.

Sometimes I talk to myself (or is it G-d?) either out loud or silently while using this technique. I'm sorry, self, that I'm not always as mindful as I could be. I'm sorry that even though I teach others about improving their eyesight naturally, I am not always practicing what I preach! Please forgive me for being so humyn often and rushing around without remembering to slow down and nurture my body, mind, spirit, and soul. I love you. Thank you for not giving up on me and for reminding me endlessly so many times each day to slow down, come back to my breath, and come back to myself. Thank you!

on how to do this in the back of this book. (See the "Share Your Story" page at the end of book, with link to my website: EnliveningConsciousness. com.) If you are interested, let's cross-pollinate our experiences to create the more beautiful world we all know in our hearts is possible. How? We'll begin with a conversation.

Unfurling

Stepping. Stepping. Scurrying, Prancing, Dancing out of the existing
paradigm(s) into the newness of our selves connected to Source.
Stepping, twirling, curling, unfurling into the beauty of within
Stepping, walking, running into ourselves
Untold wonder lies within, once we step out
Out of our own way
We alchemize holding patterns in the cells of ourselves, the
energetic holding patterns dissipate as we celebrate our new
BEingness as waves rippling throughout the cosmos.
And our new way of SEEing is revealed untethered. Stickiness gone
Our cells, fascia, fluids, muscles, and bones
singing so many new songs
And the physical newness of Being and Seeing in new ways
Getting out from behind the haze of the crutches of lenses and Rxs.
No longer in a daze,
The Eyesight to INsight journey of our lifetimes is here NoW!
It's a new way, a new day!
Hip, Hip Hooray!

Preparation and Arriving Early!

I have been an experiential learner and lived my life that way from day one. I was there ready to be born a few weeks before my due date. Early. As ready as could BE! Often, in this lifetime, in this physical form, I continue to be early. I've learned this is part of my role. Yet right about now, I'm feeling both early and in perfect flow in these transformational moments on our beautiful blue-green planet, Mother Earth. My hope and prayer directly from Source is that with the information I share here, we're right on time.

Together as One. And so it IS!

I've realized over my years of practicing optometry that there is more to vision than 20/20 (lots more on that topic later). That said, I also realize more and more as each day passes that most in the eye care field do not talk much or educate patients about the possibility of improving their eyesight naturally. I'm planting the seed right here right now. And now that the seed is planted, let's continue this journey. It's good to take stock of where you are on your eyesight and vision path.

A Thought is a particle of light.
You can measure it.

—*The 1 Field* documentary

Time for Self-Reflection

What are a few watershed moments in your eyesight, eyeglass, contact lens, eye surgery, and vision journey? Whether or not you've ever experienced any issues with your eyesight or vision, take a few minutes or more to journal about what you'd like to learn from reading this prose about your personal eyesight and insight journey. If you have had challenges in these areas, write down one to three key visual issues you are experiencing right now that you would love to be on the road to resolving. Then write down what you absolutely love, love, love about how your eyesight and insight serve you. Keep a running list or notes in a notebook, on a chalkboard, on a whiteboard, or in your electronic device, so you can refer often to see where you've been in this exploration inside your consciousness.

Vision Journeys

Some people have wonderful eyesight and vision from birth until death. Some of these people, like my dad, take their good vision for granted. They never really think about their eyesight or vision until they are about 45 or 50 years old, when their arms seem to be too short to read books or they cannot move their electronic device's screen far enough away to see it clearly. This "old age" or presbyopic eyesight seems to happen as people's hormones shift, and they move toward menopause or andropause. This is the moment when those with "normal" eyesight may start to feel the need for reading glasses. Some people may think they have wonderful eyesight and vision until it is pointed out to them that there's more to vision than 20/20 or being able to read an eye chart across an eye examination room or a street sign on the way home.

It turns out there are ways to improve our eyesight and vision at any age, and it is possible to maintain our eyesight and visual flexibility into our elder years if we choose to. How? By awakening our awareness about the issues and then remaining active and engaged with our eyesight and visual systems throughout our lifetimes.

Throughout this book, take advantage of the Experiential Explorations and Self-Inquiries and decide, if you feel called to do so, to integrate them into your daily routines. Be curious! No matter what your visual status, this book is an outstanding way to begin your journey into better eyesight and insight and into maintaining the integrity of your visual system and entire body, mind, and spirit until the day you leave this planet in this physical form. You can be vital and vibrant and see clearly into and through maturity!

Where do our eyesight journeys begin? And what is the difference between our eyesight and insight, between eyesight and vision and enlivening consciousness? It may seem that our eyesight and vision journeys begin with the physical structure of our eyes, as these precious sensory and motor organs become measurable when we go to see our eye doctor. Our vision journeys are all varied and all our own. Our vision and eyesight journeys may begin in utero or even in the energy field of the Earth and cosmos before we are conceived in the physical plane. One thing is for sure: each one of us, and each of our journeys, is unique—as unique as can be. We'll continue to explore the overlap between eyesight, insight and enlivening our consciousness. As mentioned earlier, the way we "see" reflects how we act and how we behave in the world. And the degree to which we are awake and fully alive varies. No matter what your eyesight and vision are like, exercising or toning your eyes and visual pathway, along with the rest of your lifestyle habits, is a wonderful idea!

Our vision journey doesn't really begin with our eyeballs; eyeglasses or contact lenses; vision surgery; concussions; or other garden-variety systemic mental, emotional, and spiritual diagnoses (which all relate to vision). Parts of my vision journey follow.

My Story: The Teen Years and My First Pair of Eyeglasses

I received my first pair of eyeglasses as a midteen in ninth grade. That first eye exam was in Dr. Miller's optometry practice inside Sterling Optical, an eyeglass chain. I do not remember much about that exam other than it being conducted in a short time frame in a darkened room, with lenses flipped quickly in front of my face through a machine, as if that were a natural, normal experience.

Before I knew it, I was looking through some lenses that made the letters on the chart across the room crystal clear. It was all "better"! The world was clear when I got that first pair of glasses. Little did I know this was the beginning of a journey that continues to this day. The journey with my fight-or-flight response. Perhaps the journey we're all on in these moments as we break through the perceived shackles of being controlled by the mores of a culture gone deep into the duality of separation and otherness.

Have you ever had an eye exam? Do you remember your very first eye exam? Do you remember the first pair of glasses prescribed for you and how you felt the first time you put them on your face? Do you remember picking out your first pair of eyeglass frames? Do you remember the feeling, the kinesthetic sense, of wearing contact lenses for the first time? Perhaps you sensed widely expanded peripheral vision. Maybe you noticed the outside world "cleared up." What do you remember about these moments in your visual history? It's fascinating (or is the word *astounding?*) to me that our culture has normalized the deterioration of our eyesight and normalized getting eyeglasses at any age.

Are you a contact lens wearer? Are you postrefractive (Lasik) surgery or someone who does not want to ever wear "corrective" lenses? Do you remember the first time you realized your eyesight had declined or when you were told by your eye doc that you no longer were reading the 20/20 line on the eye chart? Do you remember when or if your visual perception shifted prior to getting your first pair of glasses? Do you remember if your interpretation of the world shifted once glasses were prescribed for you and you began wearing them? Did you wear them? Do you remember getting stronger and stronger lenses each year for a period of time?

Some might remember how clear and crisp everything was when they got their first pair of glasses. What we're not told is how these "corrective" lenses for myopia or nearsightedness (meaning not being able to "see" clearly far away) lead to addiction to lenses. In most cases, we're not offered options to move toward improving our eyesight naturally. This addiction to lenses, in almost all cases, leads to the perception of needing stronger and stronger lenses each year and to the normalization of the fight-or-flight response the lenses create. We are forced to live with a hypervigilant sympathetic nervous system. This works on our bodies in all waking hours while we're wearing the lenses and creates behavioral, postural, and energetic shifting that we've not been informed about. Why? Because eye docs like me were not taught in school, nor did we realize within our own bodies, what's really going on.

Whaaatttt?????? Normal. What is normal? What have we allowed to be normalized in this culture of ours? How do we truly See? Can an external pair of lenses bring us clarity? Or does clarity begin within? By bringing attention to the moment when you got your first eyeglasses or contact lenses, you might remember how you felt (on a proprioceptive kinesthetic level) and be able to work through and release some of these feelings and sensations if they were painful. The first step is bringing the experience into conscious awareness. Perhaps you remember feeling happy that you were able to see "clearly" when you got those first eyeglasses or contact lenses. What other feelings do you now associate with that clarity? How did you feel? Did you feel a sense of ease, joy, an adrenaline rush, or pain? If you've never had the need for eyeglasses or any visual "correction," I'm curious about your great visual habits! Let me know!

ALL ETERNAL

From working with your eye doctor
to the inner eye doctor within
The Visionary
The Luminary
The ALL-KNOWING ONE
What will you grasp onto
and where will you land
When you realize there is nothing there
Except Air
And then the air that's there
Is Nowhere
No where
Nothing to Wear
As there's nothing there
And then we come back to
our souls.
All as One.
ALL ETERNAL.

What Do You Envision?

What is Eyesight?

What is Vision?

What do you Envision?

What is your Vegan Vision?

How do we Embody our Vision?

Is it Eyesight through which you see?

Or is it something much deeper hiding inside waiting patiently?

What insights support and interdigitate with your many hats?

The compound-eyed Bee? Bzzzzz. The Ride …

Oh, TO SEE!

Vision is the pinnacle sense. What does that mean? Our eyeballs are the gateway receptor organs to our brain and spinal cord and are the windows to our souls.

Chapter 3

CONSIDERING TYPICAL EYE CARE THROUGH A WIDER LENS

What Is Eyesight? What Is Vision?

*E*YESIGHT IS CONVENTIONALLY THOUGHT OF and measured as 20/20 (or 6/6 in metric). Early in my optometric schooling, I came to the realization that this was a limited viewpoint, an arbitrary number. The 20/20 measurement of visual acuity, or VA (how clearly we can see a series of letters of a certain size at a certain distance on an eye chart), refers to central eyesight. The entirety of our sensory-motor visual pathway and beyond are overlooked.

The visual acuity of our central visual field is usually first measured one eye at a time and then with both eyes together while we gaze at an eye chart across a dimly lit room or with our heads poised inside an instrument. Then visual acuity is measured again up close, at the Harmon distance, with the elbows bent at arm's length, with artificial lighting beaming on a small card with small print on it. Visual acuity at near point could be measured in an instrument as well.

Visual acuity refers to the central part of our visual field. Our central visual acuity reflects our macular, or foveal, vision. The macula, or fovea, is the size of a pinpoint at the back of our eyeball. This area of acute central visual acuity is where the cones are located. The cones allow for the central 30-degree field of color vision. Our side vision, or peripheral vision, is possible due to our side, or peripheral, retina. Peripheral vision plays an enormous role in our day-to-day and overall

26

functioning, our balance, and our movement through space, including sensory-motor visual awareness pathways and patterns. This peripheral area of the retina allows for motion detection and peripheral vision and is where the rods are located for black-and-white vision.

The real question for me became this:

What is vision?

My current understanding is that the receptor organs we call eyes are extensions of the brain (including the optic nerves, visual radiations, and the entire visual cortex) and spinal cord. Our entire sensory-motor visual pathway allows our souls to receive, perceive, and interpret light energy directly within our body systems. This organ, and its sensory and motor visual system, is composed of nervous tissue; fascia; ligaments; muscles; and fluid of different compositions, including blood, lymph, and tears, aqueous and vitreous. Our living bones surround and protect the entire inner structure.

Over time, I've learned that the integration of our visual action system with all the other senses is rooted deeply in and emerges through our many-layered embryological, fetal, and early childhood development. Clear vision is the crown integration of our physical senses and beyond. The development of our crystalline vision reaches back in time and space into the depths of our DNA and RNA, our ancestry, and the cosmos. Vision is us as one BEing from the inside out, reaching in and out beyond all time and space known and unknown.

The input and output of this processing within our light bodies are the essence of us. Input. Output. Is that the truth? Perhaps parts of this logical model must be put on mute? Is that astute or simply a dance? After all, these past few years have been quite a prance, with many in a daze, a trance. The haze, the haze is lifting high. It's all around the deep blue sky. Whispers and shouts. Let's get it all out!

Let's Get Physical!

Vision and the Visual System

Vision, if teased out as a "sense," is our most complex one—whether or not we are "sighted" individuals. Vision is the integration of our complete perceptual motor proprioceptive, interoceptive, and neuroreceptive systems all rolled into one: our audition (or hearing), smelling, tasting, touching, and feeling. Touching Life from the inside out is the embodiment of self. Self-discovery and allowing recovery. Why? So we will Thrive in this physical form in the here and in the now!

Eyesight and Vision are learned through our experiences and actions. Vision is an integration of our senses through movement and the experience of our physical selves, including the mystery of the interaction with all else that is, was, or ever will be, all at once.

The Nuts and Bolts of Eyesight Testing at the Doctor's Office

Let's go into some classical notions in eye care that you are likely familiar with. That, in my view, at least at this moment in time, is a good place to go next.

Which is better, one or two?

What I Now Believe

Vision is the emergent. Vision is movement.

Vision is the integration of our total action system as human beings and, when expressed as a fully integrated whole, the entire expression of our heart and soul from the inside out and from the outside in—in harmonious relationship with the cosmos and all that is, was, and ever will be.

Repeat.

Which is better, number one or two?

Which is better, the first or second?

Cuál es mejor, la primera o la segunda?

Qué es mejor, la primera o la segunda?

Numero uno o numero dos?

Click, click, click. Back and forth and back and forth. Blurry, clear (maybe), blurry, clear (maybe).

The endpoints of testing just noticeable differences and the just noticeable differences (JND) themselves are confusing. Equal blur—whatever that means to a person—is the actual endpoint we're taught to work with for fused cross-cylinder testing. This is one of the "objective" tests wherein the practitioner is determining the "correction" for a "condition" called astigmatism. Astigmatism is described by some in the field of eye care as a lopsided eye wherein the eyeball, part of the eyeball, or the cornea is stretched more in one direction than the other and not spherical like a ball. I believe astigma is caused by asymmetrical fascial, musculoskeletal, and our postural or emotional holdings that become embedded habits. Remember, habits can be changed, and many eyeball issues can be reversed and released. There is so much hope for recovery on all levels of body, mind, spirit, and soul!

Questions to Ponder

- Do the questions you are asked during an eye exam confuse you?
- Have you ever wondered why the question "Which is clearer, one or two?" was being asked, even though neither one looked clear, yet the doctor seemed satisfied? And then did you wonder how eventually the lenses created clarity?

- Did you ever wonder how eye doctors determine which glasses to prescribe, when to prescribe medications, or when to perform surgeries, such as Lasik surgery or cataract surgery, to create "clarity" for you or others?

Subjective and Objective Testing

What's this all about? What is the effect of the practitioner on the "testing" results, whether "subjective" or "objective" at one instant in time? What effect does the patient have on the findings? What of the child, teen, or adult who comes to the office for an evaluation following a meal of junk food loaded with artificial colors and flavors, often including genetically modified organisms, or GMO Frankenfood, which I characterize as "pretend food"? What of the malnourished, brain-starved child, teen, or adult? What if the mood, experiences, and emotional baggage the practitioner carries wind up in an individual's prescription?

Conventional Eyesight Care

Traditional education is what I and many traditionally trained practitioners through the recent centuries are a product of. Accepted dogma is what I've come to believe much of it is. I offer gratitude for the honor and privilege of my formal education. That said, I'll list here, explain here, and go over here the clinical aspects of some tenets we were taught in professional school as truth. I'll continue explaining how my eyesight, my vision, has expanded and continued to improve since that higher education indoctrination more than thirty-five years ago.

In the United States, the layperson sometimes becomes confused when sorting out eye care practitioners. There are more specialists for the eyes and the visual system than for any other part of the body. My dad uttered these words of wisdom from the moment I began considering the field of eyesight and vision care. There are opticians, optometrists, ophthalmologists, and many subspecialist practitioners and areas of vision care.

Opticians

The field of opticianry in the United States is based in the study of ophthalmic optics, the manufacturing and creation of lenses and prisms for eyeglasses and contact lenses, including specialty contact lenses and intraocular lens implants (IOLS) for cataract surgery. Opticians use manufactured eyeglass *blanks* and create glasses by cutting the blanks and crafting them into eyeglasses by placing the expertly cut lenses into eyeglass frames. There are many styles of eyeglass lenses, including the single vision lens, the bifocal or trifocal lens, and a wide range of progressive lenses, often called multifocal lenses. Eyeglass lenses in many styles can be designed to fit a wide variety of eyeglass frames. Frames are made of metal, plastic, and composite materials. Specialty lenses may be designed by an eye care professional practitioner and prescribed, taking into consideration occupational needs. Examples of more complex lenses include bifocals or trifocals, with or without special magnification, such as telescopes or other technologies integrated into the lens or frame. There are also virtual reality glasses with all kinds of other bells and whistles!

Optometrists

Optometrists may or may not fill the role of an optician. Some optometrists place orders for eyeglasses and/or contact lenses for patients within the context of their offices. Others do not. The majority of optometrists who have studied in the United States have completed a four-year undergraduate degree prior to entering optometry school, most often in science. Following the undergraduate degree, professional education continues with an additional four-year optometry school program to study eyesight, eye disease, lens prescribing, and visual function as postgraduate education.

Most optometrists consider themselves general primary care practitioners and perform eye exams resulting in eyeglass or contact lens prescriptions. Some optometrists treat those with glaucoma and diseased eyelid or anterior segment (the front of the eye, including the cornea) issues. Some refer these patients to ophthalmologists. Some optometrists manage or comanage cases of eye surgery or disease—post-Lasik surgery (reshaping the cornea to "correct" for nearsightedness, farsightedness, and/or astigmatism), cataract removal, glaucoma, or a retinal hole or tear—with other optometrists, ophthalmologists, or other health-care professionals. All optometrists, by nature of our profession, monitor systemic diseases, such as the stages of people's heart disease, diabetes, autoimmune issues, and other chronic illnesses, by looking inside the eyes, which truly are the windows of the soul.

Some optometrists, a minority, are primary care practitioners with a specialty in functional, behavioral, developmental, or neurodevelopmental care, including optometric vision therapy and natural eyesight improvement. Functional optometrists facilitate patients decreasing their prescriptions over time if the patients are receptive to that idea.

Optometrists like myself who specialize in optometric vision therapy use lenses and prisms, in instrument, and free-space techniques (and sometimes colored lights and filters) to help their patients increase their eyesight and visual awareness capacity and move them into a more well-functioning visual system. We are happy to work with patients to decrease their eyeglass prescriptions gradually over time or to help them immediately take off their glasses and see. (See *Take Off Your Glasses and See* by Jacob Liberman, OD, and many other natural eyesight-improvement books in the references and on my website: EnliveningConsciousness. com.) This increased awareness allows patients to function more effectively and efficiently in all aspects of their lives, from more ease in reading and writing to better sports performance and smoother ability to communicate with loved ones and in the community at large and the world and cosmos!

Ophthalmologists

After completing a four-year undergraduate degree and an additional four-year medical school program, some physicians go on to specialize in ophthalmology. Some ophthalmologists remain general primary

Seeing Eye Care Differently

The paradigm we explore as developmental, functional, behavioral, integrative, holistic optometrists is one of improving visual functioning rather than being caught in the dis-ease model of care, where it is assumed that people's vision will deteriorate as they mature. The dis-ease model of care, which we were taught is "normal," is one of the real epidemics in our Western culture. Most of the classical eye care education, in the fields of both optometry and ophthalmology, in my view, is extremely medically oriented, grueling, and complete— that is, if you're willing to live mostly in the paradigm of deterioration and Dis-ease.

care practitioners for their entire careers and do not delve into surgical specialties within their field. Many ophthalmologists specialize in diagnosing and treating eye disease and performing surgery. My understanding is that ophthalmologists who choose to specialize in surgery generally become surgical specialists as apprentices to surgeons through residencies and, often, fellowships. Surgical specialties include anterior segment surgery (the front of the eyes), such as surgery of the eyelid, cornea, and lens; orbital and general oculoplastic surgery, retinal surgery, and neuro-ophthalmology; glaucoma and strabismus procedures; amblyopia treatment; and more. There is overlap, and many combinations of specialties and subspecialties exist.

Comanagement of Patients

Many ophthalmologists, optometrists, and opticians comanage their patients. For example, a person who has had cataract surgery performed by an ophthalmologist to remove a cloudy lens might go to their optometrist for follow-up visits to receive postsurgical care. This postsurgical care might include eye health evaluations and lens prescriptions. Or this person might then go to an optician to fill the lens prescription. Some ophthalmologists and optometrists comanage cases either in their own offices or in other types of settings. It is no wonder consumers of eye care can be confused!

Ophthalmologists and optometrists comanage certain cases of refractive surgeries, strabismus surgeries, and a multitude of eye diseases, such as cataracts, glaucoma, and macular degeneration, to name a few. In addition to comanaging cases within the field of eye care, many practitioners comanage patients with practitioners in other fields.

Comanagement can be a club of sorts. Certain practitioners know one another, belong to certain overlapping organizations, and tend to refer to one another. Sometimes consumers are guided to some degree by their insurance policies. In today's day and age, many consumers of health care are left to their own devices to sort out when to go to which type of practitioner.

My Dream

My dream is to know that all my professional colleagues are acting in not only their own interests but also their patients' best interests by prescribing preventatively rather than prescribing compensatory lenses and procedures that further embed patients' dissonant visual habit patterns. I'd love to see more understanding from practitioners about how to cross-pollinate their expertise with one another and with the expertise of those who come to them (patients and clients) to seek care.

Chapter 4
A LOOK AT HOLISTIC EYE CARE

The Crown Sense

The whole person approach
Looking at a BEing
Seeing
As the pinnacle, the crown, queen of the senses
The integration of our behavior
Sensing, feeling, and actions as we move
through our visual spatial worlds

What Is a Holistic Eye Care Professional?

A HOLISTIC EYE CARE PROFESSIONAL CONSIDERS the entire person, not just their eyeballs. Holistic eye care professionals work harmoniously with the person they are serving in a beautiful, symbiotic give-and-take dance. We work with patients and clients as a team to improve eyesight and insight naturally, rather than continuing to function within the existing paradigm as if the eyes and a person need stronger and stronger prescriptions. Strengthening prescriptions year after year leads down the path of progressive eyesight deterioration and systemic degradation and disease.

A holistic eye care professional may or may not offer therapeutic natural eyesight-improvement services. Ask the office or practitioners directly if they practice traditionally or holistically. Ask if they will refer you to other practitioners who can meet your needs if they cannot.

My goal here is to offer some glimpses into how an individual begins to think about not only improving their eyesight naturally but also expanding their insight. It is important that you see eye to eye (pun intended!) with your provider or those who cocreate your wellness care. It's worth the energy investment to learn something about practitioners before visiting or working with them. Once you've made initial contact with the office by phone, email, or some other way, it's important to know how to advocate for yourself during your initial evaluation and your follow-up care with a practitioner.

Let your eye doctor know *in detail*
what your visual needs are!

My Exposure to Integrative Optometry

The words *behavioral, functional, developmental,* and *neurodevelopmental*—do they all mean the same thing? These terms have been used at various times over the years to define the subspecialty of the field of optometry that I've practiced for my entire career. Each practitioner has their own background and their own contribution to caring for people. In all cases, these descriptions and the approaches are looking at the whole person. Some practitioners are more focused on facilitating improvement of visual acuity, or how clearly one can see the eye chart. In all cases, these holistic, integrative practitioners facilitate vision enhancement in areas such as peripheral vision, visual-spatial awareness, depth perception (3D vision), learning, and more.

People often come in for an eye exam before going to their primary care physician or to any other subspecialty. Why? So they can SEE, of course! But it turns out that both acute and systemic long-term chronic illnesses are reflected through the eyes and visual system. The eye doc may find other systemic issues through the history taking or through the physical eye evaluation. When a person goes to the eye doctor, they may think they're coming in for a pair of eyeglasses and leave with a referral to some other provider.

Of paramount importance from a holistic, integrative perspective is the eye doctor asking about not only ocular, or eye, history but also the overall health and wellness of the person sitting in their exam chair. When it is not possible for me to physically examine someone, I advise them about what questions to ask their respective practitioners so they can advocate for themselves during the evaluation. I often refer for proper evaluation before I work with a person individually in person or virtually or comanage their care with one or more other practitioners.

What to Consider Sharing with the Holistic (or Any) Eye Doctor

Ask yourself the following questions about your visual and lifestyle needs (activities of daily living, or ADLs).

Basic Questions

- What are my primary visual needs?
- Am I visually comfortable in all the activities I engage in over the course of the day?

- Are my eyes dry? Do my eyes itch, burn, or tear by the end of a visually stressful day?
- Do I see double?
- Do I get headaches at the end of the day?

Specific Questions about Daily Activities (To Determine Your Unique Needs and Challenges)

- Do I hold books at arm's length all day?
- Do I drive long distances at night?
- Do I drive only during the day?
- Do I attend theater performances regularly in dark theaters?
- Do I attend sports events and sit in the peanut gallery?
- What sports am I participating in (running, yoga, tai chi, swimming, golf, tennis, soccer, skiing, croquet, or others)?
- What are my sports vision needs?
- Am I exercising? In person? Remotely?
- Do I sew or cook every day or on occasion?
- Am I able to read food and beverage labels on shelves easily when shopping?
- Am I visually comfortable when in conversation with others?
- Are there any other activities of daily living (ADLs) that I struggle with visually, such as cooking, cleaning, or hygiene issues that need to be addressed? Have I considered that this struggle might have to do with underdeveloped visual-spatial awareness? (Note: *Visual-spatial awareness* is a broad term. It has to do with what's directly in front of you [central vision] in relation to what is around you [peripheral vision]; the people, objects, and spaces in your life; everything in the 3D [your

physical space]; and how you relate to others and all of space, in all dimensions as well.)

- Am I open to the idea of different pairs of glasses for different circumstances in my life?

- Am I teaching remotely or in hybrid fashion? Am I visually comfortable in this situation?

- Do I spend hours a day in front of electronic devices, researching, writing, conversing, or engaging in a variety of ways with colleagues, business acquaintances, friends, and relatives?

- What is the distance between my eyes and the various digital devices I am viewing? Take these measurements with you to the eye doctor's office, and be sure that at the end of the exam, you are shown differences in lenses the doctor is planning to prescribe with their *trial lens kit*.

A trial lens kit is a suitcase of lenses. The doctor will use loose trial lenses with a *trial frame* to create the prescription for you in the office at the end of the visual evaluation. You'll have the opportunity to look through the lenses and move around the office with them on your face. This will ensure that when the new prescription in your new eyeglasses is prepared, the new prescription will work well. In other words, you'll have a chance to experience the lenses prior to receiving the written prescription. From my perspective, trial framing is imperative in prescribing lenses and prisms. Do most optometrists have trial frames and trial lens kits? Absolutely. Ophthalmologists? I've not a clue. Do most optometrists actually use them? I'm not sure about that either. Do functional optometrists use them? Absolutely! I've been functionally and therapeutically prescribing (from a preventative and natural eyesight improvement perspective) for my entire career.

Ruling Out Pathology First, Vision Therapy Training Next!

The obligation of the health-care professional is to rule out underlying disease before embarking on facilitating the natural eyesight-improvement journey with the patient.

Critically important note: Before working with anyone in optometric vision therapy, pathology, or underlying disease conditions, must be ruled out as the number-one order of business. So with patients, I and those in the field of optometric vision therapy must be 100 percent sure, for example, there is not a brain tumor or other organic underlying cause of a person's blurry eyesight, double vision (diplopia), or a myriad of other physical or neurologic issues. That said, if a person has been diagnosed with an eye disease or other visual anomaly, is being followed by a medical professional for their issue(s), and is highly motivated, they can choose to work collaboratively and cooperatively with a more functionally oriented practitioner such as myself to ease their symptoms and possibly look forward to reversing their disease to some degree or completely or to live much more harmoniously with their existing condition.

Vision Rest Break Time

Pause. Take a breath. Look away from the printed page or through the pages of the book or computer screen or other electronic device to relax your eye muscles and fascia and more fully oxygenate your blood. Bring your blinking into conscious awareness. Flutter those eyelids for some extra hydration for your incredible eyeballs and entire visual system. Breathe, Blink, and

Be Present. Ahhh! Take Vision Rest Breaks every few pages while reading this book. Consider taking vision rest breaks throughout your day!

◆ Breathe

◆ Blink

◆ Be Present!

Visually Related Stress-Revealing Behaviors

Whether or not you've ever had an eye exam or visual evaluation or worn glasses or contact lenses, some or all of the items on the list below may describe you. Here are some revealing visual behaviors related to visual development and functional visual issues. These sorts of symptoms often appear prior to or in conjunction with a person moving into refractive error or being diagnosed with a vision-related learning issue or conditions of eye disease:

- Needing to rub your eyes, or head, often
- Burning, itching, tearing eyes
- Getting headaches after reading for short or long periods of time
- Having difficulty comprehending written material and following directions
- Having trouble tracking along a line of printed words, sometimes skipping words or phrases

- Confusing right and left hands or right and left sides of the body or having trouble following directions
- Reversing letters when writing on paper or typing
- Losing focus while reading or writing
- Having trouble with putting things in order, or sequencing, as in constructing a logical sentence or paragraph or writing a book (that's why I have an editor!)
- Bumping into things, being clumsy without apparent reason, or having poor visual-spatial awareness
- Feeling uncomfortable in navigating social situations
- Having a short attention span for subjects that do not captivate you

Remember, whether you have experienced trauma while in utero; coming through the birth canal; in early childhood; through accidents, traumatic brain injury, concussions, other physical or emotional pain, or social, mental, or cognitive situations; or while giving birth, you have the potential to regain and remain in homeostasis, or balance, throughout your lifetime. You may have noticed learning disabilities (LD) and dyslexia are not mentioned here. These terms are not descriptive from my perspective. The list of issues above overlaps with the diagnoses of LD or dyslexia. Some or all of these behaviors disappear with optometric vision therapy and with supportive therapies as well.

Thriving in wellness is a wonderful way to live life! If you are someone who would love to maintain your vibrant vision or improve your eyesight naturally, feel confident that you can learn to be an expert in the ways of self-healing and in advocating for yourself to be sure your treatment is optimal.

Visiting a Holistic Eye Care Professional

A visit with a holistic eye care professional begins similarly to a visit with a conventional eye care professional. First is conventional eye exam testing to make sure your eyes and visual system are healthy and functioning efficiently and effectively and to rule out eye disease. Then the practitioner will likely move into functional visual testing to determine how well your eyes work as a team. Following that, many different types of specialty testing are performed, depending on the person's needs.

My practice both for myself and with those I see as patients or clients has shifted over the years. I consider myself a holistic, integrative practitioner—sometimes a coach, sometimes a facilitator, sometimes a yoga teacher, sometimes a spiritual nutrition counselor, and sometimes a doctor. Sometimes all of the above! My backgrounds blend into one. I pride myself on meeting people where they are, and the journey continues from there.

So what is "optimal vision care" with a holistic eye care professional? For some, optometrically, the initial recommendation begins with spending more time without glasses or prescribing the most appropriate preventative eyeglass prescription to allow for improving eyesight over time. It could initially include other recommendations about how to maintain one's eyesight in prime condition through the practice of positive thinking, movement modalities, and spiritual practices. It could include therapeutic and educational tools to improve one's eyesight naturally through optometric vision therapy (with lenses, prisms, colored lights and filters, walking rails with prism glasses, and a myriad of other visual enhancement techniques) combined with other healing modalities, such as somatic (body) therapies. I work with patients and clients on the reflexes that underlie visual development as well. You can find more details on these modalities in the Movement chapters.

> Optimal vision care for both children and adults includes recommendations for the tools needed to integrate natural eyesight-improvement techniques into daily routines, so eyesight gets continuously better rather than getting worse.

The Importance of Resilience

A goal of optometric vision therapy and its expanded, integrative enlivening-consciousness view I have developed, practice, and teach involves reintroducing and habituating resilience in every moment so we can be at our optimal level of efficiency and peak performance in all we manifest in our moment-to-moment lives and in the long term.

As I have noted, the notion of eyesight getting worse each year has been normalized in Western civilization, but it does not have to be that way. I facilitate preventative care and the shifting of eyeglass or other prescriptions over the course of the visual, movement, nutrition, and spiritual therapy journey to be sure people can ease into their new way of seeing gracefully. As we shift awareness, our habits change for the better. As we begin to feel the difference of the wonder of living in our true natures, we habituate to new habit patterns and routines that serve us to move more fully into health, wellness, and peak performance, instead of into continued degradation of our human physical, mental, emotional, and spiritual forms.

The totality of the visual process includes visual acuity, peripheral awareness, depth perception, tracking ability, focusing ability from near to far and vice versa, and converging and diverging one's eyes with ease. When in homeostasis and all combined in balanced movement, the integration of these processes allows for astute visual perception.

The Whole Paradigm. Holism. Our Vision in Its Entirety as the Felt Sense of BEing as One!

The Whole Paradigm
Being
Being in the center of it all.
The Fall.
The Reemergence of Being.
As ONE.
Here we are. We have come so very far. What now?
POW!!!

When both eyes and all aspects of the visual system are integrated in the visual process, we are said to be functioning optimally with single simultaneous binocular vision, or SSBV. When the entire visual process is coordinated and seeing is easy, life itself flows more gracefully. Did you ever wonder why you see one of things you're looking at, when you have two eyes? That is because when we look directly at an object, such as a pencil or pen, a word, or a person's face, with both of our eyes pointed in the same direction, and if our visual system is working in a coordinated SSBV fashion, we fuse the two images with our eyes through our brain.

Many people of all ages I've worked with over the course of my career have not had robust SSBV. In the general population, many individuals of all ages struggle with the coordination of their two eyes as a team, with focusing, with tracking, and with depth perception, among other visual issues. Culturally, our visual systems have been stressed emotionally and physically by "modern" technology and the artificial intelligence (AI) revolution. Staring at screens of all types and playing in the virtual reality of all kinds of devices and machines challenge our naturally developed good and flowing vision and other habit patterns.

When our two eyes do not work well together as a team, our thinking can be scattered and incohesive. We may not be able to focus clearly on the task at hand. When our visual system is in coherence, our thinking, sensing, feeling, actions, and reactions in the world are more in alignment with our true perceptions. Our functioning on every level—physical, mental, emotional, and spiritual—is more effective and efficient. Living is easier and flows smoothly when our sense of vision is fully integrated.

Giving Yourself Energy through Your Eyes (a.k.a. Palming)

Rub your hands together. Then place your overlapped, cupped hands on your eyes (with eyelids gently closed) while resting your lower palms on your lower orbital bones, the bony structures just below your eyes. Notice the energy of your hands, and feel the warmth moving into your eyes.

Come back to your breath for a few inhalations and exhalations at your own pace.

Gently release your hands down by your sides, slowly open your eyelids, blink a few times, and squeeze your eyelids together. Now notice the energetic connection between your hands, your eyelids, your eyes, and the world.

Begin reading some more, either right here in one continuous flow or by dipping into the book where you feel called. Permission granted!

Refractive Errors

Classically, the term *refractive error* refers to shifts in the shape of the eyeball such that eyeglasses or another form of visual "correction" is necessary for a person to "see" clearly. *Refractive error* is the general term that refers to myopia (or nearsightedness), hyperopia (or farsightedness), presbyopia (aging eyes), and astigmatism.

From a holistic, integrative perspective, the actual reasons why a person may not be perceiving and seeing as clearly as they are capable of perceiving and seeing have a myriad of root causes. Emotions, such as fear, can have a lot to do with how one sees and perceives. The environment one is surrounded by and the inner ecosystem environment in one's gut and other multiple microbiomes inside the body are other huge factors.

What visual changes are "helped" by compensatory lenses? Sadly, the normalization of prescribing compensatory lenses, meaning lenses that "correct" for refractive "error" (nearsightedness, farsightedness, astigmatism, presbyopia, and so on), potentially creates a cycle of an individual needing stronger and stronger lenses for a period of time—an addiction of sorts.

When and how do these changes occur? Vision is learned. Our eyesight and broad integrated visual system develop beginning in utero (or maybe even earlier if you consider our DNA, RNA, and emotional bodies, but we'll let that topic rest for now) and in earnest during our first six years and throughout our lifetimes. *Emmetropia* is the term that refers to "perfect eyesight," meaning the ability to read the 20/20, or 6/6, line on the eye chart. Emmetropia generally does not refer to any of the functional visual issues referred to earlier.

Eyesight diagnoses and visual dissonance (nearsightedness, farsightedness, astigmatism, etc.) that are used as diagnosis codes in the medical profession and beyond can be a DNA and RNA legacy issue, meaning we carry habit patterns and social, emotional, and spiritual constructs from prior generations.

- The visual imbalances can develop in utero if a mom is physically, emotionally, or spiritually imbalanced.
- The visual issues can develop during a child's early years, in early development. In the first year of life, when parents or caregivers keep a child for long periods of time in the confined space of bouncers, walkers, and strollers, the child is not allowed to simply BE on the floor, exploring and naturally developing their visual-spatial world experientially by connecting and relating with their developing bodies, brains, and eyes to gravity and earth and relating with others.
- Visual issues can also manifest because in babies' first year of life, caretakers stand them up on their feet, mistaking the stepping reflex for a desire to be upright.

- Refractive error can develop in third or fourth grade, when most children begin to read to learn and have already learned to read. Reading the written word to learn (as contrasted with learning to read) involves a higher level of concentration and cognitive ability, so some children begin their journey into "refractive error" (myopia, hyperopia, astigmia, etc.) at this junction in their education.

- The issues can develop in high school or during college or postgraduate educational years, when the academics become more strenuous, with much more stress and greater amounts of reading and writing, now often on electronic devices.

- Stressful or deeply traumatic job experiences or life events can be a root cause of visual dissonance that is held in the eyes as "refractive error."

Personality, Character, and Eyesight

There are certain behavioral and functional characteristics, developmental traits, and personalities associated with, and reflected in, certain eye conditions. The development of "refractive error" refers to the need for a visual correction, such as eyeglasses. We'll discuss the refractive eyesight diagnoses myopia, hyperopia, astigmatism, presbyopia, and anisometropia. Beyond our genetic constitutions, do we wind up with certain eyeglass lenses, contact lenses, or eye surgeries due to the environment where we spend our time, the food we eat and drink, our spiritual leanings, and movement and behavior habit patterns we've developed to that point in our lifetimes? Yes, yes, YeS, yES, and YES!

The Myope: Nearsightedness

Myopia. The myope, a nearsighted or shortsighted individual, is focused on the near visual-spatial world. The well-adjusted myope is often determined, follows through, is curious, and focuses well on the task at hand. The person with a "diagnosis" of nearsightedness can be a perfectionist. It takes one to know one!

Ramifications include the following: Myopes might dwell for too long and get stuck in the story of their past. They tend to block the periphery—what is beyond their central eyesight. They may feel threatened by what is beyond their perceived orbit of control and become anxious when in situations that seem out of their control. They are hyperfocused and task-oriented, so they're great workers. Yet they tend to overwork, often to the point of exhausting themselves, and not only become habituated to this overfocused way of being but also wind up with progressively stronger prescription lenses. High myopes have overworking habit patterns that run deep and often are rooted in emotional or physical trauma, PTSD, or addictions, which can be buried in their generational DNA.

Note: When a person has Lasik surgery to "correct" their nearsightedness but does not do

What about Perfect Eyesight?

Emmetropia is the term that refers to "perfect eyesight," meaning the ability to read the 20/20, or 6/6, line on the eye chart. It turns out 20/20 is an arbitrary number. Emmetropia generally does not refer to any of the functional visual issues referred to below. What is Perfect Vision when we consider our entire visual system integrated with our body or soma? We're exploring that question throughout this book. We each have the opportunity to draw our own conclusions! Perfect? What does *perfect* mean? What is the personality of perfection? Are we all striving toward perfection in this physical form through our senses? Or are we traveling beyond our senses? Are our sense organs part of our tool chest?

any natural vision improvement prior to surgery or following the surgery, their nearsightedness has not really vanished, as their myopic behavioral patterns (as mentioned above) that were present prior to the surgery remain the same. The surgery might not "take," and more "corrective" surgeries are needed as the person becomes more nearsighted.

The Hyperope: Farsightedness

The hyperope looks into the future, has big-picture thinking, and systems thinking comes easily. The farsighted individual loves to be part of group dynamics and easily brings together large groups of people, as in fairs, festivals, and organizational structures of all kinds. The "farsighted" individual can easily see far away into the distance, predicts the future easily, and loves to move.

For example, this individual, when well adjusted, has no issue with driving, going to the movies, enjoying a ball game from a distance, or seeing a television across the room. The hyperope may have difficulty seeing up close at arm's length, as in reading a book or looking at electronic devices. Especially when they reach the age of about 40 or 45, when things start to shift hormonally and physiologically in other ways, farsighted individuals often come to see an eye doctor or visit drugstore eyeglass racks to seek out lenses for up-close tasks.

Effects include the following: the farsighted individual might not attend adequately to details necessary to complete a task at hand or might overlook nuances in personal or professional relationships.

The Astigmat: Astigmatism

What the heck is astigmatism? A stigma? I'm just now thinking about the root of the word.

Astigmatism is most classically defined as when the eye is not spherical or round but is curved differently in different areas of the entire eyeball, cornea, or lens. Light that reaches the retina does not do so in a harmonious fashion, so blur or perceived double vision can occur. As optometrists, we measure the curvature of the corneas, or the very front curved surface of the eyes, and balance the measurements with lenses to neutralize the curvature to allow for clear eyesight. What does that mean anyway?

Although a star student in the clinic, I was not a stellar student in optics—that's for sure. I never really fully understood the optical explanation of much of what I was doing during my years in clinical practice. And it turns out, most of my colleagues still don't fully understand what they've been up to. We did practice with one another and in the clinic with people, but our initial technical training in optics was mostly based on a stationary optical bench eyeball or visual system model, not a living human model. My awareness now is that the entire field of optometry, ophthalmology, and opticianry—and almost all of the medical field, for that matter—is based on compensation. Compensatory lenses. Compensatory drugs. Compensation instead of looking at root causes and educating one another about the basis of disease. Why? Because let's face it: it's much easier that way. At least that's how it appears on the surface of things.

Astigmatism develops when a person has a strongly embedded physical habit of viewing objects at a certain angle, on a certain axis or plane, and not in other areas of space. A person who sits for eight hours a day in front of a computer or reading a book may develop a different type of astigmatism than a professional golfer or an auto mechanic. Those with certain occupations may have characteristic forms of astigmia based on how they posture themselves during the day.

Effects include the following: A person's habitual postures are completely reflected in their visual systems. The behavioral characteristics of an astigmat can include having a contorted, slanted perceptual view of the world; being wishy-washy; having difficulty in making decisions; or being certain about decisions at times, though not always being happy with those decisions.

The Anisometrope

The anisometrope is someone whose two eyes are very different and has a diminished sense of two-eyed vision, with a lesser sense of 3D compared to others with more fully coordinated visual systems. One eye may be adapted for distance eyesight as some form of farsightedness, while the other eye is adapted for the near visual-spatial world, as in nearsightedness. If there is large asymmetry between the two sides of the visual system, in eye care lingo, we call this visual condition *built-in monovision*. The two eyeballs may congenitally be of different sizes. There may be an in utero developmental cause or possibly a genetic predisposition based on the energetics of the family line.

Effects include the following: People with two very different seeing eyes can be confused, apologetic, waffling in decision-making, and inconsistent. They can be creative and literally not "see" things the way others do. Every person with two seeing eyes has some degree of binocular, or two-eyed vision, but the anisometrope has a very different sense of two-eyed, or binocular vision, and often has enormous difficulties with using the two eyes together as a team. These individuals may alternate between their two eyes, suppressing much of one visual system while using the other part of the visual system at different times and for different viewing distances. They may adjust well to eyeglasses that "correct" their situation, or they may have trouble adjusting to any type of eyeglasses or contact lens prescription.

Monovision and More

What is monovision? In the eye care world, *monovision* refers to prescribing for one eye for clarity in the far distance and the other eye for clarity at close distances. This type of prescribing is most often used when people have previously had equal vision in each eye. Some people enjoy the monovision prescription. At least they appear to enjoy this type of prescription initially, as they can "see" at all distances. As holistic, integrative eye care professionals, we are interested in prescribing lenses that allow for optimal functioning for the entire visual process. When eye doctors intentionally prescribe monovision, this is the antithesis of allowing for maximal binocular visual functioning (SSBV) and homeostasis within both the visual system and a person's entire body.

Just as I feel that variable focus lenses are not wise for a person to wear as eyeglasses or intraocular lens implants, I feel intentionally prescribing monovision lenses (where one eye's visual acuity is more optimal for distance eyesight and the other eye's prescription is more optimal for near vision) in the form of eyeglasses or contact lenses or refractive eye surgeries is not wise. This form of prescribing (monovision) is not allowed for pilots for obvious reasons. Pilots must have intact binocular, or two-eyed, vision. A pilot needs to have a fully functioning binocular visual system and single simultaneous binocular vision without double vision.

Lenses affect a person's soma, or body. Prescribing to create monovision disrupts the symbiotic nature of a well-functioning binocular visual system of a person's brain. This disrupts a person's posture, as this type of prescribing affects all body systems and ripples from head to fingertips to toes. Disrupting the normal functioning of an intact binocular visual system is not something I think a licensed professional ought to promote, as it does not follow the Hippocratic Oath of first doing no harm.

The story is different when a person has naturally developed monovision (anisometropia), meaning one eye naturally sees more clearly in the distance (farsighted), and one eye sees more clearly at short distances (nearsighted) for one reason or another. Rest assured, there is a story! If someone has what I'm referring to as built-in monovision, what is the reason? While the child was in utero, was mom working at a desk or at another job where there was a consistent asymmetric posture held for long periods of time? What was going on emotionally for Mom and Dad or other caregivers while their child was in utero?

How was this person handled as a child? Were they kept in a crib against the wall in their first year of life and, therefore, likely lying on one side of their body more than the other side? Was this person bottle fed by a parent or caregiver feeding the child while holding the child in a certain asymmetric body posture themselves? Was the child often placed in a bouncer, crib, or walker? Was the child held in emotionally trying circumstances, being forced to listen to arguing parents and trying to avoid paying attention by suppressing or turning off the visual system on one side of the cortex or the other and eventually developing a very asymmetric system? Was there a physical developmental issue or movement patterning where, for whatever reason, the eyeballs developed physically asymmetrically?

Any or all of these situations could be causes for a person who has anisometropia or one of many different eye conditions mentioned above. There could be many other causes as well.

Eyesight, Presbyopia, and Aging

Many of us never need eyeglasses until we hit the level of maturity of age 40 or 45 or sometimes 50 or 60 or older (like my dad)! This is often when presbyopia, or elder eyesight, sets in. Then we go to the drugstore to experiment with which power of reading glasses we need, beginning usually with a plus-one (+1.00) or plus-one-twenty-five (+1.25) when we're around age forty or forty-five and progressively using stronger and stronger prescription lenses until we reach the plus-two-fifty level (+2.50) at around age sixty-five. Our hormones have shifted throughout our bodies, and our eyesight has shifted right along with our eyeballs. Menopause occurs in women, and andropause occurs in men. But is that the whole story? Does the story have to play out in this way?

No, it does not! Your presbyopia (classically defined as aging eyes) prescription does not have to increase year after year. If you choose to shift your awareness and use the tools of natural eyesight improvement, you can minimize or eliminate the need for eyeglasses or other types of visual compensation. This approach involves shifting into healthy lifestyle patterns. It involves moving through, letting go of, or burning up (zero pointing) old, outdated habit patterns. In other words, it involves some work! What has your story been, and what are you choosing your story to be as you move into the future?

Breathe, Blink, and Be Present!

Whew, time for a Vision Rest Break!

Ahhh, remember to bring your Breath to conscious awareness, Blink consciously a few times, and Be Present in your body!

Blinking lubricates your eyes and is usually done unconsciously. By bringing blinking to conscious awareness, you can reestablish a more normal blinking pattern. Blinking patterns are often disrupted when one is doing a lot of reading and writing or concentrating for extended periods of time in classes, in person, in phone or Zoom (especially Zoom) conversations, while sitting in front of a computer screen or other electronic device, at work, in conferences, or in back-to-back meetings.

Reading the history and descriptions of techniques is one thing, and practicing these techniques experientially with consistency—making them your own, habituating them, and then ultimately modeling them to others—is something completely different and necessary if you are into making changes within yourself and in the world around you! Breathe into that. Blink. Be present. Take a moment to gaze out across the room into the distance. And know that you are just where you need to be in this moment. Ahhhh.

◆ Breathe

◆ Blink

◆ Be Present!

Vision-Related Learning Issues

In optometry school, I learned about the specialty field of pediatric optometry and how that department in our eye clinic was working with children who were medically diagnosed as "learning disabled." Pediatric optometrists classically work with children with all kinds of functional visual issues, such as difficulty with both eyes tracking across a line of print in a book or on an electronic device. When a child has trouble focusing their eyes and moving their eyes in a coordinated fashion, using their two eyes together as a team, they also have trouble focusing on the printed page and very often have trouble learning to read. If this same bright child (as all children are bright!) has struggled to learn to read, they will likely have trouble maintaining attention for the extended periods of time required in most schools. The child may then withdraw into themselves and spiral into poor self-esteem or depression, or they might become the class clown or disrupt the classroom in some other way. Then they will be awarded the diagnosis of LD (learning disabled), ADHD (attention deficit hyperactivity disorder), or one of the other DDs (dissociative disorders). In some cases, if they've been pushed hard enough by the dysfunctional system, they may wind up not only with eyeglasses to "see clearly" but also with a physical disease or mental health diagnosis. From teenagers to the elderly from all backgrounds and all walks of life, many have undiagnosed vision-related learning issues. You may have noticed yourself in some of the descriptions above. Any of us, if put in certain circumstances, could be characterized as having vision-related learning issues.

I'll never forget the service and clinical trip I took as an optometry student to examine inmates in a jail close to Philadelphia, Pennsylvania. The young people I examined that day had excellent distance eyesight, meaning they could see and sometimes read the eye chart across the room at a distance. Their visual and other reflexes, such as their reaction times, were outstanding. But "seeing" letters, objects, or anything up close to their faces was next to impossible for most of them. They had a variety of functional visual issues. Easy convergence, meaning using their two eyes working together as a team, was not easy. This diagnosis of convergence insufficiency means they had double vision when they looked at printed material up close to their faces, within arm's length. No wonder so many gifted and talented young people are illiterate, wind up struggling in school and life, and sometimes end up in jail. Undiagnosed eyesight and visual issues have become an epidemic in our world.

These functional visual issues apply to people of all ages. I had no clue that natural eyesight improvement was a possibility, until I became familiar with what I now call *integrative optometrists*.

The reason a recharacterization of learning disability terminology is so sorely needed is that the way we speak about and document "disabilities" has had an enormous impact upon how these issues are treated in our current-day (now crumbling) systems, including, but not limited to, the educational, medical, corporate, legal, and business systems all around the world. And the way we speak about and handle these issues as individuals based on the cultural constructs is a big deal.

As mentioned above, it turns out children aren't the only ones who have these visually related learning issues. These issues are common in adults. Perhaps it's an unseen (pun intended) epidemic? I say absolutely!

Most holistic optometrists and practitioners in other disciplines work with those with the diagnoses listed above. The Optometric Extension Program Foundation (OEPF) publishes a pamphlet containing a chart comparing vision-related learning issues to ADD, ADHD, PDD, autism, and more, to distinguish one from the other. There is a lot of overlap in these diagnoses, if you believe in these labels at all. Lori Shayhew, MA, founder of the organization the Gifts of Autism, helps individuals of all ages who have been labeled as autistic to live their gifts.

The Relationship between Optometric Vision Therapy (OVT), Vision, and Movement

Vision therapy is a specialty in the field of optometry that involves the use of lenses, prisms, and colored filters prescribed to facilitate changes in the way light enters the body. When lenses are placed in front of a person's eyes, their entire body, or soma, is affected. Shifts in both movement patterns and visual awareness occur. That's one definition from this practitioner's perspective. Then there is the definition from the other side. How does the person act upon the lenses? This brings up the following discussion: What is a lens? What is a prism? What is the purpose of using lenses, colored filters, and colored lights? As posed earlier, what effect does the practitioner have on the patient or client and vice versa?

As I studied to become an eye doctor, there were many courses in optometry school in primary optometric care. There were also many courses in systemic disease and eye disease and in visual function from both the anatomic and physiologic perspectives. And there were courses in refractive "error" and in complex visual issues, including a course in strabismus, or crossed eyes, meaning eyes that look in different directions rather than in the same direction. Another course was on amblyopia, the inability for an eye to be "corrected" to 20/20. These teachings included the presumed causes of these visual conditions and specialized treatment using lenses, prisms, and optometric vision therapy for these diagnoses. Although classic disease issues were not often discussed relating to vision therapy, these conditions may also be helped by visual enhancement strategies. We learned all about developmental visual testing. I've come to understand that because the eyes are extensions of the brain and the entire nervous system, with OVT, we are truly working with the brain, the nervous system, and the connections to the systems in our entire body.

All these different tools and techniques in optometric vision therapy are designed to help people awaken, enliven their consciousness, and shift their visual-spatial awareness and movement patterns (and, hence, their bodies, minds, spirits, and Beings). Additional testing is added for an expanded visual evaluation in preparation for optometric vision therapy. In later chapters in the movement section, we'll explore some basic and rudimentary movement analysis and techniques I use as an integral part of, or used prior to, enrollment in a full optometric vision therapy (OVT) program. Practicing these movement techniques is fundamental to reintegrating our body systems that underlie visual development, and therefore, grounded movement practices help to facilitate fully developed, easy vision.

Movement analysis refers to looking at the whole person during a complete holistic and integrative visual and movement evaluation. On a physical level, it refers to looking at their body, or soma, and at how a person cares for themselves. Does the person have enough self-love to take wonderful care of themselves? On a mental, emotional, and spiritual level, it refers to overall functioning. How do the individuals interact with others in their families and serve in their chosen professions, their communities, or the world?

Because movement development is the basis of visual development when vision is defined broadly, looking at how a person moves through space is critical to understanding their total visual action system and how they are functioning in the world. It is why I've always integrated movement modalities into the vision experiencing (some call it *work*) I facilitate, whether or not a person pursues OVT.

Moving Beyond 20/20

As mentioned earlier, optometric vision therapy is not necessarily directed toward natural eyesight improvement when eyesight is defined just by the measurement of visual acuity, or 20/20. When we look at vision in a broader context, we include all the components of eyesight and vision: eye movements; tracking ability; near and far focus; depth perception, or stereopsis; visual-spatial perceptual awareness; auditory visual integration; cognitive processing, including sequencing, following directions, mathematical abilities, and logical thinking; and more.

Holistic optometric vision therapy provides a wonderful solution to the abovementioned and may also include improvement in visual acuity. With optometric developmental testing as an add-on to a conventional evaluation, this integrative approach is a superb, holistic whole-person solution to some, and sometimes all, of these issues.

Would you like to gain awareness about your entire visual system and the visual process and gain insight into who you are? If you are dedicated, consistent, and persistent with the process, some of your visual skills will surely become more integrated. You will become clearer, more efficient, and more effective in your life path!

There are additional types of therapeutic interventions I and others offer to get to the root of preserving and improving visual acuity. These modalities are influenced by the elder behavioral optometrists on whose shoulders I stand and many others, including the natural eyesight-improvement work of ophthalmologist William H. Bates; Janet Goodrich, PhD; and Alexander practitioner and EyeBody founder Peter Grunwald, among others.

A Multitude of Vision Pioneers

From many different fields, vision pioneers have risen. In the field of optometry, the late doctors A. M. Skeffington, Frederick Brock, Robert Kraskin, Mort Davis, Paul Lewis, Amorita Treganza, Marilyn Heinke, Gerry Getman, Harry Wachs, Bruce Wolff, and John Streff are just a few of the shoulders on which the current generations of optometrists stand. People enter the natural eyesight-enhancement arena in many ways. Many disciplines integrate natural eyesight improvement into their teaching. The late Darrell Boyd Harmon, an educator, and Samuel Renshaw, a psychologist, are examples of two luminaries who collaborated extensively with optometrists. Natural eyesight practitioners have become prominent, building on the work of Bates, an ophthalmologist in the early part of the last century; Janet Goodrich; Aldous Huxley; and, in the later part of the century, optometrists Ray Gottlieb, Jacob Liberman, Sam Berne, Sarah Lane, Brenda Montecalvo, Marc Grossman, and many others.

Improving Eyesight and Insight Involves Change

We humans have developed all sorts of adaptations in our lives for one reason or another. Our environments—physical, social, mental, spiritual, and emotional—and the way we interact in our environments affect our eyesight and vision in a myriad of ways. Our behavioral patterns—physical, mental, emotional, and spiritual of the entire family, community, and world structure—affect how we see moment to moment and how embedded our eyesight, visual, thinking, feeling, and acting habits are. Improving one's eyesight naturally involves change. Sometimes we humans can be resistant to change. As we change our view, our vision naturally improves, our peripheral visual fields widen, and our single simultaneous binocular eyesight morphs into deeper insight and deeper vision. We "see" things that have always been right in front of us, literally and figuratively, that we never noticed before.

Working with Soft Neurological Signs

Each individual on this planet has both masculine and feminine characteristics and hormones in differing quantities. Our hormones and physiology affect the way we are in the world. The culture in which we were raised also plays an enormous role in how we behave in our daily lives and in our career choices. I have sometimes seen the medical mainstream as practiced by all genders as extremely hardhanded and coarse. The sensitivity of feminine sensibilities has so often been overlooked both unintentionally and intentionally or discounted.

My understanding is that both researchers and those the research is being conducted on to this day are most often white men. Female researchers are still relatively rare, and female research subjects are rare as well, especially female research subjects with vague but consistent complaints that are often described as idiopathic (unknown) in cause. I personally have not seen the issue of gender and research addressed much, at least not in the disciplines or professional journals I've been aware of thus far in my life. This does not mean gender studies do not exist. I know university programs across the United States have courses and departments diving into this subject.

In the book *What We Will Become*, author Mimi Lemay mentions in a few sentences the science behind hormones and gender identity. It's a topic I'm not very familiar with but one I've become aware of more recently. There's no question in my mind that hormones and the development and maintenance of our vision are connected, and the stress of gender identity issues surely can have a role in the development of eyesight and vision in the form of refractive error or other disease states related to our whole bodies and visual systems.

My main interest has always been prevention of illness, working within the context of vibrancy, vitality, and wellness. I sincerely believed I would learn mostly about preventative vision care in professional school. We learned that the prescribing of compensatory lenses and prisms was the way to go!

As a young female undergraduate biology major with my four-year degree in hand, I found myself matriculating in 1982 into the Pennsylvania College of Optometry (PCO), now Salus University, and soon to be part of Drexel University. Our optometry school class was the very first with 51 percent women and 49 percent men. Still today, in 2023, there are more practicing male than female optometrists in southwestern Pennsylvania, where my family currently resides. Worldwide, the picture is likely the same.

Why care about whether a man or a woman, or however the person identifies, sees you as a patient or client? This is tricky territory, but I will attempt an explanation. There are many categories along the spectrum of what has classically, in Western culture, been described as the gender male or female. Our culture at large has been guided into a male-persona-dominated hierarchical structure that has affected every single aspect of our culture. However a person identifies gender-wise, we have all, in Western culture, been affected by this construct. From my feminine perspective, it's a good idea in the field of wellness care and prevention to work with a practitioner who has a well-developed feminine side, no matter how the person identifies.

The analysis of dis-ease in mainstream medicine, in my experience, continues to a large degree to be centered on end-stage disease, such as heart disease, cancer, diabetes, autoimmune illness, and others. This seeming "knowingness"—this confidence in having all the answers to "treat" already established, diagnosable dis-eases—is, in my view, a hard-core, unbalanced way of viewing disease states. In contrast, the idea of identifying and then working with soft neurological signs is a concept that is still not known widely as a thing to be concerned with. What is a soft neurological sign? And what does this have to do with the feminine side of all of us and gender? Are women more likely to notice subtle behavior-related visual changes in a person? I believe so. Both women and men with more sensitive personas as nurturers will be more likely to pick up on these subtle behavioral signs.

Soft neurological signs are multidimensional (physical and nonphysical) gentle whispers from our hypersensitive, balanced feminine and masculine souls that teach us what is going on inside our hearts, minds, and spirits. Soft neurological signs are what the field of optometric vision therapy specializes in "diagnosing" and "treating." How? By moving through and into integration from the inside out, so that a person feels more comfortable functioning within their own skin, body-mind, and emotional self. Soft neurological signs are subtle physical, emotional, social, mental, and spiritual indications that something is not quite right, not quite homeostatic, but a bit off or awry. Although some signs can be crushing or severe, often, soft neurological signs are more subtle; appear out of nowhere acutely or over time, without apparent cause; and are unexplainable. These soft neurological signs cause behavioral changes in individuals.

Having a mild headache, being unable to work for too long on the computer or at any task, losing concentration sooner than usual, finding your mind wandering, and feeling mild aches and pains can all be classified as soft neurological signs. Bloodwork may be slightly off, breathing may be slightly irregular, and coordination may not be quite up to par. Periodic headaches may be mild. A bit of foggy-headedness may be present. But you know in your heart of hearts that something is not quite right. Full-fledged headaches of all different types may develop seemingly out of nowhere but following visually stressful time periods. Trust yourself when you feel these things.

Interestingly, subtle neurologic post-COVID signs are beginning to be reported as of this writing in early 2022. A case reported by Jamie C. Ho, OD, details "how neuro-rehabilitation optometrists can optimize patient outcomes despite residual functional visual deficits following a severe acquired brain injury from COVID-19."[5] Scientific studies, when done carefully and accurately, take time. It will be interesting to

---

[5] Jamie C. Ho, "Neuro-Optometric Rehabilitation for Post COVID-19 Syndrome," *Optometry & Visual Performance* 10 (January 2022), https://www.oepf.org/wp-content/uploads/2021/12/OVP-10-COVID-Ho-Final.pdf.

see what other studies emerge over time regarding ocular sequelae to the COVID story.

As eye doctors and visual therapists, we see irregularities in our detailed optometric findings where we look for functional visual issues that affect human performance. These soft neurological sign findings can be extremely subtle. Most eye care professionals (and most health-care professionals in general) are not doing the testing that reveals soft neurological signs. There is specific visual testing for soft neurological signs. There are many treatable subtle diagnostic signs quietly whispering as soft neurological signs. But if practitioners do not do the functional optometric testing, they will not be letting their patients or clients know that there is help for these issues. Often, testing for common visual conditions that can cause headaches, difficulty tracking along a line of a printed page or on the computer screen, or issues with reading and more is not done. Convergence Insufficiency (CI) is an example of an often-overlooked diagnosis.[6] This is the inability to use the two eyes as a team.

Integrative, holistic optometrists understand how to facilitate treatment of the symptoms created by these findings. The treatment involves a combination of our own intuitive, balanced presence as practitioners and the presence and utilization of a combination of tools we have learned about from those we have been honored to work with. We use the tools and skills, lenses, prisms, and colored filters in and out of free space instrumentation (in home and in office) and other bells and whistles we have been taught about and sought out on our own to facilitate a person's rehabilitation journey.

---

[6] American Optometric Association. Convergence Insufficiency. Accessed October 19, 2023. https://www.aoa.org/healthy-eyes/eye-and-vision-conditions/convergence-insufficiency. For CI studies in the reference section of this book see Borsting et al., Rouse et al., and Scheiman et al.

Break Time!

Take a breath. Stand up. Stretch your arms all the way out to your sides. Appreciate the width of your torso and how your breath fills the spaces between your ribs and in your belly. Lower your arms to the sides of your body. Breathe again into your head and eyes. Breathe into the entire length of your spine from the root of your first chakra, at the base of your spine and perineum, all the way into the front of your corneas, the very front layer of your eyeballs. Sit back down, or continue to stand, and read on. Ahhhh!

Complexity of the Visual Pathway in Our Brains

We know that six—some say seven—of the twelve cranial nerves have to do with eyesight or vision. Cranial Nerve Two is the optic nerve; one of these optic nerves is connected at the back of each eyeball from the brain. Each person who is "normally" sighted has two optic nerves. These two nerves are part of the larger visual pathway. The electrical receptors of our eyes (one optic nerve in the back of each eye, rooted in the retina) meet in the center of the brain, where they decussate, or cross, forming the lateral geniculate bodies on the way to the occipital cortex. The visual pathway then moves into the occipital cortex at the back of the brain, just below the occipital bone at the very back lower part of the skull.

Cranial Nerves Three, Four, and Six are involved with the eye muscles that move our eyes in all different directions. Cranial Nerves Five and Seven play a role in our visual systems as well. We'll explore in some detail the development of the human visual system through embodiment and the importance of harmonious integration of the visual system into the other body systems experientially in the movement section.

This is a brief synopsis of the complexity of eyesight and the visual system. All systems of the body—including the nervous system; the ligaments, muscles, and fascia; and the endocrine, circulatory, lymphatic, respiratory, and sensorimotor systems—and, beyond the body, the soul are involved in true eyesight and vision.

Nutrition, Eyesight, Vision, and Dis-ease

Diet is an important component of care that needs to be addressed for everyone. Healthy individuals can stay healthy by eating mindfully. Who can benefit by eating wisely according to constitution and comfort? Those with diagnoses of systemic diseases, including hypertension, heart disease and diabetes, autoimmune disorders, and post-traumatic brain injury, such as stroke or concussion, as well as those with visually related learning issues, trauma-induced somatic pain issues, and mental health issues. How many health-care professionals have taken the time to educate themselves and care for themselves in this area of wellness?

When eye doctors look inside a person's eyes with an ophthalmoscope, we see the front, middle, and back of the eyes, magnified. We can see all the way through the cornea, lens, iris, and pupil, all the way to the very back of the eye. We can even see the optic nerves and the retina. Magnificent indeed! The health of our eyes, our visual system, and the visual process reflects the health of our entire bodies. There are systemic disease processes with ocular manifestations. Or is it the other way around? Things in the 3D multiverse look different depending on the angle we're looking at them from. Function affects structure, and structure affects function. It's a circular, spiralic dimensional situation!

As part of treatment plans for a variety of diagnoses (including, but not limited to, common nearsightedness [myopia]; farsightedness [hyperopia]; presbyopia [aging or mature eyes]; astigmatism; other visual-spatial distortions [such as strabismus or amblyopia]; functional matters causing learning issues; recognized chronic illnesses that affect the back of the eye, such as heart disease and type 2 diabetes [adult onset]; and the others mentioned above), there is help! I have become comfortable recommending lifestyle shifts, including dietary lifestyle changes. The whole-food, plant-based (WFPB) lifestyle, or recommending elements of the WFPB lifestyle, is one example described in the nutrition section. This sometimes involves trying a meatless Monday or one meatless meal a week to begin with. It all depends on what a patient or client is receptive to trying.

In my area of tertiary specialty, optometric vision and movement therapy, assisting patients in minimally stabilizing and, often, lessening or reversing their myopia, or nearsightedness; hyperopia, or farsightedness; astigmatism; traumatic brain injury symptoms, such as concussion or stroke; and vision-related learning issue symptoms, I've recommended the WFPB or other versions of plant-based dietary interventions as part of the treatment plan as well.

The idea is to meet people where they are comfortable and then go from there. That is the context a practicing therapeutic health-care professional like me works in. In this book, my hope is that a wide range of people from all walks of life will be interested in the perspective of this one health-care professional (who is also a spiritual nutrition counselor; a permaculturist; someone with a background in ballet, modern dance, flamenco, somatic movement therapy, and yoga;

a wife; and a parent of two amazing young women). My hope is that this will be interesting and instructional in some way and that you will use this information to shape, form, learn, and copy in your own life to live a more vibrant and wildly satisfying life of joy, balance, and love. The stories, suggestions, or comments in this book may seem foreign or take you out of your comfort zone, but that's okay. Be with those feelings, and if and when you feel ready, read on! In other words, be calm, and carry on.

Our vision quests continue! There are many stories of incredible positive results from patients and clients I have seen over the course of my career. For children and adults, reports of improved clarity, expanded awareness, and increased comfortable productivity are the most common experiences after working with my colleagues or with me.

Here is a small sampling of some people—not my patients and mostly folks in the public eye—who have reversed visual issues, including myopia (nearsightedness), presbyopia (often referred to as inevitable in "old age"), astigmatism, and other eye conditions:

- Christine Northrup, MD, reversed her refractive eye issue with huge doses of vitamin C.
- The founder of MindValley, Vishen Lakhiani, has a fascinating story about reversing his astigmatism.
- Jacob Liberman, OD; Sam Berne, OD; Steve Gallup, OD; Marc Grossman, OD; Janet Goodrich, PhD; and Peter Grunwald of *EyeBody* fame, among many others, reversed some or all of their myopia and other visual issues. Some incorporate dietary interventions, including diet and supplements, and all use other techniques and lifestyle changes that could include optometric vision therapy and a variety of visual, physical, emotional, and spiritual techniques.

- Kevin May, author, community organizer, and transformational coach, has taken an active role in controlling his type 1 diabetes with the whole-food, plant-based lifestyle, or close to it!
- Ocean Robbins (in the fabulous Food Revolution Summit he cofacilitates with his father, John Robbins, son of Robbins of Baskin-Robbins) has presented many testimonials of people whose eye conditions have improved once they've committed to a plant-based diet.

There are many books and articles written on control and reversal of chronic illnesses that affect the health of our eyes. Examples include heart disease, adult-onset diabetes (type 2), obesity, and cancer. Many more autoimmune diseases that are often classified as "without cause," such as fibromyalgia and lupus, are included. See *The China Study, Defeating Diabetes, The Kick Diabetes Cookbook, Goodbye Lupus*, and many more books. Check out the works of Caldwell and Rip Esselstyn, Gabriel Cousens, John and Ocean Robbins, Will Tuttle, Victoria Moran, and on and on. The chronic illnesses mentioned above that develop over time often have negative impacts on our eyes and our entire visual systems. Eyesight, insight, and vision issues must be reversing themselves on a fairly consistent basis along the way when people step into a healthier lifestyle. Where are the studies? Are you waiting for the studies to shift your focus?

Reversing Changes in the Back of the Eye Related to Adult-Onset Diabetes (Type 2) and Hypertension

Plant-powered-author Rip Esselstyn showed me some stunning ocular fundus (back of the eye) photos one day, following a book signing of his I attended. He showed me these photos because we had been chatting about my background as an eye doctor, and he thought I'd be interested. The stunning images were incredibly revealing. Rip opened his laptop computer in the entrance and exit lobby of a Whole Foods Market in Pittsburgh, Pennsylvania (he was on his way to catch an Uber), and showed me two retinal photos of the back of the same person's eye—before and after being on the diet he recommends, a whole-food, plant-based (WFPB) diet. The first photo showed a very diseased eye, showing changes that occur in the back of the eye as type 2 diabetes progresses. The second photo was taken of the same eye after a period of time on the WFPB diet. The second photo was of the same, now very healthy, eye, which was free of blood vessel bleeding and free of other retinal changes that occur with this chronic disease! I was completely amazed and delighted at the same time!

In conversation with Dr. Michael Klaper at the 2023 North American Vegan Society (NAVS) conference in Johnstown, Pennsylvania, I learned about Dr. Walter Kempner's work in reversing both diabetic and hypertensive retinopathy. According to Dr. Michael Greger, "The reversal of blindness due to hypertension and diabetes with Dr. Kempner's rice and fruit diet demonstrates the power of diet to exceed the benefits of the best modern medicine and surgery have to offer."[7]

Reversing Meibomian Gland Dysfunction

This is a story of the miraculous reversal of meibomian gland dysfunction (MGD). The meibomian glands are small openings—lots of them—on the rims of our upper and lower eyelids, at the base of our eyelashes. Sometimes these glands, which create part of our tear

---

[7] https://nutritionfacts.org/video/can-diabetic-retinopathy-be-reversed/, accessed July 16, 2023.

film that lubricates our eyes, become clogged up and do not function properly. When this is the case, a person can notice dry eyes or burning, itchy, sticky, watery red eyes; have intermittent blurry vision; feel as if they have something in their eyes (foreign body sensation); be more prone to styes (chalazions); and be light sensitive. This eye issue is caused by stressed-out eyes and a taxed visual system, which cause many functionally related eye distress symptoms as well. Yes, vision therapy can help to reverse these situations. But people often reach out because they have an acute situation, so the acute situation is addressed first, using conventional treatments.

I know of a beautiful woman (not my patient or client) who had a major case of meibomian gland dysfunction, or MGD. She had "tried everything" to reverse this troubling condition. This woman had been to a myriad of eye doctors and other types of practitioners. Nothing seemed to help her recover from her MGD. And she was not interested in using the conventional treatment of ointments, warm compresses, or steroids for the rest of her life. Miracles are occurring at Hippocrates Wellness (formerly called Hippocrates Health Institute, or HHI), in West Palm Beach, Florida. During the course of the three-week Life Transformation raw, organic living-foods program at Hippocrates Wellness (which included spa treatments, exercise, and many other types of detoxification modalities, including eating raw living foods and drinking shots of wheatgrass juice and other green juices and salads daily, as well as sessions with the resident wellness psychologists and group sessions), her MGD completely disappeared. She was absolutely thrilled!

At the annual Kraskin Invitational Skeffington Symposium (KISS) in January 2023, my esteemed optometric colleague Samantha Slotnick, OD, commented, "There are a lot of ways we feed ourselves, and light is one of the ways we feed ourselves." We hopefully feed ourselves with sunlight in many forms every day. The biophoton light energy we ingest directly from the sun is one way we absorb light. Another way is through the food we eat. In the nutrition section, we'll explore some of the ways to increase our intake of biophoton light energy through what we eat and drink!

Holistic and Integrative Approaches to Enlivening Consciousness

For most of my solo career, prior to 2020, I was a doctor and optometric vision therapist seeing patients mostly one-on-one in my physical office space. For me, that approach to patient and client care has changed in recent years. Are the reasons obvious as to why? I now work mostly virtually, sometimes in a hybrid fashion. In working with patients and clients, I collaborate with colleagues from all over the world to advocate for those I work with to be sure they are carefully cared for from the inside out.

What if one is not inclined to launch into a full vision therapy program? What then? Over these past few years, I've helped people ease into vision therapy often called optometric vision training or neuro-optometric visual rehabilitation. My approach most recently has been to offer some of my services in an educational format. That way, a person can ease into their awakening slowly and comfortably over time. They can include daily practices little by little, mindfully integrating these new habits into their lifestyle.

There are many levels and layers to shifting our visual awareness and enlivening our consciousness. Shifting visual awareness with grace and ease follows developing flexibility within our total body action system. The process continues throughout our lives. The appropriate eyeglass prescription, lenses, prisms, syntonics (color and light therapy), and other tools and techniques used to facilitate change in a person's visual-spatial world are a large part of what is offered in the field of total holistic vision care. For now, I've been working with colleagues through referrals back and forth on that part of the equation.

Change rises from within us. Flexibility and shifting levels of awareness of both a motivated practitioner and a patient or client play a critical role in the ultimate outcome of how we express ourselves in the world and cocreate the more beautiful world we all know in our hearts is possible!

MOVEMENT

- ❖ Moving within through movement explorations
- ❖ Developmental movement patterns that underlie vision development
- ❖ Somatic movement therapy and education
- ❖ Feeling ourselves from the inside out and outside in

Chapter 5

MOVING WITHIN

Movement

We are all movers and shakers
Movement is natural
In stillness, there is movement
Moving Beyond Sit Still!
Moving into the excitement of what's inside.
No more hiding
What has been waiting so very patiently
Unfurling
Uncurling
Opening to the signs of the
Divine

Birthing Embodiment and Movement

*H*OW DO WE ENLIVEN OUR consciousness by moving back inside to feel ourselves, to *embody* ourselves from the inside out, remembering who we are? From swimming about in the womb to moving through the birth canal—we move our bodies in our environments. Many move freely from conception, in utero, through and following birth, and throughout the first year of life and childhood. If we're lucky, on our way to standing up, we easily creep, crawl, sit, and bear-walk (among many other movement patterns) while moving through the patterns underlying standing on our own two feet (verticality). In our early years, we experience, through movement, fundamental interwoven patterns that set the stage for future development. We then walk, jump, hop, and skip through our visual-spatial world.

Some of us are not so fortunate. We are confined in ways that do not allow for freedom of movement. We may habituate unhealthy patterns and become disconnected from our own body sensations. The ease or difficulty in self-embodiment and deep, balanced connection in our visual-spatial worlds after birth and throughout our lives depends on many factors, including the physical and emotional state of our mothers, caregivers, and families and our relationship with cultural mores and the world at large.

Your Movement Influences List

Would you like to explore expanding your movement vocabulary (not just in words but in actions) to connect more deeply within? If so, birth a list of what you feel may have influenced how your body moves through space in these present moments. Then experience some or all of the movement explorations in this section.

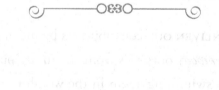

Beginner's Mind Movement Exploration

The experiential movement exploration that follows is for the beginner. Let's consider ourselves all beginners. Whether you've been a mover and shaker your whole life or you are just becoming involved in the movement world on any level, this activity is for you! The inspiration for this sequence comes from my nursery schoolteacher at the University of Maryland experimental nursery and my kindergarten schoolteacher. Both created nap times for us little ones. We were instructed to roll out our mats and lie down to take a rest.

Your Turn!

Find a comfortable space on the ground. Roll out a blanket, a yoga mat, or your choice of padding on a flat, welcoming surface. Lie down on your back. Place a folded blanket, a pillow, or another thin layer of cloth beneath the back of your head so your face plane is parallel to the sky and your chin is not pitched upward. Feel yourself fully supported by the earth. Scan your body. Feel your body, your soma. Release. Relax. Feel the tone of your body.

Listen to what your body is telling you. In the stillness of your inner ecosystem, notice the curves in your spine and the natural curve of your occiput (at the lower part of the bottom of your skull) as you rest on the smooth surface. Visualize and feel the incredible strength of your bones and all the beautiful curves in your spinal column resting on the floor, supported by the earth. Remember your delicate spinal cord coursing through the inside of your spinal column. Then let go of your thoughts, and feel your insides swimming. Remember the fluids, the ocean within you, the fascia (connective tissue), and the ligaments.

Take time each day to rest for a few minutes, or twenty minutes or more, on the back of your body.

At One With a Tree

Visualize yourself standing and leaning the back of your body against a tree, being fully supported from the center of Mother Gaia through the soles of your feet to the tips of your toes and heels; all the way to your tail and head; through your arms to your fingers; up through your torso and neck to your mouth, nose, ears, and eyes; and through the top of your skull out into the cosmos. Feel your strength and connectedness to the universe All Ways! Then turn around and hug that tree. Feel the connection from your naval chakra (your belly button area) to the strong tree trunk, the energy of the soles of your feet reaching down through the deep tree roots to the center of the earth, and your crown reaching up once again to all corners of the earth and out into the cosmos. And so it is.

The BEcoming

The depth of movement
for me
goes beyond words
from vibration
in sound
comes the word
yet, beyond words
Becoming
Movement
The expression of our souls
through
Dance
Singing Sounds
play
cartwheels
walking
running
and
in silent vibration or
in the unity of community

dancing some more!

For me

in my experience

Movement is words and actions

yet transcends

through inner and outer vision

into

Be ing ness

A Practical Experiential Introduction to Somatics, or the Sense of Feeling Ourselves through Our Feet!

Following the recommendation of my eldest daughter, Laura, I went into a local outdoors shop one day to look for some walking and hiking shoes. I'd been trying on shoes of that sort for many months to replace my two pairs of decades-old hiking boots. A young woman named Madeline began to assist me. And what a fun experience the outing became!

Madeline showed me several pairs of comfortable shoes— comfortable enough on my feet. But then I stood up, and my feet and body rolled forward, so I told Madeline those shoes were like standing on rocking chairs. She told me she had recently run 10 miles in those shoes on the Rachel Carson Trail. I explained I did not want shoes that told me what to do or how to move my body. I wanted shoes that listened to me and allowed me to move the way I liked to move, so my natural coordination could shine through. Then I mentioned that I had just participated in and spoken at a four-day conference with others who were certified in somatics and that I was incredibly sensitive to my soma, my body, in that moment and wondered why so many shoes were so hard and inflexible. She told me people liked solid, inflexible soles, which made them feel solid, safe, and in control.

"Whhaaaatttt?" I said. "That explains *everything* that's going on in our culture and world right now! The rigidity. The stiffness. The disconnection from our selves and the earth. It explains all of the cognitive dissonance."

She laughed out loud! I sure did enjoy her light spirit while I was looking for shoes that day. Next, I told Madeline I was interested in shoes with *flat*, flexible soles. She began talking about how most of the shoes were designed with a half-inch drop. *Drop*—that was a term I'd never heard before. I told her I didn't like high heels. I'm a tall woman, and high heels mess with one's poise, posture, and soma, no matter a person's size. More chuckling followed!

Then I asked her if she'd ever heard of Earth Shoes. She had not. Have you ever heard of them? Those shoes, introduced in 1970 three weeks before the first Earth Day in New York City, had heels that were lower than the metatarsal. My husband said he had a pair of them in college and loved them. Then Madeline taught me about the hard plastic plate currently placed in the arches of most hiking-type boots—to be sure one is "supported" and does not get poked by rocks or other unknown sharp objects on hiking and running trails. In my imagination, I saw and felt my bare feet on the soil, grass, or sand or flipping through the water.

This story illustrates that our culture at large is simply not somatically aware. In this section of this book, we'll explore some didactic and experiential detail about the meaning of movement in our lives and the lives of all generations to follow.

Some Movement Herstory

Forms of writing, forms of listening and hearing, forms of SEEING, and forms of visualizing and processing are all forms of BEing in movement.

I've explored and embodied many movement forms in my life thus far. A partial chronology follows, beginning with my formal movement experiences with specific vocabularies. My movement training began with the formal movement vocabularies of Ballet, Israeli Folk Dance, Modern Dance, and Flamenco.

Here I mention some of the teachers I've crossed paths with and with whom I've learned to experience flow in movement and grace throughout life. In the late 1980s, I took a weeklong developmental movement course with the incredible Bonnie Bainbridge Cohen at the School for Body-Mind Centering®, or BMC®. We were on the floor in a huge gymnasium with about a hundred others and lots of physioballs all around us. In between the deep work, we had so much fun flying across the space, moving from one physioball to another without touching the ground! Flying amid the depths. Right where we are now in these movements. Pause. Breathe. Blink. Be Present. BE. Ahhh!

The developmental movement BMC week was a pivotal moment in my life and work. It was the beginning of a time (that continues to this day for many of us) of deep recovery from formal academics and formal movement modalities. The Body-Mind Centering (BMC) experience was like none of my other somatic experiences. Even now, at age eighty years young, Bonnie leaves time in Zoom class for questions but says she hopes she does not have any answers. She hopes the questions trigger us to practice. Experience. Learning through Doing and BEing with the material. She emphasizes her discoveries that have come through her own self-inquiries over more than the past sixty years. She emphasizes the importance of patience; self-inquiry; studying with family, friends, and colleagues; and learning from all of it. She has been researching her own embodied self for sixty years! In this time, she has generously shared her work with thousands of people all around the globe.

More recently, I've become certified as a somatic movement educator and therapist through the Center for BodyMindMovement and the amazing Mark Taylor, the school's founder. And I've been studying with the incredible Lisa Clark, founder of EmbodiYoga™ and the director of the newly formed Body-Mind Centering® Yoga Immersion Series. Mark Taylor and Lisa Clark were both trained as Body-Mind Centering teachers at the School for Body-Mind Centering.

Incorporating developmental movement practice into my optometry practice for self-preservation of my and my patients' eyesight and insight and for the good of the collective became me.

Most recently, I've had the honor of crossing paths with the Association of Hanna Somatic Educators (AHSE), first by presenting at their annual conference in April 2022 on "Vision and Somatics" and then becoming certified in Hanna somatic yoga with the legendary Eleanor Criswell Hanna, whose late husband, Thomas Hanna, coined the term *somatics*.

What Is Somatics?

Soma, the root of the word *somatics*, means "body." Many health practitioners, such as functional, developmental, behavioral optometrists, chiropractors, osteopaths, occupational therapists (Bonnie Bainbridge Cohen), homeopaths, and other integrative practitioner movers and shakers, worked within the context of the body, or soma, throughout the twentieth century. Some of these practitioners were integrative practitioners before "integrative" was a thing. For example, some worked with both conventional and alternative (not well known in mainstream culture) modalities, such as spinal manipulation, herbalism, and homeopathy. Because of my deep love of movement and my understanding of many movement disciplines, I have been integrating developmental movement work into my own daily practice and as a foundation for natural eyesight improvement for decades.

In my view, those early wellness practitioners, on a conscious or subconscious level, were rebelling or revolting against the normalization of Victorian-era nonmovement, or stillness. For example, a child moving around in their seat in a classroom setting was, and is now, frowned upon. I'm referring to the ants-in-their-pants syndrome. A "good" little girl or boy stayed still and in line by following directions and not deviating from the straight and narrow. This was what brought, and currently (often) brings, reward to an individual.

Embodied somatics is the study of the movement patterns of the living body, the study of how we sense ourselves from the inside out. Maintaining flexibility and resilience in our bodies throughout our lifetimes is imperative for us to move comfortably and easily during our daily movement (a.k.a. activities of daily living) and to age gracefully. Staying active and mobile and moving easily from head and eyes to fingertips, pelvis, tailbone, and toe tips are essential ingredients in our day-to-day activities and a wonderful way to preserve our eyesight and vision until the day we pass into another realm!

I have been questioning the true roots of the field of somatics. The field is based on the movement patterns of the plant and animal kingdoms that are naturally programmed within the cells of our bodies, in our RNA and DNA. The great masters of the past and present have deeply studied movement patterns in the physical and sometimes ethereal (nonphysical) world to reach their conclusions and teach their discoveries through their own deep experience of embodiment, their somatic experiencing, the experience of deeply sensing, feeling, and knowing their own bodies from the inside out. Each person's soma (body) is unique, and each person on the planet will consciously or unconsciously develop their own rhythms in life to either simply survive or thrive.

From my perspective, the study of somatics grew out of the study

An Origin of the Term Somatics

Thomas Hanna wrote a book called *Somatics* in 1988. Hanna's work was based on the work of both F. M. Alexander and Moshe Feldenkrais. Hanna studied with Moshe Feldenkrais for three years and was a certified Feldenkrais practitioner. He participated in and directed the first US Feldenkrais Method practitioner training in 1976. Thomas Hanna coined the term *somatics* in 1976 and specifically worked with reversing what he called sensory motor amnesia, or SMA. SMA is forgetting—and not sensing or feeling—the movement capabilities of our body. We form unhealthy habit patterns in our neuromuscular structures and beyond. These improper, uncomfortable, self-sabotaging habit patterns (including social, emotional, and spiritual patterns that are unresolved) are reflected in and through our somas and create pain!

of plant and animal development and unobstructed natural and normal human development and through the study of movement, ritual, and dance in indigenous cultures. Somatics is now threaded through the dance and movement world and now, in our day, reveals itself (is taught) through the sensibilities of some, both professionally trained and not, in the fields of health and wellness.

Embodiment, Somatics, and Movement Disciplines in a General Sense

The terms *embodiment*, *somatics*, and *movement* are tricky to define in words, as they are experiential in nature. What does it mean to be the embodied version of yourself? To feel yourself from the inside out? How do we BEcome ourselves, our embodied selves? The movement patterns in our bodies, beginning in utero and as part of our DNA and RNA genetic natures, are both intrinsic behavioral reflex patterns and learned through the experience of interacting with the world. The experience of our true natures, the felt sense of ourselves, comes from taking the time we need to experience ourselves. Quietly. Experientially.

Movement Explorations—Coming Back to My Soma and Grounding by Moving through the Woods

I had just come out of the woods. Earlier that day, our family had attended a funeral. The ninety-eight-year-old matriarch of my husband's mother's side of the family had passed into the next phase of her BEing. Bless her soul.

To reharmonize myself with myself, others, the earth, and the cosmos, I took a walk in the woods. Why reharmonize? Why take the time on a daily or, ultimately, moment-by-moment basis to come back to yourself? Why remind yourself of what complete and total harmony with self feels like? Because that's how we're most in touch with the self we're meant to be and how to be in our highest vibrational octave, our highest ability to serve. I walked mindfully, sometimes leading with my toes, my tiptoes, stepping gently on the soft earthen path, and then wrapping my arms around a few favorite deciduous trees, first an oak and then a tulip poplar. I felt the physicality of the beautifully textured bark, breathing, blinking, BEing with the tree. Breathing with the tree. Condensing and expanding, arching and flexing with the rhythm of the xylem and phloem of the central core of the tree, flowing with my breath through my spine.

What do you do to reconnect with the ground of your BEing?

Union, Birth, and Development: An Exploration

We Are Born: Our Development

As Sentient Beings, as Human Beings, and Visually, our development is spiralic and continuous in the universe from birth to death to rebirth. The cycles continue. On and on and on.

We begin on the physical plane with egg and sperm. Then comes the dance of the union of sperm with egg. With penetration and fertilization, we become the zygote, the first of the union of our being. And then the blastula becomes the embryo and fetus. So much development is occurring during these early moments. The emergence of many of the primitive reflexes is rooted in our early in utero development.

In our early development in utero, our bodies are in the form of three layers: the endoderm, the innermost layer; the mesoderm, the middle layer; and the ectoderm, the outermost layer. The front of our bodies (front body) arises from the endoderm, the middle part of the body arises from the mesoderm, and the back of our bodies (back body and nervous system) arises from the ectoderm.

The Emerging of a Humyn Being

When born vaginally, we emerge through the birth canal and birth process using the movement patterns of (through expression of) the early reflexes we have developed in utero. In utero, we develop the movement patterns of pushing against the walls of our mother's womb with feet, tail, back, head, and hands, experiencing the deep *yielding* into the womb waters and *pushing* and then yielding back into the tonicity of ourselves within the protected, watery womb space.

We move, preferably headfirst, through the yielding and pushing experience into the first inklings of *reaching and pulling* headward through the birth canal. With the energetic movements of our mother and Source, we birth ourselves, emerging into the air and earth space outside of our mother's womb. As land BEings, we pull back into our fetal pose, with our hands fisted, for a long while, coddled, hugging inward, and sleepy, as we recover from our birth. We Breathe. In the beginning, our eyes stay closed for many hours a day.

∞YIELD YIELD YIELD YIELD YIELD YIELD YIELD ∞
∞PUSH PUSH PUSH PUSH PUSH PUSH PUSH∞
∞REACH REACH REACH REACH REACH
REACH REACH∞
∞PULL PULL PULL PULL PULL PULL PULL∞

An Experiential Moment—to Move into a Sense of What It Was like When You Were in the Womb

Being Development.
Being on this planet.
Doing.
On this planet. Inside our Mother.
In these moments. Being inside ourselves.
The cells, the fascia, the bones, the resilient stories of our hearts.
Softening. Into Gel. The gel-like substance of just below our skin.
The primitive streak, the head and tail revealing themselves
are the first gleaming glistening gleanings of our Selves.

The Importance of Floor Time

The time we spend on the floor, on all sides of our bodies, during our first year of life is critical to our whole-body development and critical to our visual development. Bonding with the earth on all sides of our bodies—back, belly, and sides—is absolutely critical. Tummy time is really a thing. An imperative! Time on our backs, sides, and bellies is not just for babies but for all of us at any age and in whatever shape we are in.

Many of us were not placed on the floor, on the earth, in the grass, or in the sand often, if at all, during our babyhood years. Why? Germaphobia? Did we think it was best to hold our children always in

Floor-Time Tip: Belly on Earth

Of utmost importance is being sure your baby spends lots of time on the floor with belly grounded to the earth, preferably with you on the floor right with them. Look at them directly in the eyes, and engage them with visually interesting stimulation, so they develop their entire visual systems symbiotically with their body tone with homeostatic ease.

Look into their eyes, and play! Rock and roll on the ground, all around with visual targets: soft toys, your pets, bugs, and the dust balls! Okay, so maybe not the dust balls. Clean those up.

Give your child the gift to Be and to Play while supported by Mother Gaia! Laying children gently on the earth, sand, and uneven surfaces is also an experiential imperative. What follows naturally? The development of a strong central core, resilience, and much less likelihood of development of "refractive error" (and all kinds of other visual issues), as it's classically called in the field of eye care.

At any age, we can move back onto the floor on a mat, blanket, carpet, or other soft surface. Take time to witness yourself, and breathe. Breathe fully. This connection when slowly and mindfully moving from one side of your body to the next, making contact with Mother Earth, is primal and brings us back to our somas to reconnect with ourselves and others more authentically.

an upright position so they could "see" what was going on and so we and others could see them? Did we not understand the importance of time to simply be on the ground? Were you placed in a bouncer or walker as a child? Were you held for your entire first year because you were a colicky child and would not settle down unless held? Were you often in a playpen?

If we were not given time and space on the earth to connect to the ground, explore, and play as babies, it's not too late. It is important to spend time on all the surfaces of your body in many positions daily. At all ages, we benefit from spending time on the floor, bonding with the earth and exploring our Inner Vision!

Experience the Four Sides of Your Body Each Day!

What you notice in your movement may be very subtle. And that's fine. Take time each day on each of the four sides of your body. Begin on the back of your body for a few minutes. Then gently roll onto one side of your body, make yourself comfortable, and bring your breath to conscious awareness. Then roll onto the other side of your body and repeat. Then roll onto your belly, resting your forehead on your stacked hands, and come back to your breath once again. Roll gently back onto one side, yield, and press one or both hands into the earth to sit up. In under ten minutes a day, you will become a new person over time!

How long do I continue with this ten-minute activity, you ask? Well, for me, it's been such a satisfying activity with infinite variations that it's an activity I do every day, often many more times than once a day. And I love it. As I've mentioned, most recently, it's taken me back to my nursery school days, when we were gifted blissful nap time on mats. One day, while doing this deeply grounding activity, I became a nursery school student once again. I felt the energy of being a small child held by Mother Earth very deeply. It was and is profound as we move back home inside ourselves in relationship to our mother, Mother Earth!

Traveling More Deeply into Embodiment through Your Breath and Eyes

Take some time right now. Put down this book or the electronic device you're reading from, and be there on your back on the surface of the earth, either on a mat, directly on the floor, on the carpet, or on a blanket. Feel yourself there. Notice your breath, and breathe naturally. Without judgment. Simply Be there. Bring awareness to your inhale and exhale. Your natural rhythm. Appreciate yourself in these precious moments. Yield the back of your body into the earth. Then release your weight to the earth a little bit more.

Observe your breath. Perhaps notice the condensing of your unified diaphragm (thorax from clavicular area to pelvic region) with inhalation and the expansion of the organs inside your torso with each exhalation. Or do you notice the expansion of the front of your body—your belly, your thorax, your throat, your head, and your eyes—with each inhale and the downward movement or flow of your front body, including your eyes, with each exhale? What sensations do you feel? How are you breathing? What are you noticing? What feels most natural for you? Is there a right or wrong way to breathe?

What is your experience of breathing at different times of the day or night? How do you experience your breathing when you are around different groups of people or different individuals? How about with your loved ones?

Inhale. Exhale. Continue consciously breathing for a full minute. Notice the rhythm of your breath without judgment. Close your eyelids gently, and inhale and exhale. Do you notice if your breathing pattern changed in any way? Now squeeze your closed eyelids gently. Did that affect your breathing pattern? Open your eyes, and look around. Flutter your eyelids. What do you notice? Ahhhh!

Movement, Exercise, Health, and Wellness

The dear late Tasso Spanos, trigger point myofascial release therapist extraordinaire, understood how important it is to move in all the planes of the body. He taught me about the work of physicians Janet Travell, MD, and David Simons, MD, who wrote volumes about trigger point myofascial release. Releasing trigger points releases congested fascia and fascial knots, and this allows for reoxygenation and increased blood flow in static tissues. Tasso encouraged those he worked with to move through a series of movement exercises daily.

Consider designing for yourself a daily movement routine to keep your body temple supple. My father understood this too. One of his favorite phrases was "Keep moving!" So very important!

Stasis (inactivity) over time leads to dis-ease. Stabilized retinal images fade. When we are static and devoid of movement, we die. When our eyes do not move, we don't see.

Toe Walking as Many Children's Stories

It seems that toe walking and unintegrated developmental movement patterns are intrinsically related. I continue to wonder where children's and adults' toe walking comes from. How old were they when they began walking? From the moment they began to walk, did they toe walk? Does toe walking have to do with how much time children had on their bellies, sides, and backs, connecting to the earth with torso and limbs, in that first year? How does limited ground-exploration time tie in with toe walking? How often were the children being held when they could have been on their backs, sides, and bellies, kinesthetically exploring their connections to the ground with their newly landed soul?

Can toe walking be an extension of a hyperactive startle reflex habituated from trauma in the womb, trauma during birth, or postbirth trauma? BEing confined to a "playpen" cage? And what does early development have to do with ultimately developing refractive error? What might this have to do with developing winged scapulae and a "straight" spine? I'd say the total load theory is a factor in developing asymmetry and synchronous movement habit patterns. An accumulation of troubling movement habits can be seen as gifts to be shifted through once one's life practices become rooted in embodied movement practices.

Embodiment (Musings)

What is it to FEEL yourself in each waking moment?
And how does that transfer to our behavior, to our Being here Now?
But wait—if we are awake and aware and feeling
ourselves in each waking moment,
what does that mean, anyway?
The possibilities are infinite!

Being
Conscious
Consciousness
SUCH A GIFT!

Eyesight and Movement: The Interweaving

Those formative years and who we become. How does our eyesight develop as we become? And what do the conditions in the classroom and on the playground have to do with our visual development? A lot!

Questions to Ponder

- Where are we in our somatic development as adults or young children or older children or elders? Why should we care?
- Why is it important to move a lot each and every day we are alive?
- How can we get moving?
- What kind of movement is best for us at various stages of life?
- What does movement and how we move and carry ourselves have to do with eyesight and vision?

My particular interest most recently has been with educating those in the somatic world about the connection to vision and educating those in the vision world about somatics.

Chapter 6

EMBODYING OUR EYESIGHT AND VISION THROUGH EXPERIENTIAL EMBODIED MOVEMENT AS THE BASIS OF VISION DEVELOPMENT AND NATURAL EYESIGHT IMPROVEMENT

In 2022, I presented at the Association for Hanna Somatic Educators (AHSE) Conference. In this presentation, both didactic and experiential, I emphasized how our entire body system—our active somas in body, mind, and spirit—is the basis of natural eyesight improvement.

Eleanor Criswell Hanna, during the Q&A, reiterated, "So are you saying that the somatic work is the basis of natural eyesight improvement?" She then reinforced with the participants of the conference that the practice of embodied somatics is indeed the basis of natural eyesight improvement. Eleanor's PhD dissertation was dedicated to eye movements and visual processing.

As we consider and embody the entire visual system, we include visualization and the embodiment and integration of our nervous systems with all the other body systems. These other systems include but are not limited to the organs, blood, lymph, sweat and tears, muscles, bones, glands, hormones, cells, ligaments, skin, proprioception, interoception, and exteroception. From our groundedness in embodiment, we move confidently through our visual-spatial world, our environment.

What other systems of our bodies, minds, emotions, and spirits would you add to the list? Add to the mix. You have so much to add!

Waking Up

Waking up
To the understanding
That how we see is rooted in movement
We must move freely
In our bodies
In each moment
In order to See clearly!

What Is the Relationship between Movement, Eyesight, and Vision?

Mindful movement is an imperative for enhancing verbal communication and preserving overall fluidity, ease, and grace of movement from head to eyes, through the visual pathway, to tail, toes, and fingertips throughout your lifetime. When we reawaken our full body movement patterns, we enliven our eyesight and vision, including our awareness and insights into who we are and what we are here on this planet for in these incredibly powerful, transformational moments.

Fixational eye movements (moving our eyes as we look from one spot to another) relate to our overall body movements. Our eye movements are multifaceted and include vergences, smooth pursuits, saccades, the vestibular-ocular reflex, fixation, and more. Stabilized retinal images fade. In other words, if our eyes were not moving (which they always are, at least at the level of micromovements), we would not be able to see.

When our visual systems are integrated with our bodies, minds, and spirits, we lead our movements and actions from the wisdom of our eyesight and visual systems. This integration includes gross and subtle eye movements; visualization and insight; and the integration of our senses, our feelings, and our actions. We literally learn to see shape and form and understand the context surrounding shapes, forms, and patterns over time through movement. So moving—being allowed to move and allowing ourselves to move—is critical in humyn development.

This entire movement section is an introduction to experiential movement practice that works at the root of human eyesight and visual development. Perhaps you have not "seen" eyesight and vision from this perspective yet.

There are many movement patterns and sequences to explore. We'll begin with a series of movements that benefit the reestablishment of body integration and visual awareness. If you are not familiar with movement vocabulary and yoga poses, you might want to skip this section!

We'll begin by working with our midline, from tail to head and head to tail. This is the imaginary line that runs up and down our bodies and is ultimately the center line of our verticality once we stand up, usually sometime in the first year of our lives. Movement toward and away from our belly in this vertical-body-dimension orientation of our body is referred to as *homologous movement patterns.*

A Developmental Movement Series Based in Homologous Movements

The upcoming series of homologous movements (symmetrical movements of both arms, both legs, and upper and lower body) begins to:

- support integrated overall body movement patterns
- rock and roll our eyes and visual system (moving eyes up and down, in and out [toward and away from our bodies])

- enhance eye coordination along our midline, looking from our bodies out into the distance and vice versa (near-to-far focus and vice versa)
- enhance, develop, and preserve depth perception and visual-spatial awareness

There are many movement patterns that are both therapeutic and excellent for daily practice to keep our bodies, minds, and spirits tuned. What follows is a thumbnail sketch of a series of movements I developed as a blending of movement modalities I've studied and, often, become certified in over the decades. I share details and detailed combinations of these developmental movement sequences with those I work with (individuals and groups) to varying degrees, depending upon where a person is in their development for whatever reason.

There are many developmental patterns, including sponging and navel radiation and prevertebrate, that are called basic neurocellular patterns. In the 1980s, Bonnie Bainbridge Cohen called them basic neurological patterns. She researched, named, and organized her somatic BMC body of work beginning in 1963, when she first read that there were four vertebrate patterns: spinal, homologous, homolateral, and contralateral. Yield-and-push and reach-and-pull are also processes she identified and named. See Bonnie Bainbridge Cohen's book *Basic Neurocellular Patterns: Exploring Developmental Movement* to explore further.

I know that you are opening
the door for many people.

—Bonnie Bainbridge Cohen

The facilitation of natural eyesight improvement through visual toning and visual awareness is based in developmental movement and reflex patterns. Overall, it is an incredible sequence that helps both with full body, mind, and spiritual development and redevelopment and with maintenance of lifelong resilience—depending on how it is used and how it is offered to you. Preferably, a program is offered as a one-on-one, individualized clinical series. Individuals work with the series in different ways with different entry points, depending on where in the sequence need arises.

I created this series over the course of my career and was greatly influenced by my experiences in the world of developmental movement practices and my observations of my babies and other babies.

The Basic Movement Sequence

This particular series begins with visual awareness while rocking from head to tail and from tail to head in a loose form of the fetal position known as child's pose in yoga. We then move onto our bellies and through a series of belly-down yoga poses, including a gentle belly-down backbend (integrating eye and hand movement patterns). Then to all fours. All throughout the sequence, we bring attention to our eyes and visual system in various ways. This is an introduction to a full developmental movement sequence. There are infinite possible variations to explore on all sides of one's body and in all levels and dimensions in space (somatic exercises and yoga postures) along the way. There is no specific end to the series—other than eventually getting up to walk and ultimately exploring space through jumping, hopping, skipping, running, dancing, prancing, and more on two legs, sometimes moving back and forth between different levels in space (swimming in place on the ground [lizard], table, cat, or cow moving into crawling, creeping, down dog, bear-walking, and more) with visually directed movement patterns. Often, this series is introduced very gradually over time. Sometimes the series is introduced all at once if a person is comfortable with the sequence of movements.

Allowing yourself to rest in between each part of the sequence for as long as necessary is part of the process so that you can eventually travel through the movement patterns with more confidence, ease, and grace.

As mentioned, throughout this movement sequence, we add eyesight and visual integration and include homolateral (one side of the body and then the other side of the body) and cross-lateral (a.k.a. contralateral) movement patterns, such as rolling slowly on the floor. We move through other patterns and eventually stand up on our own two feet! I'm happy to explore any of this work with you through consultation or through my other offerings.

Prepare your space with ample padding on your hard floor, mat, rug, or earth. Stack a few blankets or, if available, a mostly deflated Coregeous ball in the area where you'll be gently placing your head. Begin on the floor, with your belly facing the earth in a loose, elevated-from-the-floor embryonic or fetal position of your choice. Be aware of your breath throughout the series, and move as slowly and mindfully as possible.

Head-to-Tail Rocking

Begin in some form of the fetal child's pose, moving gently, with your belly down and facing parallel to the earth but not yet connecting to the earth. Where do you feel your breath moving through your body? Does your breath get stuck anywhere? Slow down. Be with that feeling on some or any level without judgment. Feeling this deep connection from head to tail can bring us back into the feeling of the womb space. Being breathed from within.

I like to begin in a version of the fetal (child's) pose with the front of my body facing the earth, my body folded with bent knees below my torso, and my tail in the air. (You can find child's pose and other yoga poses I refer to in yoga books or online.) When you arrange yourself in child's pose, be sure you are comfortable. If you cannot move comfortably into child's pose, be sure to begin in a modified position you are comfortable with by tucking in a combination of blankets and pillows or bolsters so your body is not suspended in midair but fully supported.

Release your forearms, and rest them down to the blanket, mat, rug, or earth in a comfortable position by the sides of your body. From the yielding and pressing of your forelegs, rock forward from tail to head as you gently lower your head to the floor. Adjust so you can easily rock onto the top of your head, connecting the celestial crown at the top of your head (the reflex point for the mammillary glands at the top of the head, terminology I learned from both Bonnie Bainbridge Cohen and Lisa Clark), the crown chakra, with the ground, the earth, gently through your spinal cord, softly, being aware of the fullness of your breath. Rockaby baby in the womb space …

Feel your organs deeply, including the

Assuring Your Comfort in Balasana (Child's Pose)

If you need to widen your knees, do so. Settle in deeply. Pad with blankets or other props if there are areas of your body, such as your ankles or knees, for example, that do not flex or bend easily yet as the front of your body bonds with the earth. Place a blanket between your bottom and your lower legs if that's where the padding is needed. Place a mostly deflated, spongy ball, such as a Gertie or Coregeous ball; a pillow; or a blanket on the floor where you will be placing your head.

105

organs of your eyes. Breathe into the bones of your head, including the bones surrounding your orbits, and breathe into the organs of your eyes.

Feel the connections throughout all your body systems from head to tail to head as you slowly and gently continue to rock back and forth from head to tail and tail to head. Yield and press into your forelegs, reaching and pulling with your head initiating. Yield and press with your head into the earth, and then reach back with your tail. Stay within your easy range of movement. Yield, push, reach, pull. These explorations can go on for portions of days, each time exploring different combinations of the numerous body systems in different combinations. Take a few more breaths. Then take a break by moving more deeply into your breath, noticing your inhalation and exhalation at your own pace. If that is enough movement for you, stop here, and rest back into child's pose with your breath. If you're ready for more movement, continue as detailed below.

Moving onto Your Belly

Head-to-Tail Rocking to Connecting to the Earth, Moving through Inchworm (Ashtanga Namaskara) and into Baby Cobra

From here, we can move directly onto our bellies; then into a baby Cobra (Bhujangasana) pose, or Head-Supporting-Neck Reflex, with central and peripheral eye movement patterns added; and then into the ATNR, or Eye-Hand-Mouth sequence (a.k.a. swimming in place, or lizard), or another exploration (not all detailed here).

Begin by rocking head to tail and tail to head, as in the above sequence. Your arms are not involved at first, so place your arms to the sides of your body, resting them gently on the ground. Come back to an awareness of your natural breath. Breathe fully from head to tail and tail to head.

Now place your hands, with palms facing downward, on the earth. Next, with your hands and arms yielding and pressing gently into the earth and sliding forward, gently ease your head forward at the same time with your face parallel to the earth. Allow your nose to skim across the floor, carpet, or blanket. (Note: Sticky mats are not used for this activity, as you cannot easily move forward on your belly on a sticky mat. You'll get stuck!) Slowly, mindfully, and as smoothly as possible, inch forward toward the ground. Then ever so gently extend your body onto your belly. Ahhh.

Stack your hands one above the other, and rest your forehead on your stacked hands. Extend your legs (with legs on the ground) and toes at a forty-five-degree angle from your body (Makrasana or Crocodile pose in yoga). Take a moment to breathe deeply. Or allow your legs to remain parallel or at some other comfortable angle. Breathe fully. Scan your body from head to toe, and release and relax as much as possible.

End here by moving back into child's pose for a few rounds of breath, or continue this short series by doing the following.

Moving into Cobra (Head-Supporting-Neck Reflex)

Continuing on your belly, bring your legs back into parallel. Place the palms of your hands on either side of your torso, near your armpit chest area. Yield and press (push) into the earth with the palms of your hands, gently raising your torso, leading with the crown of your head (the celestial crown) and eyes. Find something of interest to look at in front of you. Are you leading your head movement with your eyes or allowing your eyes to follow your head movement as you gaze beyond your nose along your midline? Try the movement both ways, and compare. Are you initiating the movement from another part of your body? Are you initiating from your entire torso? From your tail? Your feet? How are your eyes and visual system involved?

Gently lower yourself back down to the floor. Move in and out of this (cobra pose in yoga) sequence, breathing consciously a few times, sometimes initiating from your torso, all the while noticing if your eyes are leading or following the movement of your nose and head. Now, as you inhale and rise into the air, with your eyes, trace an imaginary line moving from your body away from yourself, and find something of interest to gaze at directly in front of you. As you exhale and move back down to your mat, rug, or blanket or the earth, follow that imaginary line again, moving toward your body. Notice how your body feels as you bond with the earth. Notice how and where your eyes settle. Notice how you feel.

Stop here, or move into the next section.

Table Pose

Next, move to all fours with your hands, knees, and forelegs in contact with the floor. Begin rocking headward and tailward. Rock gently. Gently. Ever so gently. Rock forward and backward slowly and mindfully, feeling the deeply parasympathetic head-to-tail connection. Deeply relaxing and deeply releasing. Head to tail. There's so much to explore head and eyes to tail that emerges from the primitive streak so very early in embryonic development. This original head-to-tail axis continues to develop in our fetal posture in utero, in the watery womb, and then outside the womb following birth.

Feel the connections even more viscerally as you slowly, luxuriously, and mindfully move between the cat and cow yoga poses. Move even more deeply into your parasympathetic (relaxing part of the) nervous system.

Now move back into extended child's pose (or supported child's pose with lots of padding so you feel fully supported) by extending both of your arms in front of you, yielding the front of your body into the earth, and then pressing your hands into the earth and reaching backward with your tailbone back toward your heels. With eyelids gently closed, breathe deeply, and appreciate the feeling of this relaxing position with the front of your body fully supported, your legs tucked under you, and the back of your body long and wide, from head to tail. Now release your arms, and place your arms by your sides. You are back in the womb space!

Begin by spending a few minutes in each part of the sequence. Increase the time frame to your level of comfort.

Our Early Development, a Recapitulation

What physical and behavioral factors affect our development in the womb and in the first years of our lives?

Defining Developmental Factors

- What were our mothers' movement patterns when we were in utero?

Powerful Mindful Micromovements

Eyesight and visual integration awareness micromovement patterns can be integrated into the movement sequence at any point. Don't overdo it. When you explore with your eyes and your vision as part of overall movement patterns or independently, be extra gentle with yourself. A little bit of gentle eye movement goes a long way when working with the delicate but very strong ocular (eye) muscles and the entire visual system. The eye muscles are about fifty times as strong as they need to be to move our eyes in any direction. There is a subtlety to the coordination component of the visual system, both the coordination of the two eyeballs and the coordination of the accommodation (focusing) and vergence (convergence and divergence, a.k.a. turning the eyes in and out) systems and the body, mind, emotion, and spirit components.

Eye movement and visual awareness cuing are a high-level activity, and we add these to sequences for exploration or therapeutic purposes.

- How were we treated as young babies and children?
- Were we encouraged to explore on our own?
- Were we placed on our bellies with lots of belly time or not?
- If we were encouraged to be on our bellies on the ground, were we with parents or caregivers directly across from us? Were they playing with us on the ground at eye level? Or were we placed in restrictive environments, such as cribs, strollers, and walkers, in which our bodies were not contacting the earth?
- Were we encouraged to stand by being held in a vertical position prior to the age of one and placed in walkers and bouncers?
- Did our parents or caregivers mistake our stepping reflex for our wanting to walk and position us vertically before we were developmentally ready to be placed in the vertical dimension for extended periods of time?

Resilience

Vision is learned by experience throughout our developmental lifetimes. As long as we are alive in this human physical body form, we are developing. Even when we resist and get set in our habit patterns, we are developing. We are developing in our aliveness but sometimes with huge gaps as we are living in conscious or subconscious inflexibility. This hurts us in many ways. We may not realize that our set patterns may be harming us from lack of movement, or irregular movement, and that this lack of flexibility leads to a lack of resilience.

There was one woman who survived the tragedy of the building collapse in Florida in 2021. She was so totally sensorily and motorically resilient and in tune with her body mind and Spirit, or Source, that when she saw cracks in the walls and ceiling of her apartment unit and heard the cracking sounds, she knew to move out of the way. And fast. She got out of the way and survived. She moved on.

How do we get out of our own way and then move on? What does that look like for you? How will you begin? Are you ready to begin right now? Yes, you are, because you are here reading these words! Wiggle your toes. Close your eyes tightly, and then release them again. Now breathe fully and exhale. There—you've done something for yourself to bring visual and overall awareness to yourself from head to toe! What do you know?

Visual Resilience Is Trainable

Our visual systems and our abilities to see vary widely and fall somewhere on the spectrum of optimal eyesight at any given moment in time. We have varying levels of resilience. And this level of resilience is trainable. It takes commitment, practice, and, often, lifestyle shifting. Remember not to judge yourself. Wherever individuals are on this spectrum of developing their eyesight to improve naturally is just where they're supposed to be in the now. And if you feel you'd like to improve your ability to see, you can absolutely do so!

The ability to see consistently with three-dimensional or single simultaneous binocular vision is an inner and outer reflection of our ability to comprehend—to understand with depth, clarity, and focus—our inner and outer world. It's why sometimes holistic optometrists are called developmental or behavioral optometrists. The way we "see" is the way we "BE," the way we move through the world. Literally and figuratively! And sometimes we're called neurodevelopmental optometrists. Why? As mentioned in the vision section, we work with what I like to call *soft neurological signs.* These soft neurological signs are behaviors, including eye, head, and body movements, observed by the practitioner that are subtly visible, or they can be observations that are not visible at all to an outside observer but are evident to the person themselves in some way.

Becoming a Mom Optometrist and an Optometric Vision and Movement Therapist

Giving Birth.
The experiences of this woman's lifetime.
Metaphorically, the experience of all of us now in these here moments as we reemerge in ways we never imagined possible in this form on earth at this moment in time.
What's old is new again and again and again.

When our firstborn was about one and a half, I took time off from my profession of optometry to be more fully present with our family. When I reemerged as a mom optometrist, my practice was—and is—me. This reemergence was after I spent ten or twelve years in our home with our children, enjoying every mothering moment with my husband and our local family and friends and traveling back and forth to my parents' and cousins' homes farther east and elsewhere.

Being. Being on the floor with our children and out in nature and traveling. And teaching Hebrew school, teaching Hebrew letters and words to second graders in our synagogue, barely knowing the letters myself. Facilitating Hadassah's Training Wheels program, Al Galgalim!

I reemerged occasionally with my optometry hat to do some consulting with the local high school hockey team. Some players' moms were seamstresses and created wonderful bean bag hockey pucks out of black fabric for the players to toss around with one another on a grassy field. The team worked with these bean bag pucks off the ice to increase their visual-spatial awareness to reach effectively beyond their kinesphere (beyond arm's reach), peripheral visual awareness, and reaction time. That all-encompassing vision-training experience (including the social component), especially for the goalies, transferred wonderfully once the athletes were back on the ice in the rink.

The journey continues for me as a mom; wife; sister; cousin; friend; community volunteer; and vision, movement, nutrition, nature, and spiritual consultant. And what a ride it has been! My practice as a Mom Optometrist Vision Therapist facilitating enlivening our consciousnesses was and is me.

What Is Your Practice?

We are all BEINGS of Light.
BEINGS of Light and Love.
How brightly do we allow ourselves to SHINE
at any given moment?
How are you moving
through your physical space?

Visually Directed Movement

If you take one thing from this section of the book, understand that Vision is Movement. In other words, movement is visually directed, stemming from our curiosity from our eyes and heads with our hands and feet and the integration of the other senses, the tone of our bodies, our organs, our full upper and lower extremities, and more. From the tips of our toes to the tips of our fingers to the tips of our noses and ears and everything in between, the integrated visual process is supported by the entire system. Movement is intrinsically visually directed when we consider the integrated definition of *VISION*. This definition is both specifically and broadly expanded upon in the vision section of this book.

The labyrinthine, semicircular canals in the ears are oriented in the same planes as the extraocular muscles. We move through space as our vision is developing from the inside out. As mentioned a few times, stabilized retinal images fade, meaning if our eyeballs were ever to be still, there would be no visual image coming through us from the outside in or the inside out to "see." In other words, without a formed retinal image, an image does not form in our brains for us to see. Embedded visual habits that are not serving us well can be unlearned and changed. The integrative movement sequence described above (when practiced daily over time and mentioned here only as a thumbnail sketch) is a shining example of the beginnings of how to work through visual differences or disabilities. And then we are more able to thrive!

The detailed definition of *VISION* includes moving through space physically, mentally, emotionally, and spiritually through integration of easy visual-spatial awareness, depth perception, tracking ability, near-far focus, cognitive ability, body, mind, and Spirit! We are human BE-ings, so we are always in motion and E-motion. As our habit patterns change, our bodies change. Structure changes with functional shifting. F. M. Alexander taught and spoke of the "Use" of the body, Feldenkrais developed Functional Integration and Awareness through Movement, and Hanna developed *somatics* exercises based on his understanding of the work of Feldenkrais as a Feldenkrais practitioner. Bonnie Bainbridge Cohen, the Bobaths, Lisa Clark, Mark Taylor, and many others teach us about embodied movement and awareness through movement.

I repeat: functional, behavioral, developmental, neurodevelopmental optometrists understand the concept of visually directed movement to varying degrees in their own bodies. From this inner awareness, my colleagues with expertise in these specialties use their tools of the trade, including lenses, prisms, and colored filters and equipment (Syntonics or optometric phototherapy), along with other tools and techniques expanded upon in the vision section, to alter the light entering a person's visual system through their eyes. People's postural responses shift based on light input.

When lenses, filters, or colored lights are applied, people's postures and behaviors shift. Take a moment to absorb that last sentence! The first time I realized I was able to facilitate shifting awareness and people's posture and behaviors simply by prescribing different eyeglass lenses and other forms of lenses and filters, I was shocked. It turns out our behaviors shift based on how we carry ourselves. And how we carry ourselves affects our behaviors. Function affects structure, and structure affects function. This is why somatic and all forms of movement explorations are foundational and why movement practices are such powerful tools on the social, emotional, mental, and spiritual levels. Integrating our fundamental movement patterns with the use of lenses, prisms, colored lights, filters, and other techniques of the behavioral neuro-optometrist is extremely powerful.

There are varying responses to outside physical, mental, emotional, and spiritual input or stimulation. Functional optometrists observe people's postural and behavioral responses to see how they react to our physical tools. Sometimes we see an expected response based on optics. Other times, we see opposite responses, as somaticists see in "paradoxical" breathing. Lenses and prisms placed in front of a person's eyes affect all parts of the person's body posture or soma, especially the lower back and pelvic regions. The gift of the specialty in optometry called vision therapy is that the therapeutic tools of the trade offer the possibility of novel postural shifting in a person's soma (body) as a response to the physical therapies, the gift of the process of somatic integration, and the interaction between doctor or therapist and patient or client. Combined, these practices are even more powerful. There can be shifting in the person's soma, body, mind, and Spirit.

I am sharing these thoughts with some associated actions I have practiced and offered over the decades so that we all begin to bring to conscious awareness the understanding that even if we have not moved through the developmental movement milestones at the "proper" time in our overall development and our visual development, we can understand that it is never too late to begin again!

The Embodiment of Stress—Fight, Flight, Freeze

Could it be the crushing reactions we have to life events_that lead to a diagnosis of myopia? What do stuck emotions have to do with our physical structure? Ah, what a question. Embodiment. Letting go of strain and stress and moving through the collective trauma of the ages. That's what these now moments are all about.

Do we hold emotion in other organs and systems of our bodies beyond the eyes and visual system? Oh yes, we do. Optometrist and educator Elliott Forest wrote extensively in his book *Stress and Vision* about the fight-or-flight stress response and the ramifications of this in our visual systems in this modern era. The way we have put together our traditional systems, the educational systems, the corporate systems, and the medical systems—the way we have constructed all of these systems—has promoted and continues to promote embedding trauma into our Somas.

Embodying our Vision is all about recognizing this embeddedness of the systems in the cells, nerves, organs, bones, ligaments, and fascial sheaths and all the systems of our bodies and our souls and facilitating the letting go, moving through, and mindful reintegration of what we are here for. Are we meant to gently, mindfully, and soulfully embody and re-embody ourselves on a continuous basis in this lifetime, in this physical form? I believe so.

Moving through Trauma Experientially as a Collective Consciousness

Some are comfortable with discomfort, as it is familiar to them. Embedded trauma of the collective is being released right now in many ways all around the globe and into the cosmos, up and down the food chain, as I type. The domain of the food chain. Rearranged! Zero-point judgment around what others are Being or Doing. Be yourself. Move into your authenticity. Sprout boldly!

Begin where you are. And go from there. Be with where you are for as long as you need to before venturing into the next step, the next stage. Take the time you need to integrate with grace. There are many systems within our human physical form to work with: bones; muscles; fascia; organs; lymph; blood; sweat and tears; the nervous system and endocrine system; and the entire fluid system as one, including mucous, lymph, neuroendocrine, and hormonal. Oh my!

Redeveloping after Injury

I clearly remember the redevelopment of hand movement following the shattering of the radius bone of my wrist long ago. My unified hand movement began again first in my pinky. This movement progressed across the fingers of my hand, from pinky to ring finger to middle finger to pointer to thumb, until the dexterous nature of my complete hand (and my human nature) returned with the miraculous movement of my forefinger reuniting with my thumb. My opposable thumb and forefinger connection returned in this sequential way. And that is the same way dexterity in hand development occurs in babies, moving from pinky to thumb. This relationship between the development of our eyes and hands; our entire visual systems; and our heads, tails, and limbs occurs symbiotically and systematically, in a specific spiralic order. Ahhhh!

Take Time for Vision Rest Breaks, Physically, Mentally, Emotionally, and Spiritually!

Allow yourself the creativity, flexibility, and resilience to take vision rest breaks. An Embodied Vision Rest and Reset Break can include taking a conscious breath and looking out the window to relax the focusing mechanism in your eyes, brain, and consciousness. Do we have to look out the window, or can we simply close our eyes and visualize the movement out the window and then come back to the plane of regard close to us? Can we transport ourselves and our cells to other spaces and other places without physically moving? The answer through the quantum field is an absolute yes.

I think of Thích Nhất Hạnh, who has passed into the next phase of existence since I first wrote these words. I know that he is timeless and ageless and that in every now moment, he took time in all time to flow in the Now moments. His books and teachings are simple, with no need to BE a certain way. With beautiful writing, font, style, artwork, and space. No need to read and read. Space and time to think. Imagine that. And take off whatever hat it is that you wear. Dare! Dare to sing, dare to dance, and dare to move out of this deep trance we've been in as a collective for ten thousand years. Whoa, I said it. Imagine that. That is a big hat to take off!

Developmental Inquiries

- Take time to feel the organs of your eyes from the inside with your eyes open and then closed. When you move your eyes, do you feel them touching your eyelids? If not, can you imagine that?

- How do the organs of your eyes relate to your eye muscles and the bones of the orbit (eye socket)?

- Have you noticed how your eye movements are related to your head and hand movements? How about connections to your breath? Your sacrum and tail?

Chapter 7

CONNECTING WITH OUR DEPTH AND DIMENSIONALITY THROUGH OUR VISION

Embodying Our Vision in Enlivening Consciousness: The Integration of Vision and Movement 2

*T*HIS IS WHAT BOTH EMBODIMENT and embodying our vision are all about:

- ✓ Feeling ourselves from the inside out and outside in
- ✓ The development of eyesight and vision through movement
- ✓ Connecting with our three-dimensionality through our vision
- ✓ Embodied movement as the basis of vision development and natural eyesight improvement
- ✓ Embodying our vision through grounded, connected movement
- ✓ Mindfully acting in the world with underlying ease and awareness of our total-body action system led by visually directed movement
- ✓ Clearing the path for the divine to shine through us

I share embodying our vision based on the work of early pioneers in visual development combined with explorations of the developmental movement practitioners and Indigenous elders I have been honored and blessed to glean wisdom from over the years. We learn and relearn together how to be embodied and empowered to rise into the BEings we were meant to be through feeling ourselves from the inside out and allowing the Divine to flow through us. Life unfolds without us Doing. We can simply BE.

Optometric vision therapy and movement tools and techniques used in the field of neurodevelopmental, functional, behavioral optometry abound. As mentioned repeatedly, lenses, prisms, colored lenses, filters, and free space and in-instrument techniques are the core tools of the advanced practice of natural eyesight enhancement. Developmental movement explorations underlie the full expression of the visual process. These tools and explorations, in combination with facilitation of an experienced practitioner or supportive group dynamic, can be instrumental in recovery from a myriad of troubling situations. For those with traumatic brain injury to birth accident sequalae to stroke to visual issues to learning disabilities, including those "smart" in everything but school and on the ADD to Autism spectrum, natural eyesight improvement is possible.

We are all part of the enlivened rejuvenation and rehabilitation story. We may be enhancing already wonderful sports or other performances, tuning up our abilities in activities of daily living, or recovering from injury. We have the capacity to improve our life performances gracefully, gently, and gradually. All of us are on the continuum of enhancement and recovery on some level at some point. We are all disabled, and we are all geniuses in our own way!

The grandmothers and grandfathers on whose shoulders I and my colleagues stand developed body-based technologies, both with and without lenses, prisms, colored filters, simple and complex. We play with and experience moving into harmonious single simultaneous binocular vision (SSBV). Indeed, the degree to which we are binocular (meaning when our visual systems are functioning harmoniously and integrated into our total body, mind, and spirit action system) has a lot to do with how we behave and why we behave and interact the way we do.

Let's wind back to the notion of eyesight and vision as integral parts of the human action system. The relationship between movement, breath, nutrition, eyesight, and insight is undeniable. Our eyeballs are simply the external (visible to others) portion of the upper part (headward portion) of the nervous system. Our eyes are the energetic receptor organs (hard) wired to our brain and spinal cord. We've been exploring the electrical wiring of our beings and how the wiring expresses itself as the BEings we are BEcoming! This wiring and the entirety of our somas are malleable and flexible and can change with attention and intention.

Connectivity with Fascia and Blood

Fascial sheaths intertwine and communicate throughout our bodies. They are part of the complexity of our visual systems. Our billions of cells are in constant communication as the symphony of our BEing. The interconnectedness of all the senses—including but not limited to vision, smell, taste, touch, and hearing—is multidimensional. Through our fascial sheaths, our cellular pathways are fed and remove waste efficiently and effectively. As we continue to move through our fascia, our blood moves, and we detoxify our bodies.

Full and complete blood flow delivers robust amounts of oxygenated blood to the vessels and tissues of the eyeballs, to the visual pathway, and throughout the entire body. This is critical to allow for the maintenance of stellar eyesight. The blood vessels in the eyes are the most delicate of the entire body. That's why what we eat has a huge impact on our eyesight.

Clarity in the physical structure of the neuroretinal vasculature from the eyeball through the retina and entire visual pathway creates what we know of as the miracle of crisp eyesight and vision. The visual pathway reaches to the back of the skull in the occiput, or occipital bone.

Light energy travels along the visual pathway from the tip of the front of the corneas at the very front of the eyeballs through the brain and throughout the cerebrospinal fluid of the spinal cord, all the way to the tail. Maintaining the healthy, integrated integrity of our physical nature and our physicality, our movement patterns in relationship to a resilient visual system, is key to thriving in wellness.

Duplicity of Organs

Dimension. Dimensionality. In our functioning in this human form, we've wondered about duplicity, duplication of organs and structures in our bodies. From a strict medical standpoint, the duplication is presumably for the just-in-case scenario. Just in case one organ or other part of our body is destroyed for some reason, there will be another part at the ready. Or is this truly the case? Our two-sidedness—our multilobed, multichambered, spiralic design—reflects the multiverse dimensionality of who we are.

Our two eyes, the two sides of our visual systems, originate deep in the tissues of our brain and spinal cord and column. All is connected through the bones, nerves and vessels, blood, fascia, cells, bacteria, and viral and fungal mycelial connections interwoven. This is the deep reality, the dimensionality of who we are here to be. We have paired organ systems, paired structures, and highways of paired nerves and vessels of all kinds, from head to toe and everywhere in between. Two eyebrows, two eyes, two optic nerves, two sides to the visual pathway, two ears, two nostrils, two sides of our tongues and palates, and two tonsils. Our paired teeth. We have parathyroids, the butterflied two lobes of the thyroid gland; two kidneys; two adrenal glands; two multilobed lungs; two times two, or four, chambers of our spiralic hearts; and paired ovaries and testes.

And how about the other paired parts of ourselves? The two sides of our rib baskets, both side to side and front to back. Our arms and legs with ten fingers and ten toes. Pair head with tail. Pair your right arm with your left arm and leg with leg. Pair an arm on one side of your body with a leg on the other side of your body. Pair a hand on one side of the body with a foot on the other side of the body. We are crystal balls of silver and golden light spiraling in constant, meaningful multidimensional motion.

Paired Structures Experiential Interlude

Lie on your back (supine position) on the floor, upon a blanket, a mat, or the carpet. Become aware of each eye, and truly feel into that awareness while grounded with your back body on the earth.

Pair one set of structures with another, and move from those places. Take time to play! How about pairing your eyes with collarbones or hips? How about pairing your eyes with your kidneys or your ovaries or testes? How do you feel when moving from those paired spaces in your body? Oh my! Try different combinations of pairing places and spaces. The possibilities are endless. Have fun! Enjoy playing with abandon and moving, releasing, and letting go of whatever you no longer need to hold in your orb. Clear your vessel!

What of the symmetrical paired redundancies? The paired aspect, the spiral dimensional aspect of all of us, allows for the perception of our surroundings with volume and dimensionality. In the case of eyesight, we morph here into a deeper understanding of Vision. Single simultaneous binocular vision (SSBV) has been described as three-dimensional vision, the ability to perceive depth, like with 3D glasses you are given in a movie theater.

The Deeper Meaning of Dimensional Vision

What do stereo eyesight, stereo vision, and depth perception have to do with the next level or the multilevel explanation of dimensionality and our souls? Perhaps a huge percentage of our brains and beings have to do with NOW moments that we can consciously learn how to step into. Through quieting our minds and existing in a suspended animation of sorts, we can allow Spirit to flow through us and lead the way.

These can be moments when we've crossed over into another dimension. The experience of flow. Flowing. In moments. Knowing. We are in a place and a space now to allow for the opportunity to step into the Beingness of ourselves. It's no longer necessary to live in our old stories as anchors. It's time now to truly feel the freedom of the cells of ourselves. Now is the time to live into the true dimensionality of who we are meant to be.

Revisiting Vision as the Integrative Pinnacle of Human Development: A Recapitulation

At times, learning and teaching require repetition. I love to learn and have teaching in my blood, though I've not been formally trained as a teacher. My mother and sister (may they rest in peace) were both teachers. Sometimes we pick up a concept or have an experience proprioceptively and kinesthetically, and we know it immediately. Other times, we must repeat the lesson over and over until we truly get it. It can be helpful to see, hear, touch, and experience material in a different way so as to understand it differently. Thus, understand that I may be covering ground presented elsewhere, but I want to make sure this information comes through.

The Development of Near and Far Focusing and SSBV

We have two eyes. Yet most of us see one of what we're looking at. Have you ever wondered why? When we look with both eyes at one point in space, the overlapping aligned visual fields from each eye allow for easy single simultaneous binocular vision, or SSBV. Vision is learned through experiencing the world through sensation and movement through space.

As a child is born, their body expansion from the yield and push of their feet and legs against the womb and emerging through the birth canal into the world is a divergent, expanded, and open body pattern for the first time in their existence. Eventually, through curiosity and desire (to reach for food or an object or a toy, for example), their eyes gaze into the distance, and their vision moves out into space, out into the world. The child begins to see and explore the world farther away from their body, beyond where they can reach with their fingertips or the tips of their toes. Beyond their kinesphere (the area where a person can reach with their physical body parts), with eyes, ears, smell, touch, taste, and intuitive curiosity, the child then physically ventures out into their environment beyond arm's reach. As they develop, their eyes begin to coordinate and work together as one system.

Immediately following birth, a baby moves back into a lot of condensing on the earth. In the Tonic Lab Reflex, the baby connects deeply with the surface of the earth. As the months in the first year of life progress, babies develop through the land patterns of movement.

This movement is not sequential. Rather, the land patterns unfold in a spiralic fashion. The *homolateral* patterns involving one side of the body and then the other side of the body developmentally follow the *homologous* patterns.

Babies then move through *contralateral* patterns, crossing their midlines (tracking targets beginning with Mom's nipples or the bottle nipple and Mom's, Dad's, or a caregiver's eyes). The baby moves outward into the visual-spatial world, eventually integrating all their limbs, including the bottom back of the head, or occiput; the limbs of the eyes; and the visual movement system in its entirety, including hands and arms, feet and legs, and head and tail. The land patterns interweave with one another and are seen in many different forms and in different time frames.

The orientation of the way our bodies are set up and the movement patterns we experience and create for ourselves innately underlie accommodation (focusing), convergence (eyes moving inward), divergence (eyes moving outward into space), and SSBV. These patterns are supported in our whole bodies, inside our DNA and RNA, from conception through all of the neurodevelopmental movement patterns described by Bonnie Bainbridge Cohen and others (sponging, radial symmetry, and more); in embryonic and fetal development; in the first year of life; and throughout our lives.

◆ Breathe
◆ Blink
◆ Be Present!

Natural Eyesight-Improvement Tip: Bringing Blinking into Conscious Awareness

Let's consider something we do every day: blink our eyes. Blinking is an incredibly important subconscious movement pattern that we sometimes forget completely. To remember to blink, we need to briefly bring this subconscious habit to conscious awareness.

By staring at a computer screen for long periods of time, many develop a staring habit. We are then bypassing our natural blinking pattern of twelve to fifteen blinks a minute. This behavior can put us, our eyesight, and our visual systems into an unbalanced fight-or-flight sympathetic nervous system state. The fight-or-flight response is ultimately reflected throughout our entire body and causes undue stress and strain. It can result in visually related stress headaches; dry eyes; somatic pain, such as neck and back pain; carpal tunnel syndrome; and a myriad of other chronic stress-related issues, including visual issues leading to chronic eye disease.

Bringing blinking to conscious awareness during the day is important. So while working for extended periods of time up close, doing near-point work, such as reading, looking at a computer screen or other electronic device, painting, drawing, cooking or cleaning, or meeting with people in close spaces, remember to take time to blink on a regular basis. Flutter those eyelids like butterflies, as natural eyesight-improvement practitioner Claudia Muehlenweg might say. Rediscovering more normal blinking patterns, and habituating these patterns into a regular pattern by reacquainting ourselves with our natural blink rate, is important. This can be accomplished over time by bringing our blinking to conscious awareness many times a day. Eventually, we will establish a more natural habit and not have to think about bringing blinking to conscious awareness. We will blink more normally as our new natural habit pattern is established.

Restoring Your Blink Rate

Consider timing yourself for a minute or two to see what your typical blink rate is. Then consciously increase your blink rate for a few minutes. How does that feel? Then let the conscious awareness go.

As you bring blinking to conscious awareness a few times a day for just a few minutes, you'll be integrating a wonderful natural eyesight-improvement technique into your daily routine. Eventually, you will habituate blinking on a regular basis into your daily life. This new healthier habit will serve you well in your day-to-day activities by lubricating your eyes and facilitating a longer attention span for any visually intense task.

Vision and Reflexes

Going deeper:

- What do the reflexes that underlie visual development have to do with any of this?
- What do our reflex development, proprioceptive abilities, feeling, and sensing tone have to do with how we function in the world and how we feel inside our own bodies?

The Reflexes That Underlie Visual Development

Vision is learned. In humyn BEings, Vision emerges through the embryological, prevertebrate, and vertebrate patterns. Each of these developmental and neurological movement patterns (embryological, prevertebrate, and vertebrate) is supported by and developed through the interweaving of various primitive reflexes.

There are many primitive reflexes that underlie the developmental movement patterns that form our movement patterns in life. These reflexes begin developing in utero and continue developing as we move through our first year of life and beyond. The primitive reflexes underlie the postural reflexes and remain our deep support throughout our physical lifetimes. As lifelines!

The reflexes, including the tonic labyrinthine, Moro, spinal Galant, symmetric and asymmetric tonic neck reflex, and many others, are often referred to as "primitive" reflexes. They are intrinsic and innate to our species as human beings. They are specific patterns that not only underlie human development but also are seen throughout the animal kingdom. The primitive reflex patterns are programmed into our RNA and DNA and emerge in utero. They are the foundation of the movement patterns of our entire body.

As we develop as human beings, we flow through reflex development and the developmental movement patterns in spirals, not linearly. From the moment of conception and birth, the underlying reflex patterns contained in our DNA and RNA and the pulse of the universe unfold. Patterns of tone in our various body systems develop symbiotically with these reflex patterns. These reflex patterns become postural patterns that ultimately define who we are, how we move through the world, and how we act in our physical forms throughout our lifetimes.

These patterns, if not integrated in our bodies, can create all kinds of issues with our posture; our poise; our movement; and, therefore, our human performance in the world. With poor habitual movement patterns, we can develop physical, somatic body pain as well as emotional, mental, spiritual, and performance issues. The eyes and visual system will not be optimally functional if our reflexes are not fully integrated in our early life. Sometimes we can function efficiently enough for a while, but then we can no longer compensate for our unintegrated (poor) habits. Our efficient functioning becomes dysfunction.

Our genetically G-d-given developmental patterns as humyn beings allow for the development of reflex patterns to unfold through movement through the space we are surrounded by. The patterns become habituated in various ways, depending on many factors in our overall development in our first year of life and beyond. The patterns we experience somatically are integral in the learning process in our development, including our visual development.

Primitive Reflexes, Postural Tone, and Three-Dimensional (3D) Vision

Our primitive reflexes underlie our postural tone and our movement patterns. Ultimately, when fully integrated, they lead us into one of the pinnacles of seeing: the ability to see with single simultaneous binocular vision (SSBV), or true three-dimensional stereopsis—three-dimensional, or 3D, vision.

Have you ever gone into a movie theater that used 3D technology and provided 3D glasses prior to your viewing the film? Did you know that if your eyes are not coordinated as a team, if you do not have the ability to converge and diverge your eyes based on where you are looking in your visual-spatial world, you will not be able to see in 3D, whether or not you've been given those 3D glasses? Some of you reading this will surely know, as you've been aware throughout your lifetimes perhaps that you never were able to view things with depth or in 3D. You may not have realized you were not seeing with depth and dimension until someone told you what was possible. The development or redevelopment of 3D vision has everything to do with redevelopment of the reflex patterns that underlie visual development!

Many take 3D eyesight and vision for granted. Others might be reading these words with curiosity, wondering about their own 3D eyesight and visual capacity. The smooth integration of our primitive reflexes and our postural reflexes (which underlie the ability to ultimately have easy SSBV) happens naturally for some babies and children and not at all harmoniously for others. There are a lot of reasons why some develop their vision easily and others not so much. Visual development is an outgrowth of overall development and is reflected in our entire soma, our entire body.

I often tell those with whom I work that I am not a psychiatrist or a psychologist, but the way people "see" is the way that they "Be."

I can tell a lot about how a person is functioning in the world by looking at the functional visual findings. It often seems I can read people's minds or know more about them and how they behave in the world simply because I know how to read not only their visual findings from the visual evaluation but also their behavior. That is what I do. All of us read one another in this way to some extent. It is humyn nature. I have reached a point in my career and life where I can know a lot about how individuals are visually functioning in the world simply by observing them walk or talk, including on the phone, or in other virtual modalities.

When a child is very well coordinated—say, in sports performance—it is likely they spent a lot of time on their bellies on the floor in the first year of their lives. It is likely they had the opportunity to experiment with the myriad of incredible movement patterns we develop by being on the floor during our first year of life. With an integrated Asymmetric Tonic Neck Reflex, we see in the gross motor and fine motor optometric findings wonderful tracking abilities across the midline, smooth eye movements, wonderful binocularity, and easy single simultaneous binocular vision (a well-coordinated two-eyed person who sees in 3D), meaning the ability to use the eyes easily as a team without stress and strain. On a gross motor level, it is simple for these people to cross their midlines with ease and grace (as is necessary for effortless reading, walking, running, skipping, and so on), and they may be outstanding in ball sports, or they may have superior adaptations if their underlying reflex patterns are not fully integrated.

Fully integrated reflex patterns, including a fully integrated asymmetric tonic neck reflex (ATNR), translate in everyday life into easy functioning in the world in all activities and social interactions.

Remembering Who We Are: Reflex Patterns Revisited

The deep reflex patterns underlie everything we do and everything we are. They underlie not only visual patterns but also the integration of all the developmental patterns that in some way define how we function in the physical world, the physical plane of our existence.

When children are confined in bouncers, high chairs, playpens, strollers, and walkers before they are ready to walk or are not allowed to be in contact with others for whatever reason, the reflexes that underlie all of development, including visual development, and the integration of all these reflexes are stunted or warped in many ways.

Vision Is Learned through Movement Experiences!

Vision is learned as we move through our visual-spatial world, so bad visual habits and patterns can be unlearned, repatterned, rehabituated, and then reexperienced with more clarity and grace. It may take time, or it may be possible to reverse these behaviors instantaneously. Miraculously, there are many variations as to how we heal. Keeping open to the possibilities is important. We just never know what's around the corner, especially these days!

What Happened First?

The Reflexes. Defined and Refined. With
    practice. Over and over again.
Movement patterns and combinations
    thereof in sentient beings
Physical manifestations of movement, gross,
    macro, micro, and everything in-between
The movement of prior. What came before?
    Magnetism,
Gravitational forces, yin and yang patterns,
    holography
We are a hologram within a hologram of our
    DNA and RNA Avatars
Born originals, many die as copies …
All is inside
All is outside
From one another, we cannot hide.
Though we try. When we try to be in control,
All goes awry …
And when we let go, when we release.
Clear and open to Source.
It is then that we truly Know!

Inquiries on My Mind

Some questions I pose to myself
about the primitive reflexes:
When do these primitive reflexes truly begin?
With the egg and the sperm?

With our genetic line?
With the pulsation of the universe?
With the Ooohhhhhhmmm?

Behavior, Vision, and Movement Inquiries

Here are some questions for Self-Reflection related to Habitual Movement Patterns related to Vision (maybe not so obviously related to vision):

- Do you startle easily?
- Is breathing easy for you?
- What startling or traumatic experiences in your young or present life stand out as possible moments that might be embedded in your soma (body)?
- Have you thought about sorting out why you might behave in a certain way?
- Have you ever related these behaviors with your early development or some incident in your life that might have created some hidden traumatic brain injury (TBI)?
- Were you a bed wetter as a child?
- Do you have trouble sitting still for lengthy periods of time?
- What tools presented here have you resonated with to help you move through these issues? Would you consider using some of these tools, such as bringing blinking to conscious awareness, or enrolling in a more extended program of movement integration to move through some of these issues?

Questions to Ponder More Directly Related to Our Eyesight and Vision

- How do whole-body movement, flexibility, and resilience affect our eyesight? Our insight?

- What are a few movement techniques we can use in daily life to preserve and enhance our eyesight and enhance our vision?

Developmental Inquiries

- Do you take time to play with movement, to dance, sing, and move all at the same time? How often? Daily? Weekly? Monthly? Never?
- Were there traumatic times in your life when you remember being incredibly shocked? If so, have you considered working through these traumas through movement therapies?

Let's Continue the Journey

All of the experiences you've had and participated in by reading through or listening to this prose have had an effect on your soma, your body; your eyesight; and your vision. Let's journey together into the next section!

NUTRITION

❖ Integrating our vision by moving
into self-care through diet

❖ Move at your own pace while considering moving
into or toward the plant-based or vegan lifestyle (and,
ultimately, the raw living-foods lifestyle for resetting
your taste buds, detoxifying, and building immunity)

❖ Become a plant-based eater, vegan-curious,
vegan-leaning, or vegan to raise your vibrations

❖ Suggested recipe ideas

❖ Your curiosity is paramount to behavioral change!

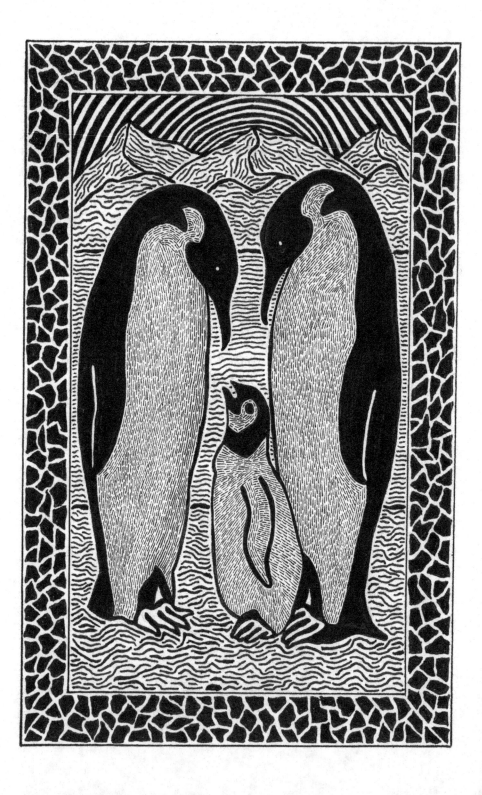

Chapter 8

CONSIDERING PLANT-BASED FOODISM AND THE VEGAN LIFESTYLE

Harvesting Light Energy by Eating Plants and Daring to Raise Our Vibrations!

PLANTS HERE, PLANTS THERE, PLANTS, plants everywhere! I am in love with the plant queendom. I love the smell of the forest in the rain. I love the smell of the forest anytime. I love to walk barefoot on the welcoming earth. I love feeling the soles of my feet connecting with the soft ground and ocean sand. I love to eat wild edibles from the earth after it rains. I love nature, and nature loves me back. How about you?

There are clear advantages to eating plants. We are literally eating and drinking light energy and creating within ourselves a clear inner ecosystem, including a fully functioning surface (or skin) microbiome and inner microbiome, clear blood vessels, and clear fluids in the body, which equals healthy organs, including healthy eyes and dis-ease-free living.

You begin digestion with your eyes. You see the food. Then you smell the food. Then you put it in your mouth and you chew it. Some who don't smell it just eat it. They're doing a disservice to their bodies.

—Stan Beck

The nutrition section is primarily about bringing real living food into your soma (body) in ways you may not have thought possible. How? By moving into or toward plant-based nutrition and a vegan, or mostly plant-based, organic lifestyle.

Defining what *vegan* means and how a person moves into the vegan lifestyle became important questions for me. Why? There are health and wellness, philosophical, and environmental reasons, including all living Beings on the planet and the planet and cosmos themselves. The foundation of my inquiry was a knowingness that all animals are sentient beings who have the inalienable right to live their own lives without humans eating them and that as humyns and other Beings on this planet, we have the right to clean and living fresh water; fresh air; and clean, real, whole food.

Moving into Eden—Diving or One Step at a Time?

Are you vegan-curious already? Do you eat a vegetarian diet? Are you a complete carnivore? Where are you on the spectrum of transformation? Are you listening to Spirit? How often? Are you ready for a deep dive? There are many ways to move into dietary shifts. Here we go into an exploration of some of the levels and layers of the plant-based and vegan lifestyle.

Veganism with the seasons and body types (kapha, vata, and pitta, the Ayurvedic construct) and moving toward a more raw living-foods lifestyle could be a diet to save our souls and Planet Earth at this moment in time. Or maybe that's not for you. And that's okay!

Emerging into the vegan lifestyle is unique to each individual and truly amazing. Some begin by gradually weaning themselves from foods other than plants. Some begin with a Meatless Monday (a plant-based diet every Monday) and stay there for a while. Some begin with plant-based foods a few days a week. Some dive right into the full vegan lifestyle.

The common thread is that at some point, we just begin, and once we see the dynamic changes in ourselves and others and how the world is changing around us, there's no going back. You may think you've failed if you can't do it all. Or if you adopt the lifestyle, you may digress from the dietary aspect of veganism from time to time by eating a cookie with some milk or egg in it or taking a bite of chicken you thought was tofu, but you'll get back on track. You might stray from the vegan lifestyle when you decide plastic is not vegan and keep and wear some of your old leather shoes. Why will many of us continue to move more fully into the vegan lifestyle? It seems our divine nature and inner guidance give us the message to get on board. As long as we are listening!

There are some basic advantages to eating in this new way. Perhaps you're starting by introducing one new vegetable onto your plate each day or one plant-based meal a day. Whether taking a gradual approach or a whole-food, plant-based dive or a dive into raw living veganism and foodism, you are on your way to improved stamina; better blood, sweat, and tears; more clarity of thought; and greater ease of living mindfully, full of energy and spunk!

What if you have not one morsel of interest in eating and drinking only plants or even more plants? No worries. Hey, skip this section completely if you wish! Or, if your curiosity overtakes you, pick one of the steps below, and dip in somewhere! And read through the nutrition section to "see" if something—anything—piques your interest. Oh my!

Possible Steps along the Way

- Adding one more vegetable to one meal each day
- Trying one plant-based meal a week
- Going to a vegan restaurant once or once a week
- Hanging out with a family member or friend who eats a plant-based diet

- Committing to the 21-Day Vegan Kickstart (https://www. pcrm.org/vegankickstart)
- Considering living in a community that models anything from whole-food, plant-based eating to raw living foodism and the modern living Essene way of life

Each of us will have our own journey with its own nuances. There is no cookbook. In fact, the purest journey does not involve cooking at all. One of the deepest dives would be to step into a raw living organic veganic lifestyle in which you grow your own and live in intentional regenerative community. How about being a full-fledged Raw Rewilding Living Foodist all the time? Does that sound ridiculous to you? Imagine eating from the earth in the woods all day long! If that's too much for you to process right now, no worries. Begin where you are, and go from there. Move in a direction. One bite and one sip at a time! Wherever you are on the spectrum is fine and where you are meant to be.

From Vision to Veganism and the Vegan Lifestyle: Journeying as a Plant-Based Foodie and BEcoming Vegan in Body, Mind, and Spirit!

Our eating journeys vary based on our life experiences. The way we eat often shifts over the course of our lifetimes. Here we dive into the idea that eating lower on the food chain is good not only for humans but also for all aspects of our precious blue-green planet and way beyond.

As you now know if you read the vision section, vision is more than one thing. As we shift paradigms, as the world and cosmic paradigms are dissolving and re-forming right before our eyes, we all have the opportunity to go with the flow. What we consume—the food and drink we put in our mouths and digest on a daily basis—is an area to consider for sure. As we clear our sacred body temple, we clear our consciousness.

What does veganism have to do with eyesight and vision? As we move into lifestyles that are in harmony with nature, our eyesight and insight become more fluid, resilient, and flexible. As we become more connected to our inner nature as human beings, our entire systems begin to clear. And our eyesight and vision are part of the whole process as we move into deeper spiritual development, becoming grounded and lighter Light Beings. Living the vegan lifestyle becomes a huge part of your existence once you take the leap!

In this nutrition section, we'll dive into a plant-based ride. As a new way. A new day. Perhaps you'll consume just one more bite or drink of a plant-based substance. Maybe much more! Ready. Set. GO!

What's Your Motivation?

Whatever your motivation is to move toward veganism doesn't matter. What does matter is to take a step in the direction of the New Earth, the regenerative future. It is important to begin. Begin mindfully and with pure intention. Let's consider your motivation.

Do you

- want to look good?
- want to lose weight, but none of the diets you've tried have worked?
- want to prevent acute or chronic illness or reverse a chronic illness?
- realize our worldwide cultures have normalized what is upside down and backward?

- realize that war, the slavery of self-abuse, rape, child abuse, child trafficking, other heinous crimes, and discrimination on all levels are all, in part, based on following twisted cultural norms occurring because we are still eating Frankenfoods, flesh foods, and the milk fluids and eggs of animals meant for their own young and to produce their own young?

Do you

- care deeply about animals and have an awareness that your love for dogs or cats is no different from loving cows, pigs, chickens, and fishes and that not eating them is how you demonstrate that love?
- want to act in a way to leave the earth in a better place than the earth you were born into and realize you've got some work to do regarding cleaning up yourself, the air and water, and other aspects of the community around you?
- want to know all your neighbors and see everyone on planet Earth treated with equal respect, dignity, and civility?
- want to connect more deeply with yourself and those around you?

In any case, this nutrition section is for you!

This is written with the understanding that all of us are different and at various stages of development as humans on this earth and in this universe, and each individual has variable dietary styles and lifestyle ideas. We are all on this journey together into spiritual awakening. Some people reading this book continue to include eating cows, sheep, deer, other mammals, chickens, dogs, fishes, and the fluids and eggs of animals in their diets. If this describes you, please forgive me for changing the vocabulary about how I refer to the animals I ate until 2012. We are all in recovery, and we are meant to hold one another on this wild and wonderful journey! The language we use in popular culture to refer to the flesh foods we eat has pulled the wool over our eyes and kept us in the dark and ignorant of what we've been up to as human beings these past five to ten thousand years. And for good reason. The gory details of animal abuse on many levels and how this abuse has been affecting our collective consciousness for eons are stories for another day.

You Are Beautiful, You Are Powerful, You Are Strong, and You Have *Got* This!

On one level, we are going through and have gone through a variety of pandemics like the world has not seen before. On another level, we are in the days of awakening, and this is a path of transformation. What's next? Let's plan to thrive for the rest of our lives. Are you in? Let's journey together. There are many ways to move into veganism as a road to spiritual awakening. Gabriel Cousens, MD, is fond of saying, "You cannot technique your way to G-d." Ultimately, the way you are in the world is up to you.

Here are some ideas about how to Rise in Spirit, beginning with veganism as a baseline. Let's clear your body of toxins so your brain, heart, and soul can be wide open for what's to come—that is, Pure Eden and the realization that we live in heaven on earth. As Bruce Lipton said recently (paraphrased), "What if this is heaven? What if we live our lives knowing this is heaven?"

Health Benefits as Part of Moving into Spirit Gracefully

The miracle of remaining healthy and vibrant from infancy through maturity into your elder years and reversing chronic illnesses, which conventional wisdom says is not possible, *is* truly possible. Some stories and tools are shared here. Ideally, our parents and grandparents understood how to take optimal care of themselves and passed those teachings and their healthy genes on to us. But if not, that's okay too, as it's never too late to begin a new way of being. By moving gracefully into a healthy plant-based diet and lifestyle, you will build the foundation for health and wellness not only for yourself but also for the next seven generations and beyond.

Wonder of Wonder, Miracles, Miracles

By working with the ideas in the nutrition section through a healthy vegan diet that is right for you, you will be:

- taking charge of your own health
- learning tips and tools to boost your own immune system through veganism
- reversing obesity (if this is an issue for you), letting go of cravings for good, and letting go of all the chronic health issues that emerge when overweight
- not depending solely on conventional Western medical "wisdom" for your own health
- tapping deeply into your own known intuitive wisdom deep within
- reversing a host of chronic illnesses—including but not limited to heart disease (Dr. Dean Ornish diet), type 2 diabetes (Brenda Davis, RD; Vesanto Melino, MS, RD; Tom Barnard, MD; Gabriel Cousens, MD; and others), fibromyalgia, lupus (*Goodbye Lupus* by Brooke Goldner, MD), and lyme disease— and recovering completely or to a large degree from stroke, cancer, or asthma

- developing a clear inner ecosystem, including a fully functioning inner microbiome, a healthy surface (or skin) microbiome, clear blood vessels, and clear fluids in the body, which results in healthy organs, including healthy eyes, and dis-ease-free living
- moving into a knowingness of your deep soul self that was hidden deep within until Now!

The benefits of moving into and ultimately embracing a healthy plant-based lifestyle are amazing. As time passes, more and more studies come out to show definitively that especially now, we must internalize that we can be healthiest and most effective in our lives with clear and clean inner microbiomes. The microbiomes, first described just in the gut, include the entire inner ecosystem: clear blood, lymph, fascia, cerebrospinal fluid, and all-vessel clarity to enhance our thinking and clear-minded actions in this rapidly shifting world.

Self-care is health care. As a basis for this reimagination of yourself, reconnecting with your inner nature through mindfully eating and practicing healthy habits throughout every day is what this is all about. Why? Once we connect with the aliveness we have inside of us, we create the more beautiful world we all know in our hearts is possible.

A Breath of Fresh Air

Bring yourself into present-moment awareness with this exploration.

Notice your breath. Become conscious of your breath. Inhale through your nose, and exhale through your nose.

Then inhale through your nose, and exhale through your mouth. Once more.

Notice if there is a difference in how you feel.

Take your time. There is no right or wrong answer here. The point is to be with yourself at your own pace.

Let your muscles and bones relax. Yield to the earth. Deeply. Feel her support. She will always be there for you. And when we listen to our kinesthetic sense of our body tone and get out of our own way, our bodies speak gently back to us by creating a sense of ease.

Visualize yourself easily transitioning into sprouting plants on your countertop, planting more plants, facilitating the planting of more plants, and eating more plants.

And so it is! Ahhhhh.

Your, My, and Our Plant-Based Foodie Journeys

What Is Your and Our Collective Food History?

I never saw myself as a foodie until now! I knew a "foodie" as a gourmet eater who ate three-course meals with lots of ingredients and complex preparations, pairing each course with the proper wine and before- and after-dinner liqueur. The "foodie" was one who explored different cuisines and ate at five-star restaurants. But then something happened to my definition. I realized I was a foodie of a different sort. I am a Plant-Based Foodie.

The Physical Aspect

Does our food history begin with the beginning of humanity and nursing our babies at our breasts? What are we meant to eat and drink? How much beyond the physical nature of food can be defined as *nutrition*? What we take in and integrate at all levels of our beings is the field of Spiritual Nutrition. The physical aspect of our food intake is one piece of the puzzle.

Moving from breast or bottle to solid foods and drinking from a cup is another early part of our eating journey. What foods and drinks were we offered, and in what form, as we developed and grew up? Throughout our childhood and teens and into adulthood and our elder years, did we think about what foods and drinks were best to promote wellness? Or did we accept what our parents or caregivers and community members ate and drank and provided to us as the best choices?

What recommendations, including from culturally accepted authorities, have been offered to our most recent ancestors, even to this day?

The Toxic Inner and Outer Ecosystem Aspect

When we eat *highly processed foods*, they do not satisfy our appetites and create physical addiction. The food industry, as it turns out, is well aware of the addictive qualities of the processed foods they create devoid of nutrition and laced with additives. This "food" creates cravings for more food. The

How do you build your plate?

The Physicians Committee for Responsible Medicine (PCRM) created the Power Plate, also known as the New Four Food Groups: three or more servings a day of fruit, two or more servings a day of legumes, five or more servings a day of whole grains, and four or more servings a day of vegetables! See ThePowerPlate.org for details.

In contrast to the recommendations of PCRM, the US government has different ideas. The myplate.gov four food groups effective 2015–2020 included fruit, veggies, grains, and protein, with a sidebar showing dairy. The veggie and protein pieces of the pie shown are larger, and the fruit and grain pieces of the pie are a bit smaller. The myplate.gov now effective 2020–2025 shows vegetables and grains as the largest parts of the pie, and the fruit and protein pieces of the pie are a bit smaller, equally sized, also with the sidebar showing dairy. It's fascinating how opinions differ and how things change over time in different dimensions of what is considered real and true! Full details about myplate.gov are found on the myplate.gov website.

artificial chemicals in prepared foods, in combination with the chemicals in our brains and bodies, create a toxic stew of our inner ecosystem. We can let go of this toxic, addictive stew by changing our lifestyles.

Who knew that our sugar addiction was being nurtured with all the refined sweetness of nutritionally depleted, processed food desserts and snacks, such as HoHos? Who knew that processed snack foods, such as Doritos, Fritos, and chips, contained quantities of salt and chemical food additives that caused one to crave more and more? Who knew processed foods, even if vegan, were junk food and had additives that caused addiction and a desire for alcohol or other depressants or stimulants?

Who knew we were brainwashed into believing we needed meat for the protein content and who knows why else? Those living the whole-food, plant-based vegan lifestyle get plenty of protein from plants and grains themselves.

Some of my female friends in my college years in the 1980s began eating only plants. Then they stopped getting their periods. In retrospect, I realize these friends may not have understood how to eat full, nutritionally based plant-centered meals, or the dining hall food was simply not nutritious enough to support full plant-based nutrition in the correct way. In the 1970s through today in these current moments, many college cafeterias continue to serve pesticide-laden, refined foods stripped of their full nutritional content and grown in depleted soils. From the 1990s to this day, genetically modified foods, known as GMOs (biotechnology), have become more and more normalized.

Rachel Carson's epic, groundbreaking book *Silent Spring* was published in the 1960s. Yet in the 1980s, many people still did not make the connections between air and water pollution, agricultural pesticide pollution, our diet, and our overall health and vision. This understanding is now included in my broad view of what vision is and the relationship between diet, wellness, and both inner and outer vision. Cognitive dissonance resolved!

Eating to Live or Living to Eat?

We all have food and diet stories rooted in our upbringing, culture, and experiences. What are your food stories? We all must eat to live, but have you ever wondered how much of what you ingest is due to mindless consumption?

I realized at some point that many people are addicted to different forms of what we consider in our culture to be food. In fact, these processed, chemical-laden, GMO-containing items are not in their natural form, and many are designed for long shelf life. Their nutritional qualities have often been stripped out. Are you addicted off and on to refined sugar? Oh, it's "healthy" all right. Unrefined, organic. You know the rap! Food addiction is a big deal and a big issue in our Western culture. Need I say more about addiction to sugar, fat, and MSG (an umami taste)? How does food addiction relate to other types of addictions?

TruthinLabeling.org addresses the MSG issue in almost all processed foods in one form or another. It explains what catch-all phrases on ingredient lists, such as "natural flavors," really mean and what those ingredients contain. MSG in foods and drinks is disguised in dozens of ways.

I'll stop this rant in a moment, but first, I'll refer you to the Environmental Working Group (EWG.org) so you can print a copy of the dirty dozen (referring to the most pesticide-laden and GMO-laden produce on the planet and also listing the best produce to eat if it's not possible to source organically). Place this list prominently on your fridge!

We all deserve to know what's in our food, especially when not many of us have been growing our own food.

The Emotional Aspect

People make their own choices and move into plant-based nutrition in their own time, but they must understand that they have been drinking milk meant for the young of other mammalian species and eating the energy of death for a very long time. There is a mourning process involved in moving into healthy vegan eating. The mourning process is multifaceted and often wells up in me. Partially, it has to do with feeling remorse from eating so much meat and so many chickens, fishes, milks, and eggs for the first fifty years of my life. I'm mourning my own lack of awareness and the dear animals I ate because I did not see their soul energy.

The USDA food recommendations in the 1970s looked just like what I ate. Remember that earlier plate put out by the USDA with the four food groups (groups similar to today's)? Milk, Meat, Fruits/ Veggies, and Grains? We must recognize that what has been normalized is NOT normal or healthy!

For the first fifty years of my life, I had no knowledge of the plant-based lifestyle, nor did I know anyone who ate or lived that way. It never crossed my mind that I was eating other beings. Imagine if schools taught about how different cultures around the world eat, and imagine if all of us in Western civilization were exposed to and experienced these lifestyles as we grew up. What kind of world would this be? No worries. We are now in the position to create the world we want to see. No time to waste!

How Do Our Eating Habits Develop from Infancy through Maturity and throughout Our Lives?

What food consumption stages did you go through over time to this present moment? Were you affected by food trends over the recent decades? Does any of this look familiar?

Early Years: Were you nursing or drinking from a bottle at some point? What is your early eating and drinking history or herstory or theystory or theirstory?

1970s: What was your definition of eating well in the age of bell bottoms and disco, Hamburger Helper, salad bars, pasta primavera, and quiche? Maybe not too many sweets; meat, chicken, or fish with each lunch and dinner as the "main course"; a raw green salad at least once a day; and a "starch," such as a baked potato or rice, with dinner. Eating regularly and not noshing in between meals. Now that was the way to eat!

1980s: In the time of the Walkman's and Pacman's popularity, bran muffins, and some beginning vegan trends, were you eating fast food, home-cooked meals, or some of each? Did you discover your local food co-op and

Food Stories

What is the relationship between what we learn at times in our lives and whether or not we act on this knowledge? Often, we do not act wisely because we do not know how. So now is the time to realize that acting on your own inner knowingness, your inner hunches, and your deep-seated intuition is the proper thing to do ALWAYS. Hopefully, these food stories and the other information presented here are giving you a taste, an introduction, to speaking your truth all ways!

organic food, or were you still eating refined and MSG-, pesticide-, and sugar-laden fast foods in those days?

1990s: In this decade of relative prosperity including lots of Beanie Babies and Magic Eye books, did you hear about types of eating styles and explore foods from cultures outside of those you grew up with? Had you heard about ways of eating like the one in *The Book of Whole Meals*, a mostly vegetarian cookbook by Annemarie Colbin? *The Book of Whole Meals* lays out, season by season, a series of menus, advice on how to use leftovers from one meal to the next, and the tenets of food combining, laying out the reasons to eat certain foods with other foods so our digestive systems are happiest, and exact recipes with quantities are clearly stated. The book also features a synopsis of the Ayurvedic system of eating with the seasons. For example, you learn why eating warm and warming foods, soups, and drinks in the wintertime in certain climates is ideal and why eating cooling foods, such as fruits and room-temperature drinks, is a good idea in the summer. There is an emphasis on whole foods and organically grown foods. Whole foods are unprocessed and straight from nature. It turns out this is a mostly vegetarian and pescatarian (fish included) cookbook, and my family was becoming vegan-curious at that time without realizing it!

Early 2000s: The turning of the ages for those of all ages. We are all here for a reason at this distinct moment in time.

Were you eating low-carb or fat-free or trending toward vegetarian with whole grains? Did you stick with whole foods (not whole-food, plant-based), including meats, lots of veggies and fruits, minimally processed foods, sometimes restaurant food when eating out, and a minimum of sugary foods? Did you cut out eating dairy foods, realizing that dairy was mucous-producing?

Where are you on your food journey today?

At some point, were you a woman of childbearing age? Did you have mama-bear tendencies to take incredible care of yourself in order to protect the next generation of women carrying the eggs with the primary germ cells of future generations?

You Are Just Where You Need to Be

Here's another reminder that all people move into their own awareness of how they want to live their own lives in their own time. And that is okay. We make our own choices in our own time about how we choose to spend our time on this planet. If you're interested in plant-based eating, NutritionFacts.org and the work of Michael Greger, MD, are great places to begin your journey beyond this book. Check out Stephanie Redcross West of VeganMainstream.com. See the resource section at the end of the book for more ideas!

Chapter 9

PLANT-BASED FOODIE BASICS

The Question of Plant-Based and Vegan or Not?

$\mathcal{D}$ISTINGUISHING THE NUANCES BETWEEN LIVING your life as a plant-based eater and living your life as a vegan can be tricky territory to address. Those who are whole-food, plant-based eaters may or may not be considered vegan. Why? A person who lives a vegan lifestyle is more classically defined as not using any animal products at all. Strict vegans do not wear any products containing animal parts, such as leather shoes or belts or fur coats, or use items containing animal products.

It is next to impossible in our current Western culture—or in any culture, for that matter—to truly live as a pure vegan. Do you drive on roads? Did you know, for example, that bone meal is sometimes used in the manufacture of asphalt for roads? Do you eat? Did you know there are animal ingredients (cow and chicken manure) contained in fertilizers, including those labeled "organic" for food production, including for growing vegetables. Animal products are invisible ingredients in all kinds of consumer products.

Animal products may be used in the production of foods whether or not those animal parts ultimately wind up in the final commercially produced product. As mentioned above, cow manure is a commonly used fertilizer in organic food production, including in Permaculture. Specification of *Veganic* Permaculture is necessary to be sure no animal products are used at all. But then I question, what about the use of Effective Microorganisms (EM, a homemade fertilizer) using a fermentation process or purchased commercially? EM is a fertilizer made of concentrated bacterial colonies that enhance the ecosystem and have not been genetically tampered with (in other words, non-GMO). Hmm, is this any different from using biological insecticides, such as Bt? I believe so. At least at the time of this writing! Why is the concentrated use of the bacteria *Bacillus thuringiensis* considered a biological insecticide? More details on that story later. These last few sentences foreshadow the nature section of this book! Have those who characterize themselves as vegan considered the use of bacteria in fertilizers for food that is called vegan? Are bacteria animals? Not technically. Are bacteria sentient? I believe they are, along with the entire plant queendom!

We are part of an ecosystem, both inside our bodies and on what appears to us to be on the outside of our bodies. This ecosystem contains living, sentient Beings on all levels. Not all BEings are humyn!

My belief system at this point is more moderate than in previous years. I have come to understand that we all do the best we can in any given moment and strive toward more purity as best as we know how. And that is not only good enough but a necessity so one does not go *Meshuggah* (Yiddish for *crazy*)!

The Range of Plant-Based Foodies and Vegans

I'd like to share some background related to food consumption from what I've learned over the past decade of my own vegan lifestyle. Some of these observations come from a survey I conducted for my master's thesis at the Cousens' School of Holistic Wellness (CSHW) of the University of Integrated Science of California (UISCA). The thesis explored the range of veganism—from junk foodyism to raw living foodyism. You'll see there is a lot of variety in how people are living as Plant-Based Foodies. The following are three examples along the spectrum of veganism.

Note there are many other possibilities in between, including vegetarianism. Vegetarian people include dairy and eggs in their diet. The classical pescatarian also includes fish in their diet.

All of these descriptions are examples. There are many people whose dietary intake will wax and wane between the constructed categories I'm describing below. Each individual eats in their own specific way based on a myriad of cultural and other factors. I'm offering some descriptions as examples of some of the possibilities.

Note that I am not discussing vegetarianism in detail here. Why? Well, that's not a phase I went through, and there are plenty of references on that subject! *Vegetarian* is defined as those who do not eat dead flesh foods, such as cows and lambs and dogs and cats (in Asian cultures). Vegetarians do drink the milks of mammals meant for their babies and eat their eggs, which were meant to turn into young BEings.

The Standard American Vegan (SAV) on their way to BEing a Savvy Vegan

Here I will refer to the Standard American Vegan (SAV) as the animal-loving junk food vegan. What does the SAV eat? Traditionally, those who characterize themselves as vegan (because of the monstrous abusive treatment of domestic animals in our agribusiness world) are not necessarily fully aware of the health benefits of eating a plant-based diet in a healthy way for themselves. Standard American Diet (SAD) SAVs may overdo their intake of fast foods and processed foods and can sometimes create unhealthy lifestyles for themselves as human beings.

SAD SAVs are people who take care of animals better than they care for themselves, whether their pets, whom they treat better than they treat themselves, or rescued farm animals or groups of animals. These blessed souls advocate for the fair treatment of animals without realizing they are not taking proper care of themselves. In the most extreme cases, they simply do not take their own food intake into serious consideration.

The Whole-Food, Plant-Based (WFPB) Vegan—Middle of the Road

Whole-food, plant-based (WFPB) eaters eat whole plant-based foods 100 percent of the time. They will generally eat the oil contained in whole foods, such as in olives and avocados, but not refined oils. The WFPB eater will eat sugar in the form of dates, carrots, and fruits, such as apples, pears, and plums, but not refined sugar. Salt that occurs naturally in plants is fine but no added salt. Processed foods are generally out of the question. So this rules out conventional and mainstream pastas, breads, cookies, and cakes. Sprouted breads, cookies, and cakes prepared from whole plant foods are fine. Recipes for these types of foods abound! Some eat canned goods; some do not. There are individual variations. A variety of spices are included in the WFPB lifestyle as well. Try parsley, dill, cinnamon, cumin, paprika, and sea vegetables, such as nori, in soups or dulse sprinkled on salads or rice. Which spices do you love?

Specific amounts of water intake are generally considered as part of the WFPB lifestyle. Eight glasses of water per day are generally recommended. Up to twelve glasses of water may be optimal. Depending on your dosha (Ayurvedic) composition, you will require differing amounts of water per day.

In addition, supplements can be part of the mix. If you believe in supplements, the recommended vitamins for this group of vegans (and all vegans) could include vitamins B and D and others, depending on

The Whole-Food, Plant-Based Diet

What is a whole-food, plant-based diet? Definitions vary, and there are many who model the WFPB diet with various nuances. Neil Barnard, MD, and his organization the Physicians Committee for Responsible Medicine (PCRM), among many others, provide excellent models of the classical WFPB diet. The diet includes whole plants (preferably organic), including fruits, vegetables, nuts and seeds, whole grains, and legumes. The fully plant-based eater does not eat any animal products or their derivatives. No red meat, poultry, fish, eggs, or dairy products.

It can take time to arrive and settle into the way you eat. Eating habits can change with the seasons, with your mood, and often daily, depending on what you're doing on any given day.

your state of wellness. In this group of vegans (again a sweeping generality), I rarely hear discussions around the concept of veganism (as defined in the below sidebar "What Is the Definition of *Vegan*?") or spirituality.

The Raw Living Organic Veganic Foodist (RLOVF)

The RLOVF category, referred to as a "raw living organic veganic foodist," is characterized as those eating organic, veganic living (a.k.a. sprouted) foods and pure water and living as "clean" a life as possible. Examples of living foods are wild foods, such as dandelion greens picked fresh, and freshly sprouted cultivated foods recently picked that contain close to the full life force of the plant. Kirlian photographs of plants that have been raised organically without artificial chemical inputs and veganically—that is, without intentional animal inputs, such as cow manure—show an amazingly beautiful, colorful, life-giving aura around them before these foods are cooked. In contrast, foods raised in the agribusiness model with heavy chemical inputs, even in their raw forms, have a compressed, congested, and small aura that does not look alive.

There is a range of how people eat a raw diet. Nutritionist and author Brenda Davis, in

Becoming Raw, mentions that a raw diet can consist of anywhere from 60 percent raw and 40 percent cooked foods to up to 100 percent raw foods. Dr. Gabriel Cousens's Spiritual Nutrition raw diet, detailed in his book *Conscious Eating*, is a special type of raw diet including layer upon layer of additional lifestyle elements. Some of these elements of right living on many levels include being in loving relationships; living in community; meditating; receiving *shaktipat* (prayers from a spiritually enlightened individual); working with a spiritual elder; exercising in the form of walking, dancing, yoga, or tai chi most commonly; and being in service to the local and world community and environment, to name a few.

Here are some more ideas for getting started:

- Think about one bite at a time, then one meal at a time, and then a few meals a day or week—you get the idea!
- Some prefer the all-or-nothing approach. If that's your style, more power to you! Remember, we all must go at our own pace and do what feels comfortable for us.

Adding More Plant-Based Foods into Your Diet

If you do not plan to take a deep dive into the plant-based lifestyle or full-fledged veganism all at once, consider adding more plant-based foods into your diet one bite at a time.

What Is the Definition of *Vegan*?

Vegan defined: you do not use or enjoy any parts of animals or their fluids (think milk) or eggs to eat; you do not use animals to entertain, as in zoos, animal parks, and circuses; you do not wear animal products, including leather, silk, or animal skins; and you do not use animal products in home-care items, cleaning supplies, body-care products, and the like. (Note: There are exceptions, such as using pigskin grafts in the case of cancer or heart valve replacements or using leather items you previously owned rather than giving or throwing them away.)

- Look up Veganuary's 31 Day Vegan Challenge to explore the plant-based lifestyle.

- There's no right or wrong, good or bad. You are where you are in these moments. That said, be inspired by local vegan family and friends and groups and sources on social media, such as Kris Carr, Jane Unchained, Chef AJ, 10,000,000 Black Vegans (https://10millionblackveganwomen.org/), the Happy Pear from Ireland, and Brittany Jaroudi.

- If you're feeling hard core, read the books *LifeForce* by Brian Clement, *Conscious Eating* by Dr. Gabriel Cousens, *Survival in the 21st Century* by Viktoras Kulvinskas, and *Diet for a New America* by John Robbins.

- If you're seriously wanting to take a deep dive, read *Spiritual Nutrition* and *Rainbow Green Live Food Cuisine* by Dr. Gabriel Cousins, and put these books under your pillow! Then find a supportive spiritual community who understand what real food means as a springboard for spiritual enlightenment, and spend time with them.

- Start with one vegan dessert recipe! You can start with the dessert recipes in this book. Mmmm. And on YouTube, you'll find Dave and Steve (of the Happy Pear) demonstrating, in three and a half minutes, vegan peanut butter chocolate chip cookies. Search for "Easy Vegan Oatmeal Cookie Recipe + YouTube." (For the ebook, go to www.youtube.com/watch?v=Ps9XCJdSDNc.)

- A plant-based juice or smoothie to start off your day will provide wonderful energy! See my idea of a great green juice a day in the Juicing section. Check out KrisCarr.com, and Victoria Boutenko's *Green for Life: The Updated Classic on Green Smoothie Nutrition* for more great juicing and smoothie ideas!

Adjusting to Eating More Plant-Based Meals

Some feel eating more beans causes a gas issue. Bottom line: If you sprout beans by soaking them overnight before cooking them or by soaking them overnight and rinsing them for several days without cooking them (see the sprouting section) and eat way more fiber (all vegetables have fiber) than you are used to, there's no issue with gas. The issue generally resolves itself. Fruits, veggies, and beans have lots of fiber. So many simple solutions that they're hard to believe!

Eggs, fish, and meat do not contain any fiber. John Robbins told an interesting story about the amount of fiber consumed in a whole-food, plant-based diet. He and his son, Ocean Robbins, sponsored a vegan nature retreat. Those supporting the trip commented that they had to provide more facilities for poop. Why? Because when you make the full transition into the WFPB vegan lifestyle, you'll easily be pooping two to three times a day, minimally once a day. And that is normal! As our daughters used to say when they were little, "It slided right out!"

Wherever you are, begin there. For example, if you are already eating a vegetarian diet, prepare a meal without dairy. Go gradually at your own pace if that's your style. A friend of mine has been eating a vegetarian diet for decades and is resisting moving into veganism. So I mentioned to her to start somewhere. But where? When I felt into her process, I asked if she chewed her water. She said her grandmother had done that, but she was not clear what that meant. She said, "I haven't figured out the difference between sipping, swishing, and chewing." We benefit from chewing our food thoroughly. Chewing everything we put into our mouths before swallowing is a wonderful idea. Simply considering other ways of doing things is a start. You are stepping into a more wholesome lifestyle one sip, one bite, and one chew at a time. Wherever you are, begin there!

General Suggestions for Eating and Drinking as Plant-Based Foodies

Ahhh. Delicious plants. First you see food. You smell it. Then you taste it! Yor vision guides your eating, so the presentation is important. It's art. You eat with your eyes, then you smell your food with your nose, and then you taste it with your tongue in your mouth.

Eat until your stomach is 80 percent full. Many of us get carried away and eat until we feel full. Often, this fullness means we can feel our stomach stretching out, and sometimes we might feel as if our stomach is going to burst open. As we eat more slowly and mindfully, once we take the time, the food will travel through our mouths and down our digestive tracts, and we will simply know intuitively when we are finished with our meal. When you chew your food to a pulp and chew your water, this intuitive sense will rise from within.

Remember, digestion starts in your mouth. Your mouth is the top of your digestive tube. So if you chew your food to a paste, the digestive enzymes in the saliva in your mouth will combine with the food in your mouth as the first part of absorbing nutrients into your system. When you chew your water fifteen to thirty times before swallowing it, your whole digestive system can get ready to receive this fluid and will be much happier. Your digestive process overall will be much smoother. By the time the liquid reaches your stomach, it will have been processed to a certain degree by the rest of your system to really be ready to be integrated along the ride through the circuitous intestines, through your organs, and into your cells to carry away waste products ultimately through the bottom part of your digestive system, the anus and exit hole, much more easily.

There's a wonderful story in the book *Your Body's Many Cries for Water* about a man who lived through a war. While living under awful circumstances, he took the time to mindfully chew his water before swallowing. His friends did not chew their water. When asked why he chewed his water, his answer reflected that this chewing of the water became part of a meditative process to pass the time. This man lived much longer than most of his friends. He lived to joyfully tell the story.

As I reflect on the question of why to chew your food to a pulp and why to chew your water before swallowing, I realize the act of eating is a metaphor for the full circle of life. We begin by expressing gratitude before we eat the food in front of us. We chew and swallow. We share the sprouts and other food we've grown mindfully in our yards or in our community. We pay attention to which watershed our water comes from. We track where leftovers and food "waste" go when we are done eating. We may pay attention to the processes of growing, selling, preparing, eating, and excreting the food. We are diving deep into creation.

Mindfulness in Eating

In your meditations and prayers for gratefulness, include the entire family of people, animals, plants, and all of life that made your meal possible. Include the planning, seeding, planting, tending, caring for, and harvesting the food. The vibration and rhythm of life are contained in each bite and each sip.

Sit down with friends or family. Leave distractions behind! Turn off your phone and all electronics, and say a prayer of gratefulness before taking the first bite. My father, who lived to the ripe old age of 103, always sat down to eat. He removed distractions from the table. In other words, he cleared the table of newspapers and mail. Do you remember when newspapers and mail were only in paper form?

Mni Wiconi: Water Is LIFE!

Clients sometimes ask me, "What is the best water to drink, and what about tap water?" It could be that for some people whose systems have strong detoxification components, tap water works. The long-term effects of pollutants—including fluoride, heavy metals, and other toxins—in local municipal water systems are rarely publicized. In my view, filtered tap water is preferable to unfiltered, fluoridated city water.

Ideally, you would collect your own water from a well, spring, or stream if you know the source is pure. If collecting your own water from a safe source is not possible, use a distiller, or drink filtered tap water, using a reverse-osmosis filter and then remineralizing the water with a pinch of noniodized salt.

What are the best ways to remineralize water? Perhaps with well-sourced trace minerals.

Note: If you live in an area where there is legacy industrial pollution, such as acid mine drainage, or current toxic industrial inputs, such as from hydraulic fracturing, a.k.a. fracking, have the water tested, no matter what the source is, before drinking your water.

When I think about water, my mind immediately goes to Standing Rock and the year 2016. That was the year of the historic gathering of more than three hundred Indigenous First American tribes and other supporters coming together to bring awareness to Energy Transfer's plans to build the Dakota Access Pipeline across tribal land in North Dakota.[8]

The Lakota saying *"Mni Wiconi"* means "Water is Life." Water is the lifeblood of our precious Mother Earth. We are made of water, and we must honor the water of this planet both inside and outside ourselves. We must move back into being able to drink the waters from the streams and rivers. This topic is one for another day as well. Waterkeepers. We are all that.

Your Unique Journey

Many feel there needs to be time to adjust to solely eating plant-based meals. As mentioned earlier, how a person steps into eating plants is just right for them, on one hand. On the other hand, part of stepping into the healthy vegan lifestyle involves making up your mind that that's what you must do for whatever reason: maximizing health and wellness, dropping your blood pressure or blood sugar levels, reversing an autoimmune disease or heart disease, controlling thyroid disease, losing weight, saving all sentient beings, creating less pollution on Planet

---

[8] https://standwithstandingrock.net/mni-wiconi/, accessed July 17, 2023.

Earth, or stepping into your full spiritual expression more easily by clearing and cleaning the vessel of your body first. Whatever moves you toward embracing the lifestyle, you must make up your mind and JUST DO IT!

Each person's food journey is unique and their own. As I've repeated more than once in this prose, each person must make their own choice about how to live and how to eat. Check out the book *Vegan Voices: Essays by Inspiring Changemakers* to read fifty stories and a few poems about different individuals' journeys into veganism. You might especially enjoy the poem called "The Terrain" by yours truly!

One recommendation I have is to step immediately into the WFPB version of being a vegan foodie, as processed-junk-food veganism is not a healthy choice! Which is healthier: consuming impeccably raised farm animals or wild animals or eating "pretend" processed or genetically modified created meat or packaged vegan meats or foods made from processed ingredients? My view is to steer clear of those "pretend" choices.

Life is a journey, not a destination, and we can change our minds to step into Source energy contained within us more and more with each breath! Eating a wholesome plant-based foodie diet can be a bold first step to support your spiritual journey. It is true that not everyone on the deep spiritual journey eats as if they care about their bodies or the environment. It is also true that people have individual metabolisms. Some are much better than others at removing toxins from their systems through the pathways of processing through the kidneys, the liver, and all of the excretory systems of the body; breathing through the lungs; processing stuck emotions; and more.

Chapter 10

THE JOURNEY CONTINUES: GOING DEEPER

Launching into the Spiritual Raw Living Foodism Lifestyle

*H*OW MUCH DEEPER CAN WE go than into the depths of our digestive systems? When you first begin eating more plants, you will notice changes in your digestion. What do I mean by that? Mainly that you may notice changes in your pooping habits and the size, shape, texture, smell, and frequency of elimination. This is a topic that many people do not care to talk about most of the time unless they are having digestive issues causing discomfort or pain. Don't despair! Once things normalize—generally within a week or two (sometimes longer, depending on how you go about the transition)—you will be amazed at how great you feel and how smoothly your digestive system is functioning!

Detox

When partially or fully launching into any shift in your dietary intake, including a move into being a raw living foodist, people can initially go through a period of detoxification from whatever they have been consuming. This detox can last anywhere from one day to three weeks or more. Some choose to support the detox, or resetting, of their physicality (metabolism), emotional state, and spiritual awareness with water fasting; dry fasting; lemon water or lime water fasting; juice fasting; spiritual nutrition fasting, including meditation and more; or some combination of these or other types of fasting and lifestyle elements combined with eating raw living foods 100 percent of the time. Some include the use of enemas and other types of colon cleansing. During the detox period (usually about three days), you may experience dizziness, headache, weakness, and a bit of confusion as your body becomes readjusted to its new inner ecosystem and your new attitude.

Then there's the realization that if you can consume food and liquids on an ongoing basis that continuously assist in detoxifying your body, could it be that intense intentional detoxification regimens are not necessary? In today's day and age and with our current state of affairs, is that possible? What do you think?

Meeting the Juice Man: A Synchronistic Story (Some Might Call It Divine Intervention!)

In early 1990, I was attending an optometry continuing-education workshop with colleagues at a hotel in Ohio, USA. During one of the breaks, I wandered into the room next door and discovered a seminar on juicing. The speaker was Jay Kordich, the original Juiceman!

At the back of the room, masticating juicers were lined up, and the helpers were handing out samples of apple carrot juice in small paper cups. Those were the ingredients: raw apples and raw carrots. I was offered a sample juice. As I drank the juice, I was amazed at how simple it was to prepare and how delicious it tasted. And so very sweet. Mmmm.

I was excited to bring that energy into myself after sitting on my derrière for so many hours, listening to content I was already well versed in. I enthusiastically called my then-boyfriend, Stan, later that day and learned that he had been listening to a Juiceman Jay Kordich infomercial in the wee hours of the night before.

At some point after that, Stan bought one of Mr. Juiceman's juicers. That first juicer was perfect for juicing apples and carrots! That juicing experience was decades before either of us had any notion of moving into the vegan lifestyle.

The Joy of Juicing

Nutritious and delicious, juicing is a wonderful way to begin your day!

When you awaken, try drinking an eight-ounce glass of water with a squeeze of lemon, followed by eight to sixteen ounces (about a quarter to half a liter) of freshly prepared organic green juice. Anthony William, the Medical Medium and author of a book by the same name, recommends working up to drinking thirty-two ounces (about a liter) of celery juice each morning. The Medical Medium says this quantity of celery juice each morning is the best detoxifier to boost the immune system—especially for purging heavy metals. Some cannot drink this much celery juice at once, so do what you feel comfortable with. Also, see the green juice recipes in a few pages. These juice combinations will get you moving in more ways than one without needing coffee!

In any case, be sure to soak your produce in a peroxide water solution (one capful of peroxide per bowl of water) for at least a few minutes, preferably ten or fifteen minutes, before rinsing and peeling, slicing, dicing, or chopping. Food-grade peroxide is a wonderful natural disinfectant to wash away bacteria, fungi, and viruses.

Some people prefer smoothies for the fiber content, but I have found delicious fresh juices first thing in the morning are a fabulous way to get your own inner juices flowing—from head to toe. What better way to start the day?

Tools

You'll need a masticating juicer (slow or cold-press juicer) and the fresh fruits and veggies. Choose organic produce. As mentioned earlier, if you cannot find all organic, look up the Environmental Working Group (EWG.org) to see the dirty dozen, or the "dirtiest" veggies. The "dirty dozen" refers to the fruits and veggies most laden with pesticides, herbicides, and fungicides—hormone-disrupting chemical residues. So at all costs, stay away from all of them. Remember to lean into organic foods or grow your own when possible!

Juices as Part of the Vegan Diet

Fast-forward to my movement into the healthy vegan lifestyle. I fell in love with juicing and have created various forms of green juices almost every day for the past decade! Here are some ideas for you to fall in love with juicing too.

Juice these ingredients in the suggested recipes to judge the quantities produced. I wing it these days! You'll get a feel for quantities over time. Consider diluting the juices with 50 percent water before drinking them. Juices are tastiest and most nutritious when consumed fresh. They will keep in the fridge for twenty-four to forty-eight hours, though they are most nutritious when consumed immediately after they are prepared.

Apple Carrot Juice (variation with Cucumber, Celery, Lemon, and Ginger) One to Three Servings (if diluted)

A juice for those who love sweet, tangy tastes and have never juiced before. This juice is absolutely delicious! For me, these days, it would be a dessert juice.

1–2 apples (Green apples are tart. Try Fuji or other red apples for more sweetness.)

3–4 carrots (Juiced carrots are extremely sweet!)

1 cucumber (Peeled if waxed. I usually leave a bit of skin on there—not much!)

2–3 celery stalks

1/2 lemon (Optional but will cut the sweetness and the mucous, and citrus is so healthy!) thumb-sized piece of fresh ginger, peeled

Slice off most of the lemon rind, and then coarsely chop all the other ingredients. Slowly put them through the juicer. Enjoy!

Green Lemonade
One to Three Servings (if diluted)

3–4 stalks celery, chopped

1 cucumber (Peeled if skin is thick, and chopped.)

handful of pea shoots and sunflower shoots (Optional: You can sprout these yourself or buy them at a food co-op or some grocery stores.)

2–4 kale leaves (Chopped so they don't clog the juicer.)

1/2 lemon (Cut up with most of the rind cut off; leave some of the peel for a bit of zing!)

thumb of fresh ginger (Peeled with a peeler or not.)

thumb of fresh turmeric (Peeled with a peeler or not.)

1 green apple (Or red apple for sweetness if desired.)

Prepare the ingredients as specified. Run them through the juicer. It is helpful to juice the ginger and turmeric early in the juicing process.

Juicing Wheatgrass

To juice wheatgrass, you'll need a masticating juicer. We've used an Omega Juicer for years, but there are others. Just be sure you use a masticating juicer, and be sure the juicer works to juice wheatgrass before you purchase it.

Wheatgrass is a fabulous part of the detoxification regimen. If you are interested in growing wheatgrass to juice, that's great. If not, local community cooperatives or natural grocers often stock fresh wheatgrass for juicing. There are some companies dedicated exclusively to growing and shipping wheatgrass. If fresh wheatgrass is not available, the next best option is frozen wheatgrass juice. Another option, though last on my list, is powdered wheatgrass. Be sure that whichever product you use, it is organically sourced.

Grains and Grasses in the Raw Food Diet

Some might be curious about grains and grasses and the raw foods diet. Most raw foodists I'm aware of stay away from most grains unless they're sprouted. As mentioned earlier, when grains are soaked, they are considered sprouted. With soaking, the outer layer of the grain seed kernel softens. When you rinse the soaked seeds, you are washing away the natural coating of the seed that prevents sprouting. The hard kernel protects the seed. The combination of soaking and rinsing seeds for a few days makes digesting the sprouted seeds easier. So for example, wheat is a great grain to sprout, grow, and juice (think wheatgrass juice!). The shoots, or grass in the case of wheatgrass, are not grains. So is a seed a grain even after it's sprouted? Is the sprout a grain once it's growing? When you eat a sprouted grain, are you eating a combination of a grain and a vegetable? Now we're really getting into the weeds!

- **Sourcing or Growing Wheatgrass:** I suggest sourcing organic winter wheat seeds from your local food co-op or by finding another good organic source. Soak the seeds overnight, and then rinse and drain twice a day. The wheatgrass grows up and is ready to harvest within about ten to fourteen days (about two weeks) from the beginning to the end of the cycle.

- **Sprouting Chickpeas:** Soak the chickpeas for about forty-eight hours, and then rinse a few times a day for a few days. You'll notice the little sprouts poking out of the seed and growing longer and longer as the hours pass. Sprinkle these sprouts on salads, or put them in a food processor with a bit of parsley and a touch of salt to create some delicious raw hummus.

Tea Time

There are loads of noncaffeinated teas that are outstanding for relaxation and for medicinal purposes. Chamomile tea is one of my favorites. Details about which teas are best for which purposes are beyond the scope of this book. Know that all edible herbs can be made into teas quite simply. Use your intuition about which teas to choose. Herbs can be stored dry over the winter and used as both teas and tinctures throughout the year.

White pine tea is recommended as a powerful antioxidant and immune booster. Green tea is also known for its incredible antioxidant and healing properties.

Liquids Away from Meals

I've mentioned water and green and other juices. Remember that liquids are most easily absorbed when ingested away from meals. It's best not to drink fluids immediately before eating, as you will dilute your digestive fluids. This becomes especially important in the menopausal and andropausal years. Some advise drinking fluids at least twenty minutes before or after the meal; some prefer drinking fluids one hour before or after eating a meal. Some do not agree with this approach, but in any case, stay hydrated! This is a reminder that staying hydrated is essential for optimal body functioning. Gabriel Cousens and other sources say that pooping three times a day and urinating every two hours during the day is completely normal.

Sprouting Basics

Sprouts are an important part of the vegan diet—consider growing and integrating sprouts into your diet every day! Sprouts have the most vital energy of life. Taking these amazing plants into your being will lift your mood and make you feel very alive!

When a seed has been soaked overnight and rinsed for a short period of time or for several days, two or three times a day, it is called a sprout. So when you just begin to see the seed sprouting, that's a sprout. Seeds sprout in varying time frames, depending on their size and how firm their outside shells are. In contrast to a sprout, a shoot exists when that little sprout has grown for a few days. It will be longer but not yet fully grown to maturity.

Sprouted oat groats are delicious for breakfast. Sprinkling sprouted seeds and sprouted beans on your salads is delicious as well. At Hippocrates Wellness, Brian and Anna Maria Clement recommend filling 50 percent of your plate with sprouts and the other 50 percent with leafy greens, with a smaller quantity of toppings, such as red pepper and raw fermented sauerkraut.

Some Basic Sprouting Tips

- Buy organic seeds at a food co-op or mail order. As a start, I suggest mung beans, green lentils, adzuki beans, peas, broccoli, and radish seeds.
- The simplest sprouts for the beginning sprouter are, hands-down, mung beans. Also consider trying adzuki beans!
- You can use cheesecloth or make or purchase sprouting screens that fit on top of mason jars. The openings of the sprouting screens are different sizes for different seed sizes and for different phases of the seed development.
- Regarding soaking, rinsing, watering, and harvesting the seeds, these times vary depending on the type of seed.
- Sprinkle countertop sprouts you've grown or store-bought sprouts on salads, soup, or any vegan dish you prepare. Mmm, mmm, good!

Mung Bean Sprouting

Cover the bottom of a sixteen-ounce mason jar with organic mung beans purchased from your local co-op or health food store or online. Cover the seeds with water. Cover the jar with a sprouting lid that has small enough pores so the beans will not fall out and go down the drain when you rinse them! Soak for eight hours or overnight. The next morning, or after eight hours, place a strainer over the jar (if you don't have a sprouting lid in place already), and drain away the water. Rinse and drain the seeds two to three times a day for two to three days. Voilà! You will have delicious mung bean sprouts. You can continue to rinse them for a few more days, and then you'll have bean sprouts you'll probably recognize from Chinese cuisine.

Sprouting is a metaphor for the transformation of self into new ideas and ways of being. A recipe for life, really! Attending to an issue, considering the issue, caring for the issue by giving it attention, and harvesting the outcome with gratitude and grace! Sprouts need a lot of attention—a reminder to pay attention to what we're up to and what we're doing and BEing in our lives. I think I'll go soak some mung beans right now!

The Spiritual Juice Fast

Judy Carman speaks of "non-violence as a calling of divine love … and vegan living as a spiritual path" in her book *Homo Ahimsa*.

As we fast and purge toxins from our systems, our minds become clear. A spiritual fast, or any juice fast, can be beneficial to jump-start movement into the raw living-foods lifestyle!

There is great opportunity to clear old habit patterns following a fast of any type. Shifting patterns of overeating, addictions, and lifestyle habits that create discomfort and dis-ease mentally, physically, emotionally, and spiritually is much easier following extended fasting, especially Spiritual Fasting. I will not go into the details of the various types of fasts here, but that could very well be the subject of another book!

Stay Positive

It is important to stay positive and not to be held back by the sometimes challenging and continuous journey of moving into healthier and healthier eating habits. Still, we may slide back into old patterns at times. After all, sugar and spice and everything nice, like chocolate, sure are addictive! A fast can be helpful.

Chapter 11

WHOLE-FOOD VEGAN RECIPES (A.K.A. PLANT FOOD)

Preparing Whole-Food, Plant-Based (WFPB) Meals, Raw Living (Sprouted) Foods, and Meals for Home and Travel

$\mathcal{W}$HEN I ORIGINALLY WROTE THE nutrition section (which I thought was going to be a short e-book) a few years ago, I focused the following recipe chapter on the whole-food, plant-based (WFPB) lifestyle. Why? At that time, I thought moving into the WFPB lifestyle would be most appealing for those on the journey to more healthful living.

A sequence of wild events have transpired worldwide over the past three years, and so many yearn to build immunity from the inside out. As a result, I'm feeling called not only to mention the raw living-foods lifestyle in more detail but also to add in a few raw vegan recipes in case you're feeling inspired to try one raw vegan meal or to completely shift into the lifestyle. Like WFPB, the raw vegan lifestyle can be used to reverse chronic illness—and even more! Understandably, the raw living-foods lifestyle is not for everyone. But stepping in that direction by trying it out for a day or more is truly a life-transforming experience. I can attest to that!

Keep in mind that much of what you already eat may be plant-based and vegan. Plus, many of the recipes you are familiar with can easily be veganized by leaving out the dairy, flesh, and egg products! What follows are some vegan meal suggestions, snacks, and recipes. Most, but not all, are WFPB or raw vegan. Raw recipes are delineated with an asterisk (*). All recipes are oil free. Each recipe serves two to four people, depending on what other foods will accompany the recipe being served.

Breakfast

- Overnight Oats
- Oatmeal with Plant-Based Mylk and Toppings
- *Raw Oat Groats
- *Chia Pudding
- *Buckwheaties
- Almond Mylk and Nut Mylks
- *Salad for Breakfast (if you prefer to eat the whole veggies and fruits rather than juicing them!)

Overnight Oats
(Does not require cooking)

1/4 cup rolled oats
1 tablespoon whole buckwheat or steel-cut oats
4 ounces unsweetened soy or oat mylk
a few walnuts or pepitas (another name for pumpkin seeds) or regular
or sprouted nuts of your choice
chopped fruit of your choice
raw cacao, if desired

At night, place the above ingredients in a 16-ounce (pint-sized) wide-mouth mason jar, cover, and place in the fridge. In the morning, add 1/2 sliced apple or banana, and enjoy. For an extra superfood kick, add spirulina.

Oatmeal with Plant-Based Mylk and Toppings

1 cup of oats

2 cups of water

toppings of your choice including fruits

Boil 2 cups of pure water in a pot. Turn down the water to simmer. Add 1 cup of oatmeal and stir. Cook for about 5 minutes (times may vary). Add bananas, chopped apples, dried fruit, sprouted nuts, or any locally sourced fresh toppings of your choice. Top with homemade or store-bought oat mylk or other plant-based mylk of your choice, and enjoy!

For variety, add spirulina, an amazing green superfood that is available at most cooperative health food stores or through mail order.

*Raw Oat Groats

(Slightly modified from the Live Sprouted Oatmeal recipe of Mike Chaet, PhD, in *The Whole Health Warrior: Your Guide to Living Healthier and Longer!*)

This is the Raw Vegan Recipe Version or mixed version, as rolled oats are already partially cooked prior to being sold.

Go Local for Grains and Toppings

Keep your breakfast grains and toppings as local as possible. Oats grow in many places in the USA. Rice is used habitually in the Near and Far East. Quinoa and chia in South America. Sprouted lentils are another grain to consider. Chia and quinoa are grains native to South America. Despite regional preferences, you may find that these grains are grown locally.

Do an exploration of the grains that grow where you live, and see if you can find a local organic farmer to purchase your grain and veggies from, or join a CSA. With a CSA (community supported agriculture), you get regular shipments of local produce. Or grow some grains in your yard instead of a pesticide-treated, depleted soil field! When you buy veggies from a local farmer, there is no middle person in the process. You not only know your farmer, but you can visit the farm and see where and how your food is grown.

Explore! Learn what watershed you live in, and figure out how the bodies of water closest to where you live connect to rivers and to the ocean.

1 cup oat groats (hulled oat kernels) or 1/2 cup oat groats and 1/2 cup
   rolled oats

1 cup nut mylk of your choice: almond, coconut, hemp, or other

1/4 cup unflavored dairy-free yogurt or 1/4 cup cultured coconut kefir

1/4 cup soaked raw almonds

1/4 cup soaked raw walnuts

1/4 cup soaked raw pepitas (pumpkin seeds)

1 tablespoon powdered cinnamon

1/2 fresh apple, chopped

Soak oat groats and nuts overnight. Drain and rinse in the morning,
and add to a high-speed or other blender, along with most of the apples.
Keep a few of the nuts and apples aside to add whole to the mixture
after it's pulsed or blended for a quick moment, so you can preserve the
chunky texture! Sprinkle cinnamon on top. This is one of my all-time
favorite raw recipes when I'm eating grains!

*Chia Pudding

2 tablespoons whole chia seeds (native to South America)

2–3 heaping tablespoons hemp seeds

1 tablespoon golden or brown flax seeds

sprouted (soaked) nuts

fresh fruit, such as bananas (native to warm climates), apples, peaches,
   pears (in season)

Add 8-12 ounces of water to all the seeds. Stir, and allow to sit for about
15 minutes or overnight so the mixture will thicken. Combine sprouted
nuts, seeds, fresh or soaked dried fruit, and ENJOY!

Variations

Alternatively, to dry seeds, add 8 ounces water and 2 to 4 ounces of freshly prepared or minimally processed nut mylk of any variety. Walnut, almond, and cashew are my favorites to prepare and drink.

Or to seeds, add only nut mylk as the liquid— no water. (Nut mylks are a large percentage water!)

*Buckwheaties

1 cup sprouted buckwheat groats, a.k.a. buckwheaties
soaking water
nut mylk of choice
sprouted nuts and berries

To prepare sprouted buckwheaties:

Soak 1 cup of whole buckwheat groats overnight. Rinse thoroughly in the morning. Place soaked/sprouted buckwheat groats on parchment paper or silicon sheet in the dehydrator or oven at 110 to 115 degrees (120 degrees max). After dehydrating 1–2 hours and using in the recipe, store any extra dry buckwheat groats in a sealed container. (I like

Some Tips for Toppings

Sprouted walnuts; almonds; other nuts and seeds, such as hazelnuts, almonds, or pepitas (pumpkin seeds); and dried fruits, such as raisins and cranberries, currents, tart cherries, or apricots are wonderful additions to any of these breakfast creations.

Some say to add fruits and nuts on alternate days for food combining and optimal digestion considerations. Experiment to see what works best for you and your body!

to store seeds, beans, and grains in regular glass mason jars with metal lids. Ball jars work great!)

Serve with sprouted nut mylk of your choice, topped with sprouted nuts and berries.

*Almond Mylk/Nut Mylk

1 cup almonds
4 cups water (or 3 cups water for richer mylk)
1/2 date, optional
pinch salt, optional
1 teaspoon cinnamon, optional

Soak almonds for 8 hours or overnight. Drain and rinse. Place almonds in high-speed blender with water (and your choice of options listed) and blend. Squeeze mixture through a nut mylk bag. Save the moist nut meal for later to sprinkle on salads or to use for dessert recipes, such as Cinnamon Almond Cacao Nib Date Delight on page 195.

*Salad for Breakfast

If you prefer to eat whole veggies and fruits rather than juicing them, see more details about Salad in the Lunch and Dinner section.

Lunch and Dinner

- Tofu and Veggie Stir-Fry (Serve over rice or gluten-free noodles.)
- *Raw Vegan Salad
- Savory Black Beans served with Rice
- Red Lentil Soup (With variations.)
- Vegan Stew (Serve over rice or another grain of choice.)

- Sprouted Cooked Black Bean Burger (Serve with mixed-greens salad with cucumbers, carrots, red pepper, and princess dressing or no-oil lemon and ume dressing.)
- Salad
- Hot Pot: Miso Soup

Complete Dinner

- Black beans and rice or a tofu dish with miso soup, veggie stir-fry, and salad
- Black beans and rice, root vegetable soup, and salad

These lunch and dinner recipes can be interchanged for lunch, dinner, or even breakfast, for that matter! If you're staying with all raw vegan, build your meals from scratch with raw green salads as the base. If you steam vegetables briefly or warm them in a dehydrator (less than 118 degrees Fahrenheit) or oven, most of the nutrients are maintained. Yay! The delicious cooked recipes are here for those who are stepping into the plant-based lifestyle for the first time and aren't yet ready to dive in!

Tofu and Veggie Stir-Fry
(Serve over rice or gluten-free noodles)

8 ounces of firm or medium tofu

1/2 red pepper, chopped

1 large carrot, sliced thinly

4 leaves of kale, chopped

1 sweet onion or onion type of choice, chopped

1 clove of fresh garlic, chopped or minced

thumb of fresh ginger, chopped fine

1/4 cup pure water

Place water in pan. Heat. Sauté onion in the water for about 5 minutes. (Note: The WFPB diet does not include refined oil. As mentioned, if the oil is part of a whole food, such as an avocado, it's fine!) Add carrot and red pepper. Sauté for a few more minutes. Add the rest of the ingredients. Stir. Cover pan and simmer on low heat for 2 more minutes. Serve over rice of your choice or gluten-free noodles.

*Raw Vegan Salad

See the Salad section on page 191. Salads are raw unless you add cooked ingredients!

A Note on Seeds, Beans, and Grains

When a seed, a bean, or any grain is soaked, it is then called *sprouted*. Sprouting has many advantages for us herbivores. According to Milton Mills, MD, as humans, based on our physiologies, we are designed to eat mainly plants.

For some of us, for optimal digestion, soaking seeds serves us well, especially if we've not yet taken the time to do some systemic detoxifying. Without soaking beans, some people get lots of gas and will shy away from beans altogether, not realizing why they are suffering from sore bellies loaded with gas!

When beans, such as green beans, are fresh, they are considered a vegetable and have nutritional properties of a vegetable. When they are mature and become dry before harvest, they are considered a form of grain and have nutritional properties of a grain. There are many fine distinctions that are beyond the scope of this book.

Savory Black Beans

1 cup dry black beans soaked and sprouted
   or one 15-ounce can organic black beans
   (For the latter, skip the soaking and
   boiling steps.)
1 sweet onion, chopped
1/2 bunch kale, chopped
1 fresh tomato, chopped if in season, or an
   8-ounce jar of tomato product of your
   choice (I like marinara sauces in glass jars
   for this purpose.)
1/2 teaspoon salt, optional
water to cover beans for overnight soaking
fresh water to cover and cook beans in

Soak black beans overnight. Drain. Rinse.
Place presoaked sprouted beans in a pan with
fresh water. Simmer for 1 hour or until tender.
Or open a can of organic black beans and put
the beans in a pan to heat. In a separate pan,
sauté the onion in a few tablespoons of water
for about 5 minutes, stirring occasionally,
adding more water if needed. Sprinkle in salt,
chopped kale, and tomato product of your
choice. Simmer for about 5 minutes. Combine
with cooked beans, and serve over cooked
organic brown rice or rice of your choice.

A Note on Pressure Cookers and Microwaves

Some people cook with pressure cookers or microwaves. Some find that using a pressure cooker with beans, rice, or any foods, for that matter, creates a glutamate response in their body. That may also be the case for you, and you may not yet realize it. Glutamate reactions can include headaches, brain fog, dizziness, heart palpitations, and nausea.

What about MSG?

Monosodium glutamate (MSG) is a food additive commonly used in almost all processed foods. According to truthinlabeling.org, MSG, free glutamic acid, and glutamate-mimicking food additives are disguised in more than fifty different ways. Look at the list on their website: https://www.truthinlabeling.org/names.html. Ingredients such as hydrolyzed vegetable protein, citric acid, and many more create the glutamate effect in our bodies.

I first discovered this glutamate response in myself when eating Chinese food in restaurants. Our family consistently requests no MSG when in Asian restaurants, as MSG is sometimes a common added ingredient. It turns out that was just the tip of the iceberg. In all cultures and most food that is spiced (and even not necessarily spiced but likely overcooked), there are combinations of spices and foods that can mimic the glutamate response in a person's system.

Optional

Before serving, sprinkle beans with a topping of your choice, such as vegan cheese (yes, yes, that's processed food) or gomasio, a combination of sesame seeds and salt (yes, that's extra salt). Use your judgment!

Red Lentil Soup

This basic and incredibly delicious recipe was inspired by Frank and Silva, Middle Eastern chefs, caterers, and former restaurant owners—I've been preparing this soup for many years now with lots of variations!

1 cup organic red lentils
6 cups water

Add lentils to water. Bring water to a boil, and then lower to simmer. Simmer for 45 minutes to 1 hour, stirring occasionally and sending loving and thankful energy into the soup!

There are many variations to this bare-bones, basic soup recipe. I find simple is best, especially when first diving into this way of life. Often, if a recipe is not simple enough, you may not try it. Try this recipe. You'll be amazed! And don't be discouraged. As time passes, you will become more and more confident in your abilities as an awesome vegan chef!

(Note: Lentils can be sprouted and used raw in recipes but are generally not soaked prior to cooking.[9])

Lentil Soup Variations

When adding lentils to the pot, add another 2 to 3 cups of water, and add the following root veggies: one chopped carrot and other root veggies (based on availability), including but not limited to 1/2 celeriac (celery) root, 1/2 rutabaga, 1 turnip, and 1/3 piece of parsnip. Add any spices you love. Experiment! Consider adding cumin, salt, a bay leaf, oregano, parsley, sage, rosemary, and/or thyme.

This red lentil soup recipe, with a few variations, is the basis of my vegan chykyn soup recipe. Check out the blog on my website, EnliveningConsciousness.com, for all the details and variations!

In addition to combinations or individual spices causing the reaction, I get the glutamate swimmy-brain feeling when food is slow cooked or cooked in a pressure cooker. The MSG response, for me, feels like a woozy feeling in my brain. Sometimes the room can begin to spin, so if I'm not sitting down, I feel as if I might fall down, though I never have. One time, my husband had such a strong glutamate response from eating in a vegan fast food restaurant that he almost drove our car off the road. Luckily, my brother was in the passenger seat next to him and guided the wheel back onto the road. Often, we do not even realize this type of feeling is caused by what is in our food. We may feel sick, get a headache, or feel immediately hungry after a meal due to this response or another type of food allergy and not attribute these feelings to what we just have eaten.

Take it from me, this is the TRUTH, and it is common—much more common than anyone cares to admit.

---

[9] Katherine Gillen, "How to Soak Lentils: A Step-by-Step Guide for Soaking Pulses (and Why You Might Want to in the First Place)," PureWow, https://www.purewow.com/food/soaking-lentils.

Watch Out, New Vegans!

In the vegan world, often, those who cater to new vegans use multiple spices to try to mimic the tastes of meat and meat spices. I am not a fan of this type of cooking. In desserts, far more sugar is often added than in typical desserts. I prefer to eat whole raw foods if possible, with minimal addition of spices and zero refined sugar.

When the food is raw, sprouted, grown, and prepared with love, spices and extra sugars are not necessary, as the food itself is so full of amazing deliciousness and wonderful energy. Sometimes excessive spices are used to mask rancid food or to mask the bland or yucky taste of food laden with chemicals or the weird, tasteless energy of GMO Frankenfood, such as corn, potatoes, beets, and many other veggies that, if not organic, are now polluted by the agribusiness giant Monsanto.

Vegan Stew

(Served over rice or another grain of choice)

This recipe was created by Rachel and Laura Beck, my daughters.

1 small onion
2 carrots, peeled
2 celery stalks
3 small potatoes
1/4 teaspoon salt or to taste
1/2 teaspoon paprika or to taste
1 1/2 cups water

In a medium-sized pot, sauté diced onion in vegetable oil (or water) until translucent. Add coarsely chopped carrot, celery, and potatoes. Season with salt and paprika. Add enough water to cover vegetables (about 1 1/2 cups). Cover with lid and simmer for about 45 minutes, or until potatoes are soft. Serve over your choice of rice or other grain. Mmmmm!

Sprouted Cooked Black Bean Burger

1 (15-ounce) can organic black beans (Or soak 8 ounces of beans for 8 hours or overnight, rinse, cook, drain, and use in this recipe. The beans expand with soaking!)

1/2–3/4 cups oats

1 "egg" made of ground chia seeds (see below)

1/4 teaspoon baharat (Middle Eastern spice blend), optional

1/4 teaspoon curry powder, optional

To prepare the chia seed mixture:

This is a good egg substitute for vegans.

Add 2 tablespoons chia seeds to about 3 ounces of water, or use the bean water from the can. Stir and let sit for 5–10 minutes.

Pulse beans and oats very briefly in food processor or high-speed blender. Or mash beans separately. Combine all remaining ingredients, and stir. You can add seasonings of your choice (cumin, cinnamon, salt, pepper, etc.) to the mixture as well if desired. Form into small cakes. Place on baking sheet, and bake at 350 degrees for about 20 minutes or to desired consistency. Top with lettuce, tomato, "special sauce" (mixture of vegan mayo and ketchup), ketchup, and pickle relish or any toppings of your choice.

*Salad

Salads are incredibly versatile and are raw vegan by definition. Consider eating a salad as your main course for at least one meal a day. Begin building your salads with romaine or other green or purple leaf lettuce. Then add sprouts (up to 50 percent of the volume of your salad is especially desirable for raw living foodists), parsley, chopped carrots, cucumbers, or purple cabbage. Fermented foods, such as sauerkraut, olives, pickles, or kimchi, are more wonderful choices. Be careful: kimchi can be extremely spicy—a great food if you love spicy foods!

You can top the salad with rice, beans, or tofu. If you're on the raw

Our Soils

Soils are depleted. That means we are not getting the nutrition we need like we used to from the foods we are eating. Technology and GMO crops are not the answer. Putting hands and hearts to Mother Gaia is the answer I prefer! Depleted soils are a FACT, especially in the USA. If you need information about what to do to feed yourself and the entire ecosystem well, go to the myriad of resources on the importance of biodynamic soil and Permaculture implementation (David Jacke, Bill Mollison, Darrell Frey, Michelle Czolba, and many others).

vegan journey, leave off the cooked items, and add a variety of sprouts.

For salad dressing, try a squeeze of lemon and a few shakes of umeboshi plum vinegar purchased at a local food cooperative. Often, no dressing is necessary, as the toppings, especially raw sauerkraut, and the delicious flavor of fresh ginger, a spice I use often, seep through.

Basic Salad Ingredients

Lettuces

Kales

Sprouts

Cucumbers

Carrots

Celery

Add dandelion greens or other freshly picked wild edibles, such as scallions, seasonally if you're sure they do not have any kind of synthetic lawn-chemical pesticide; herbicide; fungicide; or spray, such as Bt, on them. If you're feeling really wild in the springtime, add yellow dandelion flowers—that's before they go to seed!

Hot Pot: Miso Soup

8 cups water

1 (14-ounce) package udon or other long noodles

1/2 cup diced carrots

1 cup sliced zucchini

1/2 cucumber, cut into thin, round slices

1 celery stalk, cut into small pieces

1/4 daikon radish, cubed small

3 tablespoons black bean, chickpea, or other miso paste (or follow recommendation on package)

gomasio (sesame seeds and salt) to taste

seaweed of choice to taste

Cook noodles following directions on package, or make your own noodles and cook them, or use raw zoodles (use spiralized raw zucchini to make this a partially raw recipe). Prepare carrots, cucumber, celery, and daikon radish. Place carrots and celery in the water, and bring to a boil. Simmer for 3 minutes. Add chopped zucchini and simmer for 2 more minutes. Turn off heat, and add miso paste. Stir. Add cucumber and daikon radish. Sprinkle with gomasio, or add other seaweed and enjoy!

Consider installing a hoop house (a type of greenhouse) in your backyard or on the roof of your apartment building (talk to the landlord first, unless you own the building!) in colder weather. Think about installing and maintaining a garden as part of or instead of a lawn. Imagine food, rather than grass, surrounding your home or apartment in the warmer months. Grow some or all of your own food, and share some of your bounty with neighbors. See the book *Food Not Lawns* for more information. The time is now to explore Permaculture (permanent agriculture) and get busy caring for your own needs. Look up Bill Mollison, who wrote *Permaculture: A Designer's Manual*, or Darrell Frey and Michelle Czolba's book on food forest gardens. Minimally, begin with some herbs on your windowsill and some countertop sprouting!

Sauce

Creamy Vegan Sauce

My daughter Laura Beck and I created this recipe.

3/4 cup raw cashews (soak for about 3 hours, drain, and rinse)
1/2 cup water
1/4 cup vegan mylk of choice
1/4 cup chopped celery
3/4 cup butternut squash, cooked
1/2 cup chopped red pepper
salt and pepper to taste

Blend ingredients in high-speed blender or other blender, and serve with pasta of choice.

Variation: In place of squash, use 6 ounces tofu, 1 teaspoon paprika, and 1 clove garlic.

Desserts

- *Chocolate Mousse
- *Cinnamon Almond Cacao Nib Date Delight!
- Vegan Lemon Cream Pie

Chocolate Mousse
(Made with avocado and dates)

3 ripe avocados
4 medjool dates, or any variety of dates you love

1 ripe banana

1/4 cup filtered water

2 tablespoons raw cacao powder

a sprinkle of sprouted nuts of your choice

Mash the avocados and banana, and finely chop the dates. Combine these three ingredients. Gradually add the water to desired consistency, sprinkle cacao powder into the mixture, and enjoy. Top with soaked (sprouted) nuts of your choice.

If you prefer a smooth texture with the consistency of mousse, place all ingredients (after removing the avocado pits and date seeds) in a high-speed blender and blend to desired consistency. For an extra sweet treat, enjoy it topped with coconut cream and a bit of maple syrup.

*Cinnamon Almond Cacao
Nib Date Delight!*

1 cup (8 to 10 ounces) almond mash (left in the nut mylk bag from homemade blended almond mylk)

3 tablespoons of organic cacao nibs

1/4 teaspoon cinnamon

3 medjool dates

Avocado—Fruit or Veggie? Food Combining. What Do You Think?

Is an avocado a fruit or a vegetable? Avocado is considered a fruit botanically but is considered a vegetable in the kitchen. Some say combining avocado with nuts and seeds in the same meal is not recommended. Some individuals who are sensitive to this combination of foods choose not to combine them in the same day. Some disagree with this segregation completely!

Mash the dates, and mix with almond mash. Stir in the cocoa nibs and cinnamon.

Enjoy this amazing treat, which I cannot stop eating once I make it. It's wonderful for adding to breakfast creations and desserts as well. It stands alone as a dessert too! Feel free to adjust the quantities of these ingredients to suit your taste. Hey, that goes for all of these recipes!

Vegan Lemon Cream Pie

First Layer

2–3 tablespoons chia seeds
2–3 tablespoons hemp seeds
2 tablespoons flax seeds
1/4–1/2 cup water

Stir all first-layer ingredients. Pour into pie pan. Set for 15 minutes or until the mixture gels.

Second Layer

1 (16-ounce) package silken tofu
juice of one lemon, plus the zest
1 avocado
1 banana
1 tablespoon maple syrup

A Word about Sweeteners

Refined vegan sweeteners include stevia, maple syrup, and date sugar. Pure whole dates are a wonderful natural sweetener. Bottom line: When you eat organic whole foods, the natural sweetness of the foods shines through when the items, such as sweet potatoes, yams, delicata squash, apples, peaches, and pears, are in season. Green beans harvested from the vine can be wonderfully sweet as well.

Combine all second-layer ingredients in a bowl one at a time and mash. Pour on top of the first layer.

Topping

Line edge with sliced apple and chopped medjool dates. Sprinkle top with a handful of pepitas (pumpkin seeds), cacao nibs, and berries.

Enjoy!

Snacks for Home and Travel

Dehydrated snacks in travel packs can be all raw (meaning not exposed to heat above 110 to 118 degrees Fahrenheit—that's approximately 42 to 48 degrees Centigrade).

- **Dehydrated nuts, seeds, and berries.** It's said that the shapes of foods reflect the parts of the body or the organs they support. Walnuts look like a mammalian brain and are wonderful food for our brains. Kidney beans look like kidneys, and carrots sliced in rounds have characteristics that look like eyes. There you have it.

- **A word about almonds.** I used to eat a lot of them. Due to the dire

The Dehydrator and Raw Foods

The dehydrator is a wonderful tool when one is transitioning into veganism. As long as the temperature of the food is not raised above between 110 and 118 degrees (opinions vary), the food is considered a raw food suitable for a raw living-food vegan diet.

Some raw foodists miss crunchy foods. Dehydrated kale gets crunchy in the dehydration process and is quite a delicacy, especially if sprinkled with a little bit of salt and nutritional yeast! Dehydrated sprouted nuts and seeds are very crunchy and last much longer than raw nuts. All these items are perfect for a snack.

While not a snack but worth a mention, raw vegan lasagna (made with tofu, walnut chyze, zucchini slices, and tomato sauce) can be warmed up to a more palatable temperature in a dehydrator rather than being eaten at room temperature. You can use the dehydrator as an oven of sorts for many snacks, especially if it's chilly!

situation with bees and pollinators in general as a result of habitat destruction and the overuse of herbicides, pesticides, and fungicides and other endocrine (hormone) disruptors, I try to stay away from raw almonds and other almond products as much as possible. Recently, however, I've not been able to resist making almond nut mylk from scratch. It's completely delicious.

- **Good transition food.** Sprouted and dehydrated nuts and seeds are great when moving into the plant-based lifestyle, as they are more nutritious than many other snack foods, and they store longer, so they are especially great when traveling. In addition, sprouted nuts and seeds are easier on digestion and allow the nutrients in the foods to be assimilated more easily. Dehydrators can be purchased online.

- **Preparation of dehydrated nuts.** Soak them as long as necessary (times vary with type of nut), and then put them on the dehydrator trays for the specified time frame. Pack them with some pepitas (pumpkin seeds) and raisins in a container, and voilà! You're good to go!

- **Spirulina crunchies** from the superfoods supplier Vivapura rock. The Raw Food World, HealthForce SuperFoods, and many others supply spirulina. Spirulina and chlorella are amazingly nutritious, chock full of protein, and immune-boosting, and they can be added to juices, smoothies, stews, and salads— really a great addition to any food.

- **Chia seeds** can be made into **chia pudding** as a quick superfoodie snack by soaking 1–2 tablespoons in about 4–6 ounces of water. (Another recipe is also in the Breakfast section.) Add in some dehydrated nuts and seeds, hemp seeds, flax seeds, and dried or fresh fruit, such as blueberries, raspberries, or foraged elderberries; stir; and let sit for 10 minutes. The seeds are extremely easy to carry along with you and, hydrated, make an incredibly delicious snack or breakfast packed with protein. Try ground chia for easier digestion, and see if you enjoy the whole or ground version better. Look for chia seeds at your local health food store, natural food markets, or any of the online sources listed previously. Remember to source organic foods always when possible. Our purchases drive the market, not the other way around. Enjoy!

For ease in traveling, use any of the snack ideas, along with the suggestions below.

Try regular oats, overnight oats, or a salad:

- Overnight oats with spirulina (one tablespoon or to taste) and nuts, seeds, or fruit to taste
- Salad for breakfast if you prefer to eat the whole veggies and fruits rather than juicing them
- Chia pudding

For Supplements, Be Mindful of the Source

When you travel, remember to pack supplements!

A note about sourcing supplements, including food supplements, such as spirulina: There are reputable and not-so-reputable sources for supplements. It's important to order from an organic source you trust.

Chapter 12

MOVING DEEPER WITHIN, INTEGRATION, REFINEMENTS

What Does a Person Need to Eat?

*T*HIS IS A LOADED QUESTION, and the answer is, it depends. Your needs are based on your constitution; the season; the time of day; and your physical, mental, emotional, and spiritual state of being. Needs can change with a woman's blood moon cycle, the season, and the time of her life. There are specific foods recommended based on your Ayurvedic type—Vata, Pita, Kapha—or a combination of types, which most of us are!

As we begin to listen to our bodies more deeply, the answers come to us. What to eat, how to eat, where to eat, when to eat and drink, and with whom can become significant parts of our personal journeys.

Is It Easy to Eat What's Best for Your Constitution?

It's not always easy to know what to eat or drink. Even if we think we are following our intuition, we may not be following our intuition. Why? Because our cultural conditioning can interfere with our intuition. We're all in recovery from our cultural upbringing. Many of us were bottle-fed or weaned earlier than optimal for prime immune system development. It is okay and desirable to nurse a child for three or four years without shame!

Some I know, and probably some you too know or grew up with, eat or ate foods that most of us clearly recognize as full of poison—and no, that is not an exaggeration!

Hamburger Helper, white wheat breads and pasta noodles with all nutrients stripped out and then synthetic fortified vitamins and minerals placed back in, and various bottled sauces and spices, such as Ac'cent, composed of monosodium glutamate (MSG), are not true food by my definition. Those "foods," sauces, and spices were an integral part of the created culture of convenience. Our parents' generation in the 1950s and 1960s were fed the convenience story of Pop-Tarts for breakfast and Pecan Sandies with a glass of milk as a staple treat for school lunches and after-school snacks. This culture of convenience was sold to us as being better than what our grandparents' generation knew.

Now we realize that as humans, we are experiential beings. Meaning comes through experience. The experience of our elders just a few generations before us included connecting to themselves through the cycles of the moon and sun and waters and to one another in community. The connections to self and others manifested through earth-based or other religious or spiritual rituals. These rituals were sometimes monotheistic (one G-d) or earth-based.

Other religious or spiritual rituals and traditions connected people to the land through social interaction, wild food gathering, and then growing (with the advent of agriculture creating "permanent" places to live) their own food for themselves to eat and to share with others. And so the circle of life continues.

Building Immunity and Your Food Choices

Some strive toward eating 90 percent raw and 10 percent cooked foods. That goal is not for everyone. Each person is here for a specific reason and has their own path. And perhaps our commitment to ourselves to be the best we can be in this humyn form ebbs and flows at times!

Practicing the raw, organic, veganic, complete living-foods lifestyle, in my view, as a basic lifestyle choice, is the absolute best way to stay healthy, peaceful, and deeply connected to Spirit. By detoxifying your body twice a year, or more, for seven days in the spring and in the fall—using green juice fasting, wheatgrass juicing (some use enemas or colonics periodically), meditation, and yoga or other gentle movement modalities—and incorporating breathing techniques, walking, right relationships, spiritual observance, strong community ties, service, and charity into your life, you can BE, and Live a life that is, consistently vibrantly healthy from the inside out.

Eating a whole-food, plant-based diet, and following the twice-a-year detoxification plan, is also a wonderful choice if you're not ready to step into the raw living foodist lifestyle.

Building and Maintaining Immunity

According to one of my most recent mentors and spiritual guides, Gabriel Cousens, MD, a 100 percent organic, vegan, raw foods diet is the best way to consistently build your immune system and maintain health in our most interesting world. Supplementing with vitamins B and D and zinc is essential. Vitamin D protects your respiratory system, and Zinc is an excellent antiviral. You will be strong and resilient and better able to weather all the storms—physical, emotional, and spiritual—you might encounter in your life on earth, even during a pandemic!

Michael Greger, in his book *How to Survive a Pandemic*, mentions that the COVID-19 pandemic was not the first, nor will it be the last, pandemic. So it's time to boost your immune system to be prepared for what is coming next! In any case, pandemic or not, staying healthy and well physically, mentally, emotionally, and spiritually with your own amazing immune system in mind is the best way to not only survive but also thrive!

Creating a strong inner ecosystem is the best way to stay resilient no matter what is going on all around us. Holding positive thoughts and staying committed to love and gratitude for ourselves and for all people and all of life are the best ways to be vibrantly alive!

If you are not moved to practice raw living foodism, don't fret. You'll be fine as you move in that direction. Stay positive, and know you are heading the right way. Positive thoughts have incredible power to keep the immune system strong and reverse many chronic and acute illnesses.

There is so much to learn as we shift our dietary intake to move into the consciousness of building our immune systems and keeping ourselves in high vibration and strong on a moment-to-moment basis.

Q&A on Being a Plant-Based Foodie

Some questions commonly asked of those eating a plant-based diet include the following:

- What do you consume?
- Do you take supplements?
- What do you recommend your patients consume?
- What do you consume energetically, and what does this have to do with the vegan lifestyle?

What do you consume?

There is a wide range of what people consume when characterized as *plant-based eaters* or as *vegan*. I do not like labels, but to understand the range of how people eat and live a plant-based or a vegan lifestyle, it can be helpful for clarification purposes. Eating habits and lifestyles can be referred to in a variety of ways, depending on whom a person is interacting with. There are many subtleties.

A whole-food, plant-based eater might define their intake as eating whole foods; both vegetables and fruits; some grains, nuts, and seeds, preferably sprouted; and beans some of the time. Brenda Davis, in *Becoming Raw*, classifies raw foodists as those eating 60 percent raw and 40 percent cooked plant foods. Fascinating. I mistakenly thought that when one characterized oneself as a raw foodist, that meant 100 percent of the time! Dr. Rabbi Shaman Gabriel Cousens defines the optimal raw diet to support one's journey into spiritual enlightenment as 95 percent raw living foods and 100 percent vegan, preferably 100 percent organic veganic if possible.

Do you take supplements?

Opinions vary regarding the necessity of supplements. Supplementation is an extremely individualized subject. When taken with the advice of a nutrition and medical professional combined with one's developed intuition, for some people, supplements can enrich their inner ecosystem. The supplements are compensating for the worldwide vitamin- and mineral-depleted soils our food is grown in and our own individual body system microbiome insufficiencies because of our polluted external ecosystem.

A person may take supplements regularly or sporadically. For some, supplementing with appropriate amounts of absorbable forms of vitamins A, B, C, D, and K on a regular basis can be important. For most everybody in Western civilization—whether the person is eating a plant-based diet or not—due to lifestyle, supplementation, at least on a temporary basis, can be extremely important. Many of us do not get enough sun exposure to boost our vitamin D levels, nor do we eat dirt (B12 is made by microorganisms living in soil and water).

Vitamin B12 is an important supplement for those living the vegan lifestyle. I believe it's an imperative for everyone, as most of the Western population is deficient in all B vitamins and vitamin D, no matter their dietary intake. But as vegans, we are told to be sure to supplement especially with the proper ratio of vitamin B6 and vitamin B12. For those of us who live close to the earth and literally eat some healthy dirt, as when we harvest a carrot and eat it without washing it, we might get our proper amount of B12. Other than if we literally eat dirt (and I'm not recommending this), most of us are deficient in B12.

The supplement question is a great one and is individual. It is important to have your vitamin B and vitamin D blood levels checked and to take supplements if the levels are below recommended levels for your sex and body weight.

In addition to vitamins A, B, C, D, and K, other vitamins and herbs can be beneficial, depending on many factors too numerous to go into here. The specificity of types and dosages of vitamins, minerals, and other supplements you need to feel and perform your best will take trial and error, listening to the advice of those you trust, and trusting Spirit to guide you to the right choice for you at any given moment in time. Levels may vary with the seasons of the year and the seasons of your life, the variety of foods you're eating, and the levels of positive energy you're creating and consuming. Levels vary based on how balanced and grounded you are on a given day.

I envision a time when the soils of inner and outer selves, mentally, physically, emotionally, and spiritually, are so rich worldwide that we no longer need supplementation! Let's visualize together as ONE!

What do I recommend my patients consume?

Generally, I recommend the whole-food, plant-based lifestyle as the best overall dietary choice. People vary, and recommendations vary, but this diet is excellent as long as there aren't health or other issues that would make aspects of this diet too difficult to follow. Supplement recommendations vary with the individual. Choosing one's own daily routine regarding exercise and loving social support are also important individual choices. The full Spiritual Nutrition paradigm includes full, heartfelt living from the inside out in all moments of everyday existence.

What do we consume energetically, and what does this have to do with the vegan lifestyle?

The energy we are surrounded by is the energy we create and the energy that is drawn to us. Those surrounding us are our mirrors. We have mirror neurons in our brains. So those we surround ourselves with reflect our energy and vice versa. Our experiences are part of our whole makeup as human beings. Spending time, ideally 95 percent of the time, with positive thoughts; meditating twice a day; getting enough sleep; being in service to self and community; repenting, saying you're sorry, and doing things to correct your ways (*teshuvah* in the Jewish faith); and taking care of yourself and Mother Earth (*tikkun h'olam*) through spiritual fasting and juice and vegetable broth fasting retreats can be of utmost importance. The physical food we eat is just one aspect of what we consume. Our human immune systems are most wholly supported by the more pure vegan diet, but there are many other aspects to what we consume and how we act for ourselves and in the world in service to humanity.

We have entered the quantum fifth dimension in this planet Earth experience. What the heck does that mean? I'm not certain myself, but I do know that we are all special, and we all have superpowers and have the potential within us to access much more than many of us think we have the potential for. The planetary, cosmic, and karmic alignments are all in our favor. The angels and our ancestors are all around us, rooting for us to live to our highest potentials as the highest expression of what we are capable of. Hence, the energetics of a vegan lifestyle are key as a foundation for enlightenment and living as the highest expression of what we are on this earth at this moment in time to be and do.

Spend time with close family, cousins, and friends you feel most comfortable with in this amazing life. Consider those you resonate with as your relatives as well. Consume fresh air, and practice exercise of varying types. Meditate. Add sunshine during the day and darkness late at night before going to sleep to the list of things you consume daily as well. If you feel called, serve those beyond your immediate family and friends and out into the cosmos and back again!

Elements of Spiritual Nutrition

As I've been taught by Gabriel Cousens, MD, the raw living-foods lifestyle is the best lifestyle to attain spiritual enlightenment. And it's not for everyone. I enjoy the Modern Living Essene Householder Spiritual Nutrition lifestyle and offer here some tangible steps (really throughout the book) to move in that direction if you choose to do so. In any case, wherever you are in your food intake and your visual, movement, and spiritual intake, following are some outstanding tips for dipping your toe in!

General Self-Care as Health Care and Spiritual Nutrition
Lessons Learned by This Plant-Based, Wise Woman Foodie

- **Cultivate Peace before you eat food or drink liquids.** Be sure you are in a place to easily digest all you eat and drink.

- **Say a prayer of gratitude** for the incredible food in front of you to G-d, Source, the Great Spirit, Buddha, or any representative of the many spiritual traditions in this world and beyond if you believe that is so. Give thanks for the soil; the water; the farmers; yourself as a recipient of the sustenance you are about to receive; and the whole food and supply chain of people, animals, birds, bees, and Source, who were responsible for that food making its way onto your plate!

- **Prepare amazing plant-based meals at home.** Doing so is a blessing and a decision to be honored in oneself and in others.

- **Sit down** to eat your meals.

- **Drink water**—about eight glasses a day.

- **Give your brain and body a rest** by finishing eating by 6:00 p.m. or sunset and taking a break until you eat the next day. This is considered a form of fasting. We all fast between the time we go to sleep and the time we wake up, and that is a healthy way of being.

- **Get eight hours of sleep each night** in clear, clean, peaceful, uncluttered surroundings.

- **Honor the biorhythms of your body and of the day and night cycles of the sun and the monthly cycles of the moon.** Sleep when it's dark, and BE awake when there's daylight outside (if you live in a location in the world where this makes sense).

- **Honor your own process**, even if you don't know what that means! We all receive information in different ways.

- There are optimal ways to present information so people can receive it. The best way is to **live your principles** and not worry about what others do or think about what you do.

- **Others will observe your joy, enthusiasm, and love**, and those who feel resonant, who feel called, will mirror your actions and move into whatever aspect of the vegan lifestyle they feel comfortable with in their own time frame. And that is A-okay.

- **Each person has their own reason for being on this planet** and will express their own unique gifts when ready to do so.

- **Work with yourself** to improve your own neshama, your own soul path, your dharma, by moving into the expression of your highest self—at your own pace.

- **Don't worry about what other people think** or how they might judge you.

- **Follow your intuition.** You know deep within your own DNA and RNA what is best for you.

Reflections on Eating as a Plant-Based Foodie

- **Is organic really too expensive?** What is your health worth? When you let go of beef, chickens, fishes, and dairy, the price points are not relevant, because you are letting go of a lot of expense.

- **Do you love animals?** The answer is always "Yes, I love animals." Well, why do you eat them then? People love their dogs and cats, their pets, but they eat cows, chickens, and fishes; drink the fluids that flow from the udders of mammals meant for their young; and eat the eggs of birds meant to develop and grow into baby birds.

- **Vegan activists have been screaming from the rooftops for a very long time.** Perhaps it's time for all of us to stop screaming. We're working through the cognitive dissonance moment by moment. The deep dark hidden from us, the truth about eating dead flesh, is bubbling up. How do we move into creating the reality of the more beautiful new earth we all know in our hearts is possible? This new reality is truly what we are creating right now in real time.

- **We humyns have been hit hard by a large dose of shifting paradigms in this pandemic.** We are showing ourselves and others how we can all rise by first going deeply within.

- **After reconnecting with our own soulful selves, we connect with our families, our neighbors, and our communities** to create edible forest garden landscapes, share food with friends and neighbors, and create the types of communities that are truly collaborative instead of living in our isolated silos.

- **Eating meat, the flesh of a dead animal** who likely lived and died in painful circumstances with a rush of hormones flooding its system at the time of death, even if killed in a kosher slaughterhouse, **is a beyond-sad situation.**

- **This commentary leaves us all in a similar situation.** We are all in a period of mourning—mourning the loss of our prior way of life that we thought was okay, thought was rich, sweet, and smart.

- **It turns out we've all been living in a dual reality, denying our deep, soulful essences** by burying the sadness and grief of eating animals. In this world of duality and cognitive dissonance, the glass ceiling has broken, and we are now wide open to the truth that how we have been living—with rape (artificial-insemination impregnation of animals at a very basic level) and abuse of the animals we then eat—has been at the root of our subconsciousness for eons. Yet we've been hiding these truths from ourselves. Even though I've been eating and living the vegan lifestyle with versions ranging from raw, organic, veganic living to whole-foods, plant-based living for more than ten years now, the mourning comes up from time to time. I also mourn the loss of habitat, the slashing and burning of the Amazon rain forest to clear land to feed cattle that people eat, and the deep disconnect between who we think we are and who we really are deep in our hearts.

Moving toward Plant-Based Eating for the Planet and Its Inhabitants

How do our food choices impact the earth?

When we eat from the earth and choose the whole-food, plant-based lifestyle or the raw living-foods lifestyle or generally move toward plant-based eating and living, we thrive! We connect with our inner microbiomes—our inner environments and the bacteria, fungi, and viruses that constitute most of our bodies! We fall in love with ourselves and

Tips Gleaned from the Online Foods Revolution Summit 2022 with Ocean and John Robbins

I attended the 2022 Foods Revolution Summit online and was blown away by all the great information shared. Interviews with the various speakers are hosted by Ocean Robbins and personally conducted by best-selling author and food-movement leader John Robbins. Here are a few of my takeaways:

- Cook in quantity.
- Make friends with leftovers.
- Plan ahead.
- Create a food shopping list, and shop from that list.
- Keep healthy recipes handy.
- Use organic foods and fresh fruits and veggies when possible.
- Eat beans, whole grains, onions, mushrooms, apples, cucumbers, kale, collards, and countertop sprouts.
- Eat out less.
- Cook at home more.
- Home cooking takes time and practice, but the more you do it, the better the food tastes!
- Healthy eating is the path of least resistance!

This is an annual event. Learn more about it at www.foodrevolutionsummit.org.

the environment we live in. We fall in love with Mother Gaia. The BEingness we are and that surrounds us!

- We protect the Amazon rain forest so that it does not need to get burned down, so the Indigenous tribes who live there are not chased away.
- Through regenerating the rain forest and bringing back LIVING soils in every ecosystem worldwide, we are all able to take responsibility to feed ourselves, and our humanity comes back with vibrancy, joy, and full health!
- We protect and regenerate living waters by creating clarity and letting go of polluting ways.
- We use far less energy and promote letting go of fossil fuels.
- We spend more time growing our own food and create more incredible community by growing together and sharing with one another freely!

How do our choices affect our spirit; our family, friends, and neighbors; the earth we live on; and the entire universe?

- We could feed the inhabitants of the world four times over if we all moved into a vegan diet tomorrow.
- We could feed the world twelve times over if we all moved to a 100 percent vegan and 80 percent raw living, organic, veganic diet tomorrow.
- We would all be much healthier, more spirited and connected, and even more amazing than we already are!
- The regenerative future—where we give back more to ourselves and our own well-being and give more to Mother Earth than we take from her—has arrived.

The Plant-Based Foodie Lifestyle

I've settled into interspersing the whole-food, plant-based lifestyle, as described by T. Colin Campbell, PhD; Dr. Neil Barnard; the Esselstyns; and many others, with the raw living-foods lifestyle, as described by Dr. Gabriel Cousens in his many books and educational retreats. Dr. Cousens's offerings include fasting and zero point retreats, many of which I participated in while visiting the Tree of Life Rejuvenation Center when it was in Patagonia, Arizona. I now participate virtually online with participants worldwide. I've been influenced by David Wolff, Kris Carr, Fully Raw Kristina, Victoria Boutenko, and other raw living foodists as well. Brooke Goldner, who maintains a 50 percent to 90 percent raw diet, is a wonderful and inspiring physician, speaker, and writer as well. It's a pleasure to share this lifestyle with you.

Where Are You Now? What Do You Want to Do Next?

How do you characterize your lifestyle and eating habits right now? What one thing would you love to shift in your eating habits and in your lifestyle? Write down what comes immediately into your mind, and put that information in an envelope. Open the envelope next week, and notice if you were able to begin making moves toward that shift. Begin small. Take a bite-sized piece!

We Are One

How do our choices affect our spirit; our family, friends, and neighbors; the earth we live on; and the entire universe? As Sally Lipsky, PhD, of Plant-Based Pittsburgh advises, "Let's all promote the shift to plant-based eating habits for healthy people to move into vibrant health with living whole (organic) foods; mitigate environmental damage from all animal agriculture, including big agriculture and small family farming; improve people's chronic health problems; and reduce costs for food and health care. How do we do this? With veganic permaculture education; basic nutritional education; food-preparation classes; ongoing support; and access to an array of grains, legumes, vegetables, fruits, and related food staples."

- Planetary healing is miraculously hatching now as we emerge from our cocoons, so let's shine our bright lights as at no other time in the herstory of this nation. There has been no other time in the memory of anyone living on the planet like this incredible moment in time.
- We've powered down.
- We've started spending more time with loved ones.
- We are taking more time in nature to nurture ourselves through Forest Bathing, meditation, prayer, saunas, detoxification, eating and drinking habits, and much more self-care time.
- We are spraying fewer pesticides and other poisons invented during World War II and getting ready to let go of these poisons completely.
- We are implementing a Food Forest Reinvention Revolution to take responsibility for growing our own food and feeding ourselves.

My family and I are excited that our decades-long next-door neighbors recently decided not to spray their lawns. We honor the other neighbors on the block following suit!

I hope and pray this introduction to other ways of eating and being has given you at least one idea to integrate into your daily routine to move toward a plant-based lifestyle as the foundation for a 100 percent plant-based-diet lifestyle. Wherever you are on the spectrum of life, you are just where you need to be. Remember that every experience, every coincidence, and every series of synchronicities is a precious lesson to learn. As Bernie Siegal said, "Synchronicity is G-d's way of remaining anonymous!" Spirit will continue to hand us the lessons until we learn them. Source will speak to us in a myriad of ways until we listen. And so it is.

The light in me sees the light in you. Shalom, Salem, Shalem, Shanti, Shanti, Shanti, and Aho.

Lifelong Learning!

The nutrition section is a general introduction to optimal nutrition for wellness and spiritual connection. A deeper exploration of more specific dietary and lifestyle choices is available through coursework, workshops, and individual consultations with me or others with whom you resonate.

NATURE

❖ Grounding barefoot

❖ Forest bathing

❖ Mycelial networks and the beginning of
the GMO story that's been normalized[10]

[10] https://charleseisenstein.org/essays/opposition-to-gmos/, accessed July 10, 2023.

Chapter 13

EXPLORING OUR CONNECTIONS TO NATURE

Question: When is the best time to plant a tree?
Answer: Twenty years ago.
Question: When is the next best time to plant a tree?
Answer: Today!

WHAT DO WE NEED TO remember about reconnecting with our humyn natures, self-nurturing, and the nature of soil?

The regenerative future—where we give back more than we take—has arrived. We give back more to ourselves, our own well-being, our family, our community, and Mother Earth. This is so very exciting! We are moving from the carbon-based era into the energy-based era. To be most clear and ready to act in this new world, we begin with the basics of how to feed ourselves—physically, mentally, emotionally, energetically, and spiritually. Once we are well fed on all levels, we offer ourselves to serve the universe at our highest vibration, and the miracles unfold moment by moment. Yes, we can work on ourselves and serve the planet simultaneously!

My intuition tells me that we're on our way into a new form of Eden. Let's join hands. We're all in this wonderful space together, cocreating our Regenerative Future now!

Two Keys to Connecting with Nature Daily

1. Grounding with Bare Feet on the Earth

◆ Step outside for five minutes a day barefoot. I dared someone to do that the other day during early spring here in southwestern Pennsylvania, even though it was 50 degrees outside!

◆ Find a local park, and take off your shoes.

◆ In deep winter, simply remove your shoes and walk around your living space barefoot. Create a textured obstacle course with towels, pillows, and various shapes and sizes of found objects you're willing to place on the floor, and step on top of them for five minutes per day.

2. Forest Bathing

◆ Walk in the woods (or a park or other nearby area with trees and plants).

◆ Breathe deeply.

◆ Take in the sounds of the birds, the bees, the mosquitoes, the crickets, the frogs, and the toads.

◆ Hug some trees.

◆ Meditate in nature!

Moving into Harmony

Aleph. In the beginning, there was light or was there the WORD?

L'chaim: To Life! On the Nature of Life.

Setting the stage for a wild and eclectic ride

It is so very exciting to move into Harmony with

Ourselves, Our Cells, Mother Gaia, and Father Sky

Nature Stories from My Early Years

If you didn't already get the drift, I love to move, especially because movement is natural and normal. Sitting or standing still in front of books, papers, or electronics in any form is unnatural. I love to move in and through nature. Do you love to move?

I adore Forest Bathing! Simply BEing in nature, especially the woods. As a child, I loved running in the woods with our family dog; wandering around our suburban Washington, DC, neighborhood; riding bikes; building forts in the woods; traveling to natural spots on overnight field trips as an elementary school student; rowing on the C&O Canal; hiking in Big Sur and Muir Woods; and traveling across the USA after high school graduation.

There are so many ways to connect with nature. How do you love to connect with nature?

Moving Back to the Wisdom of the Indigenous and Our Indigenous Natures

We are poised to move into our regenerative future. Why are we poised? How do we go about this? Perhaps we first need to take a look at what we have normalized in this era of

Witnessing a New Story

From Charles Eisenstein's essay "What Is the Next Story?": "The destiny of humanity is to bring all our gifts and powers into the service of life to create beauty and wonders, and to witness what life creates through us and around us. It starts with healing the damage done in the age of separation."[11]

[11] https://charleseisenstein. substack.com/p/what-is-the-next-story, accessed July 23, 2023.

separation. Separation from our own somas and separation from one another. And then reassemble the puzzle pieces.

What Have We Normalized?

Have you ever asked yourself this question? One thing we've normalized is the assumption that things need to get worse over time as we "age." In my optometry practice and in my interactions with others over the years, I've prided myself on referring to elders as more *mature*, not *old*! We now know we have the means to stabilize and even reverse the aging process, as described in *The Biology of Belief*. Through epigenetics, shifting our genetic expression through shifting our perceptions, we can reverse the length of our telomeres (genetic material in our DNA that is related to the aging process). How do we shift our perceptions? We do this through the power of positive thinking, feeling, and acting in ways that are regenerative. We do this by staying connected to G-d, improving our vision naturally, moving more easily, eating wisely, BEing in nature, thinking regeneratively, and trusting Spirit. So very exciting!

Through novel techniques that some perceive as "primitive" technologies, we can be awake and maximally, radically ALIVE humyns! I've threaded some of these technologies through these pages and disguised them by calling them experiential activities. These activities, when habituated, replace our old habit patterns of negativity, pain, and grief, and we get younger with each conscious and then unconscious newly patterned breath. Ahhhhh!

What else have we normalized?

- Foods coated with pesticide, herbicides, and fungicides
- Genetically modified organisms (GMOs) in seeds, foods, and pharmaceuticals

- The pharmaceutical industry
- Microscopic nanotechnology in everything from foods to cosmetics to pharmaceutical drugs of all kinds, oral, sublingual, and injectable
- Animal and plant industrial agriculture, a.k.a. agribusiness, including "organic" agribusiness
- The raping of the earth through the extractive industries
- Robotics
- Artificial intelligence (AI)
- What else can you think of that has been normalized or is in the process of being normalized in our culture?

Practicing Permaculture

I choose to move beyond the manipulation and degradation of body, mind, spirit, and soul. I choose to embrace the way of organic veganic permaculture. The practice of permaculture means permanent agriculture, where we work with the land and give back to the land. We give back more than we take. This is in contrast to agribusiness and the extractive industries that rape the land, water, and entire ecosystem of Mother Earth.

Industrial agriculture has been normalized in Western cultures. This normalization includes the field of organic industrial agriculture. What is organic industrial agriculture? It is a way of growing crops using the same or similar techniques used by agribusiness practices, such as growing large amounts of monocrops, all the same types of vegetables in a space. In contrast, the practice of permaculture is a dynamic system that intersperses and interweaves small amounts of many crops; grows food in zones, in their appropriate ecosystems; and includes farm animals in the mix. Veganic permaculture removes domestic animals from the system.

A New Mantra

"I'm reconnecting with joy, beauty, high vibration, and excitement inside my body and with all that surrounds me" is my new mantra. How about you? What new mantra will you dare to try out?

A Personal Story of a Permaculture Earth Angel

A dear friend of mine, Kate, just passed away. I have been teary these past few days while thinking about Kate and all I experienced with her, and all I have experienced with all my family and friends, over the years. She left an incredible urban Permaculture landscape behind, along with the world of wisdom contained there. I'm reminding myself and you to remember to keep sprouting and planting seeds, plants, and trees. Kate is cheering us on from heaven!

We Are All Connected as One on All Levels

The connection of ourselves to ourselves, our own interconnectedness, is easily demonstrated by looking at the interrelationships of the web of life. Our inner environment works with the same fluid nature as that of the larger ecosystem.

Said in another way, it's about us as individuals opening to the patterns of nature. Many perceive nature as something external to us. Our inner G-d-like nature, our development on all levels, is nature in its perfection!

The story of the wolves in Yellowstone National Park is the story of an ecosystem that was depleted of a keystone species and then restored to close to its original form by reintroducing this critical puzzle piece to the park ecosystem. When looked at with a wide-angle lens using both our peripheral and our central vision, this example exemplifies the interconnectedness of our body systems and the interconnectedness of all the levels and layers of the ecosystem and the connection to Spirit, or G-d. It is a metaphor for the entire book. As our eyesight clears and we broaden our vision, we will more fully and joyfully be able to participate in the renovation, rejuvenation, and resetting of our Spaceship Earth and our connection to the cosmos as it was meant to be.

The Wolves in Yellowstone National Park

This incredible story of a macroecosystem begs to be told. It's the story of the wolves in Yellowstone National Park. Wolves were perceived as a threat to the other animals in the park, and they were hunted down to the point that by the late 1920s, none were left. When wolves were looked at simply as predators, they were killed. The predator-and-prey relationship broke down. The wolf population was decimated, and the ecosystem was degraded and bare as well.

Without wolves to keep the elk and deer populations in balance with the rest of the ecosystem, the elk and deer were overgrazing and eating everything. Their populations increased beyond natural levels. Deer and elk are herbivores. They eat plants, not animals. (Yes, elk and deer get all of their protein by eating plants!) Because the elk and deer ate so many plants and trees, destroying the natural balance of the ecosystem, the population of many other species declined, as these other species did not have adequate sustenance.

In 1995, a pack of gray wolves was reintroduced to two hundred square miles of Yellowstone National Park. When the wolves returned, the ecosystem returned. The beavers, the mice, and the birds of prey all returned in more balanced numbers. Why? How did this occur?

When the wolves were reintroduced, the ecosystem came back, the courses of the rivers changed, and life rebalanced itself. Yes, you read that last sentence correctly: the reintroduction of the wolves literally changed the courses of the rivers. A balanced ecosystem returned. How is it that a group of predator animals can balance things?

We have been acting as predator animals as humans on this earth. The difference is that we have been overhunting and polluting the natural systems gifted to us for hundreds, perhaps thousands or more than thousands, of years! When wild predator animals, such as wolves, are part of an ecosystem, they do not kill other animals haphazardly. They kill just what they need to eat. No more. No waste. None. Many other species benefit when a wolf kills an animal to eat. Birds of prey, such as ravens and eagles; bears; and the soil ecosystem regenerate. And ecosystems, when left alone to weave their web, regenerate with amazing speed and grace!

How do veganism and sensitivity to our animal friends fit together? And what does the move toward eating more plants have to do with saving the wolves? When humyns do not eat dead flesh (produced by big agribusiness) and return as fully as possible to their herbivorous natures (as our teeth and digestive systems are constructed for; see the work of Milton Mills, MD), the need for livestock may evaporate.

Imagine a day when wolves are spoken of in a positive light, not as varmints who love to eat livestock. Let us think of wolves as a valuable keystone species that only kill when necessary. Let's understand that wolves do not kill randomly. Elk are their primary food source in

Yellowstone Park. A wolf succeeds in killing an elk only 10 to 15 percent of the time. Wolves, even the alpha males and females, take kicks from huge elk. These kicks often kill them. For a wolf, staying alive is hard work. Imagine humans not killing wolves that are going after livestock, because so much of the human population is eating so many plants that there is hardly a need for livestock. Then the wolves, in their keystone species role, can get back to doing what they do best: keeping the ecosystem in balance! Let's leave that job to the wolves. And let's focus on the benefits of eating more plants.

The Truth Continuously Unfolds

The truth unfolds when we look to the natural ways of nature and step back into our indigenous roots. What do our indigenous roots say about this idea? There are different interpretations in sacred texts about the directive to eat meat or not, when to eat which type of meat, and in what quantities. That topic will not be fully addressed here, but know this topic can be a contentious issue. I am not advocating an extreme position one way or the other. But I am suggesting eating lower on the food chain, starting from what you are ingesting today. That way, we can continue this conversation among all indigenous tribal peoples (the entire human population) around the globe. If you interpret within the context of your religious or spiritual tradition that eating meat is a necessity, eat less meat. Eat more plants. Examine the sacred texts carefully, and see if there is room to pay more attention to what you eat while you're at it! May we all consider embracing veganism or at least moving more in that direction as a lifestyle choice to recover our inner wellness, our Soul Purpose, and ecosystem balance.

Our Humyn Bodies: How Our Inner Natures Affect the External Environment

How do we live in our bodies, and how are the inner workings of our bodies rearranged based on use? How exactly do our behavior patterns change based on how we function? Well, I do not know exactly, but I do know that the way we use our bodies daily, how we express our physical beingness, is an expression of our patterns of behavior rooted in reflex and developmental movement. The seamless and smooth integration of all our body systems is key to our thriving as individuals and as a humyn species on this planet. Structure and function and function and structure. Which came first? The interweaving of our development emerges as a spiralic expression of our selves over time.

As I sit for a few hours a day or more in front of the computer, typing, I feel overuse in certain areas of my body and underuse in other areas. As we realize how to BE in harmony with ourselves, we create in ourselves a homeostasis, an active interplay of the full range of our human nature that feeds itself energy rather than depleting our energetics.

What we feed ourselves physically, emotionally, and spiritually is of utmost importance in the unfolding of and rising into our full, true natures. As we heal from the inside out, the environment—all of the natural world we are part of that surrounds us—heals.

Trust

Trusting that the universe is unfolding in perfect timing in our lives is a huge lesson and one I continue to work with. I am no longer waiting for the perfect time to release this book. It is meant to be an introduction to the body of work I've been practicing for my adult life, and I realize now life is an unfolding, not ever complete in the way we might expect it to be. Now is the time to enjoy a ride on the WILD side!

A Wild Experience!

What do you enjoy most about BEing in nature? Are you afraid of snakes, so you refuse to go for a walk in the woods? Or are you afraid of Being alone anywhere outside? Do you enjoy walks in the woods? Does taking off your shoes occasionally and walking on grass, on soil, or on the sand along the beach bring you joy? Do you enjoy feeling the soles of your feet striking the ground and your heels and toes sinking into the earth or sand?

Take time each day, even just five minutes, to experience nature in some way. Set your timer if that helps you to begin. Gaze at some flowers or the leaves of a tree. Watch birds fly around, and listen to them sing. Marvel at the fireflies, moon, and stars. Take time to experience nature in order to move even more fully into your true inner nature!

What of value is there to share of one's life, of one's career? How can I serve others through sharing my story? How can all of us assist others in their journeys by sharing stories? I began my career believing I was fixing people's problems. I believed there were problems to be fixed, to be mended. I worked to assist in "fixing" the person so the person could fit tidily back into the system—the educational system, their job, their family—and move through and beyond our myopia, hyperopia, presbyopia, and dis-ease states, such as hypertension and diabetes, to name a few "conditions." The fact is, we are all here in our own forms with our own issues in our tissues for specific reasons to move through our own experiences.

So what *is* my offering here?

- To inspire you to see your genius
- To move more deeply into the reason you're here in this physical form in these pivotal moments
- To celebrate our collective humanity, accepting ourselves in all our biodiversity
- To truly come to an understanding ever more deeply that we humyns *are* nature, *not* AI
- To let go of artificial intelligence (AI) and artificial genetic manipulation on most, if not all, levels of understanding

There's a significant amount of letting go of our addictions and doing recovery work involved in this process.

Machinery, and "scientific study," somehow wields authority. It hardens us. It hides us from ourselves. We can hide behind the manipulative nature of it and pretend it knows and is showing us the answers. All along, we are the ones we've been waiting for!

I've worked with a lot of instrumentation in my career. *Cuál es mejor, la primera o la segunda?* With equal blur as an endpoint, there's no telling which is really better. Why didn't we, as eye doctors, ever explain to our trusting patients about that endpoint game? I did but on rare occasions, when a person was really struggling with how to answer my question "Which is better, one or two?" Being on the receiving end of lenses being flipped rapidly in front of your face can be a real trip and a half for someone who has never experienced the phenomenon. Especially if you're a person with sensory sensitivities!

Games

There are many games we play during a visual evaluation. So many visual tricks and gyrations that allow us to "know" a person's behavior. Who are we to say what prescription a person ought to wear? As our thoughts shift, our awareness shifts, and our prescription shifts. Why harden? Why choose? Because we've been trained to believe 20/20 eyesight is the goal?

Why pick one spot on the spectrum of consciousness? Because we're human, and stability breeds perceived groundedness and predictability? My dad had a pair of glasses in every room of the house. On the kitchen table, on the end table, next to his bedside, in the living room—different readers were everywhere. My dad, a pharmacist and pharmacy business owner, never bought a pair of glasses. He just used readers people left behind at the drugstore! Flexibility as a human trait. Ahh. That was my dad!

Why do some of us continue to play the game, believing that 20/20 vision is the ultimate endpoint that eyeglasses will "correct"? Do we understand yet that our natural ways of Being will bring us back to the natural flow of our bodies, minds, and spirits and back to our state of natural eyesight, vision, thinking, moving, and acting?

Nature does not lie. Watch the unfolding with your very own eyes. Every day. Beginning with being with nature five minutes a day. You will learn more by authentically observing nature than you ever dreamed possible. And synchronicities will increase!

The Real Cows in the Room

My absolute conclusion is that the real cows in the room are what we as a collective consciousness have chosen *not* to look at. We've chosen *not* to be involved, chosen to say it's not our fight, and chosen to pretend certain topics are not there to be grappled with. Chosen to edit out! Read between the lines here, my dear friends.

Moving back into ourselves as one spirited group of amazing individuals and re–figuring out how to work together as ONE to create, re-create, and be part of the miraculous unfolding of this place that is and has been heaven on Earth, here we ARE!

And so it is, so it is, so IT IS!

Ready. Set. Let's go, humyns! The time is most certainly NOW!

The Mycelial Network

The mycelial connection among all inhabitants on Planet Earth is shifting the collective consciousness further into plant-based eating and planetary rejuvenation Right Now! The mycelial connections (the thin strands of communication that descend from mushrooms below the ground) are the nerve-cell communication highways that develop in the soil. We, as human Beings, are the mycelial energetic and energenetic connections forming deep, heart-centered connections among all inhabitants on Planet Earth. Spectacular works in process!

By shifting more fully into plant-based eating NOW, or heading in that direction on some level, we are collectively, cooperatively, and in community creating planetary rejuvenation. *Planetary Rejuvenation from the inside out is what we're all in the middle of.* Like it or not. Know it or not! I've been working for a number of years to assist those in the environmental world to see the connections between what they eat and the effects on the planet regarding the connections between individual human health, collective human health, and planetary health. Most recently, we've been reimagining together. You can form these sorts of gatherings and ecosystems in your neighborhood too!

Remembering Our Connections: Works in Process

I have been a nature lover at one with the natural world as long as I can remember. As mentioned, as a child, I tremendously enjoyed running through the neighborhood and woods with our dog and with my friends, going hiking, camping and row-boating with my cousin and other friends, and taking family trips to natural places. Fast-forward to my college days. The bulk of my studies were in my undergraduate major: biology, with an emphasis in ecology. I also spent time as an employee of the United States Department of Agriculture (USDA), working as a laboratory technician in the Insect Pathology Laboratory (IPL) in Beltsville, Maryland, close to the University of Maryland in College Park, where I attended undergraduate school.

Under the guidance of several scientists, I learned all about the bacterium *Bacillus thuringiensis*, or Bt for short. A bacillus is a rod-shaped bacterium, and *Bacillus* is the broad genus name. The species name is *thuringiensis*. These microscopic bacteria are naturally occurring in the soil and can be isolated from the environment. They have a crystal inside known to be toxic to a lepidopteran larva, a.k.a. caterpillar larva, a phase in the life cycle of the insect called a moth or butterfly. Undisturbed, these larvae metamorphosize into pupae (chrysalis cocoons) and then into moths or butterflies. Caterpillar larvae eat a lot as they prepare to metamorphose. When the caterpillars munch, they are considered pests by farmers growing cabbage, corn, and other foods. (Just as the wolves in Yellowstone were considered pests in their own neighborhood.) I understand now on a level I did not understand back then that the purpose of the research in the IPL lab I worked in was to locate and study species of bacteria that could be used in a concentrated form commercially as "biological" insecticides to rid crops of these "pests."

My job as a laboratory technician was multifaceted. I mixed up the agar-agar and plated the bacteria. Agar was used as the growth medium. On these agar plates, the bacteria grew into colonies and were used for research purposes. I spent time taking soil samples outdoors and seeing if we could isolate Bt from those soil samples in the lab. I so enjoyed gazing through the microscope and drawing the different sizes and shapes of those Bt crystals!

The scientists I worked with explained that by the spraying of this "biological" insecticide onto crops, the need for toxic chemical insecticides, herbicides, and pesticides could possibly disappear. They explained to me that the bacteria, combined with an inert powder (a commercial product called DiPel in the early 1980s), when sprayed on cabbage crops, was specific to these insect pests and would not cause any issues at all environmentally after they killed the target caterpillars.

Based on that description, I thought the idea of biological insecticides was fabulous back then. It seemed obvious that chemical herbicides, pesticides, and fungicides—the toxic, noxious chemicals Rachel Carson so eloquently wrote about in her classic book *Silent Spring*—would become unnecessary and obsolete. Think again. That's not how the story goes.

Genetically Modified Organisms (GMOs)

If you're of my generation, you might remember when Bt corn first became a thing. You might also recall that in the mid-1980s, butterflies were dying. Several years after graduating from the University of Maryland, I learned that in research laboratories, the Bt toxin was being integrated into the genetic structure, also known as the genome, of corn. I got nervous and called one of the scientists from the Insect Pathology Laboratory (IPL). She said, "Don't worry; they'll never put genetically altered corn in baby food." With that comment, I relaxed. I believed her. And I mostly forgotten about that chapter of my life—until *now*!

We are in an era of the normalization of genetic manipulation. Buyer beware! Currently, in 2023, there are many artificially genetically altered foods on the market across the Western world and beyond. Biological insecticides have been incorporated into the genome (genetic structure) of many plants eaten as food in the general population. In addition to corn, many other genetically modified plants people eat (GMO foods) have been added into our industrial food system in the United States and worldwide. In 2023, most corn, zucchini, yellow squash, soybeans, potatoes, and sugar beets, among other crops being added one by one, if not grown organically, are now genetically modified. To be sure the produce you're eating is non-GMO, grow your own, or buy organic!

The seeds for the crops mentioned above are genetically altered (engineered) so they are not killed by herbicides that would normally kill them. In other words, the DNA in the seeds is genetically altered. These plants then do not die when they are sprayed with Roundup. The brand name for the herbicide glyphosate is Roundup. You may be familiar with Roundup, as it is sprayed on the sides of highways throughout the United States to kill hearty, broad-leafed wild plants (some call these plants *weeds*) growing on the sides of roads. Regarding food crops, using soybeans as an example, this is what Robert Fraley, the chief technology officer and executive vice president of Monsanto, stated in 2015: "These soybeans [and all of the other food crops mentioned above] are tolerant to glyphosate because each soybean seed has had the Roundup Ready gene injected into it before it is planted."[12]

So to repeat myself for emphasis here, when farmers use Roundup, technically known as glyphosate, on their soybean fields, the weeds will die, but the soybean crop will not, because the soybeans' DNA has been genetically altered, and the altered soybeans are not killed by the herbicide Roundup. Many in the worldwide population are now asking

---

[12] GMO Answers, September 28, 2015, https://gmoanswers.com/ask/how-did-roundup-ready-and-roundup-develop.

Seeing the Dangers

On a conscious level and on some subliminal, subconscious, somatic level as well, I knew about the dangers of genetic manipulation. I've been intentionally eating all organic food and avoiding Genetically Modified Organisms (GMOs) and glyphosate (Roundup) in my food as much as possible for a long time. *On some other level, I let it slide by me how normalized genetic manipulation in our food system, and in many other ways on our planet, has become.*

what effect the residue of glyphosate (Roundup) has on the soybeans and on entire food systems and sentient being systems. And what effect do genetically engineered crops of all types have on the entire ecosystem of the planet and those beings in all forms living on the planet? What about our water and our air? What effects there? Zach Bush, MD, and many others are raising these questions. What questions do you have? Are you stunned to learn about this information?

OBSERVING NATURE

Observing Nature
as if
on the outside of us
and then simply
Diving Within
Witnessing
The twisting
and then
moving back into
the Spirals
the spiralic nature
of my, and our, collective true essence
with the One
as the One
Oneness
in Divinity

Chapter 14
CONNECTING MORE DOTS

$\mathcal{G}$MOs have been normalized in our culture and are rarely even talked about recently. We might see the "No GMOs" label on our food packages, but we might not even notice those labels anymore, as we're used to seeing them. What about when we eat out? Why the shift in our culture to normalizing genetic manipulation in our food system, in human and ecosystem health, and in human and ecosystem degradation?

Could it be that genetic manipulation in mostly all forms outside of a laboratory (or even in a lab) is not helpful? Could it be that intentionally altering the genes of plants and then eating those plants is harmful to our G-d-given form? Our souls are ours to protect. Self-responsibility is the name of the game from my perspective. What are your thoughts on this matter?

Supporting Our Natural Immunity as a Wonderful New Habit

Wherever we stand on these issues, as we choose to consistently raise our vibrations by building our inner ecosystems through many means, including deepening our connection with nature, we enhance our immune systems, the immune system of our soil, and the immune system of the earth. That's a big part of what Enlivening Our Consciousness and the book are all about. I've been offering how to be stronger and more human rather than being genetically manipulated to lose the connection to our G-d-given souls!

What we prepare and purchase to eat and drink daily and what we choose to put into and on our bodies in general (in the form of bioengineered cosmetics and food, polluted water, synthetic pharmaceuticals, and mRNA injections) have a lot to do with outcomes to our wellness and the health of the entire ecosystem of this planet. More people are discussing these issues publicly and acting on them in their personal lives in recent years. The polite and politically "correct" approach is to speak in generalities and simply hint at these mycelial connections. But that is not the whole truthful story. That is the old way. The myopic way. The way that is collapsing. The way of being polite so as not to hurt others' feelings. This information must be shared from our individual and collective heart spaces. From the center of our individual and collective souls. For us to consider and meditate on rather than dismiss.

I understand that some will not be able to fully digest this sharing. There are times in life when we must stop listening to certain individuals or organizations or friends because there is too much information to process. And that is okay. Although this book is an introduction to different healing modalities and contains tips and tools for enlivening our consciousness, it may not be comfortable to read too much of the text at once. It might be too much for you. And that is okay. We all live life at our own pace. It is important to thrive within the context of living in this wild world in these herstoric moments. It is important to know that healing modalities we may not be familiar with are available. This book is for that purpose. Read it in parts or pieces. Or after certain sections, perhaps not at all!

No Matter Where You Stand

On some level, we have all been participating in a huge, global GMO experiment. Still, there is great hope for regaining, maintaining, and thriving in our health, wellness, and vitality on every level. General tenets for thriving in life with incredible vitality are shared here. I'm passionately drawn to offering tools to enliven our awareness, enliven our consciousness, to move back into the amazing, sparkling, vibrant golden souls we've come here to BE! It could just save our lives.

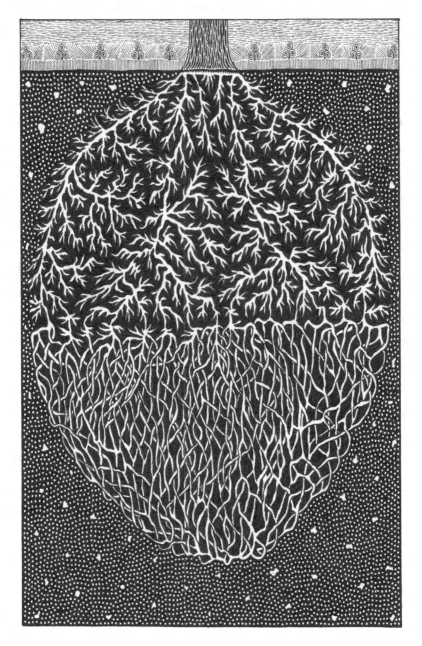

Back to the Mycelial Networks

How do trees communicate? How do people communicate? Some more roots of the story to weave in. An expansion of the mycelial network. Do you know what a mycelial network is? The *mycelial network* refers to the fine filaments, the threadlike structures or projections, the "roots" and communication system of fungi, a.k.a. mushrooms. These mycelial networks are the underground nerve- and immune-system communication networks of the kingdom of mushrooms and the soil community. The mycelial networks wrap around the roots of trees. These networks include bacteria, viruses, fungi, and billions and billions of all kinds of microorganisms. This is how trees communicate, underground. I was totally floored when I learned that trees communicate with a totally connected underground community just underneath our feet. So cool!

These colonies of bacteria, viruses, fungi, and loads of other microscopic organisms are woven like underground spiderwebs and constitute the underground biodynamic soil ecosystems of our world. These networks are the underground nervous system of the *superficial* (a scientific term referring to the top of something, not *superficial* in the literal sense of the word) energetic layer of the earth. As mentioned, these mycelial networks are also the nerve centers of the immune system of the soil.

The biodiversity of the living soil systems is what allows for the growth of hearty and healthy forests and all types of ecosystems on which all forms of life depend. I intuitively know more about deciduous and coniferous forests than deserts, bogs, or prairies, as I've been a lifelong East Coaster of the United States, and those are the microclimates and ecosystems I'm most familiar with.

The Plot Thickens! Experiences at the Insect Pathology Laboratory of the United States Department of Agriculture

In the early 1980s, Bt spores (approximately 1 percent) were added to an inert powder (approximately 99 percent), and this DiPel mixture was sprayed on cabbage crops. The little cabbage looper caterpillars ate the Bt while munching on the cabbage sprayed with the Bt biological insecticide in the carrier powder (as mentioned above, the commercial product at that time was called DiPel). The Bt crystal exploded the gut lining of the caterpillars and killed them. Mission accomplished, with supposedly no harm to the environment or any other life-form other than those lepidoptera larvae. No poison, I was told. No harm and no poison.

The hunters killing varmint wolves in and around Yellowstone Park prior to the 1920s knew what they were doing was correct, right?

Think again.

A Rude Awakening to TRUTH!

These toxic Bt bacteria work by exploding the guts of caterpillars. But what do microscopic bacteria that have now been integrated into

Our Inner Ecosystems

Our inner ecosystem, including the microbiomes of our blood, our guts, and all our organ and body systems, reflects the inner landscape of what occurs underneath the ground in the soils and waters of our planet. The soils and waters are a huge component of the immune system of the earth. The inner terrain of our fluid systems of blood and lymph, the crystal-clear flowing bodies of the oceanic system of the rivers and lakes of our inner vessels, and fluidity and solidity of our insides—this integration of all our organs and body systems—constitutes our immune systems. When our systems are disrupted by foreign substances, toxins of any sort, the homeostasis, or balance, is disrupted.

the genetic structure of the food we eat have to do with the guts of humans and other animals? Could it be that they have a lot to do with discomfort and disease issues whose causes are labeled as unknown or idiopathic? We have a lot of bacteria in our guts and throughout our body systems. Connect the dots!

Has our collective consciousness been dulled? Have we normalized and created a deep and permanent suppression of our VISION? Have we turned off parts of ourselves that we do not want to SEE or EXPERIENCE?

Could this puzzle piece partially explain how far we've strayed from our energetic, spiritual natures? Do we accept what we see in the 3D physical plane with our naked eye without question—as if this is the only truth there is? Do we have to SEE evidence on the three-dimensional physical plane to believe it? What happens when the shifting is happening outside the range of light visible to our humyn eyes? What is the TRUTH?

Discovering My Herstory

We can be affected by generational cultural experiences we may not know about—ever. As I was putting together the sections of this book and wondering what threads would weave all the pieces together, two experiences occurred in the early months of 2022 that I could not ignore.

The first is the story of how my great-grandfather died as a result of transporting a cow to a slaughterhouse. My great-grandfather was practically dragged to his death by an angry cow. He died shortly after that incident. This awareness, which was brought to me seemingly randomly through a second cousin of mine, could not possibly have been random. I needed to know that information to put together why

242

veganism has been such a prominent part of my passion over this past decade. It explained to me why the vegan experiences I've been having over these past eleven years have been pleasurable, easy, joyful, and life-affirming. It explained why I became a contributor to the recently released *Vegan Voices: Essays by Inspiring Changemakers* and was the emcee for the book launch. Those opportunities fell into my lap without my working to get them or chasing after anything at all.

It explains why I seamlessly was able to interview seven of the fifty contributors of the book for the *Journey through Health and Wellness* podcast. It explains to me why we all need to get out of our own way, get back to Source, go deeply within, and trust ourselves and the unfolding of life through us as we get more and more out of our own way.

More Is Revealed

The other story I'm sharing here, about the USDA's Insect Pathology Laboratory (IPL) and Bt, seems to be close to the final thread for now. Connecting it all together. The memory of my days in that lab started coming through to me strongly in early 2022. As I was recalling the details of the job I'd had while in college, I had the sudden realization that I had been involved with a lab that was working with what would be the beginning of the GMO story in Western culture. The understanding that the Bt toxin is now being incorporated into the genetic and genomic structure of food, such as corn, and that food crops are now bioengineered by shifting the DNA of the plants to create resistance to poisonous insecticides, such as glyphosate, began to weigh heavily on me, on my shoulders, on my soma.

Pollen blows in the wind. The corporate giant Monsanto is the producer and distributor of a multitude of GMO crops, and it has been creating genetically modified food crops since the 1990s. To repeat, biologically genetically engineered toxins (GMOs) are integrated into the genetic structure of corn, soybeans, sugar beets, yellow squash, zucchini, potatoes, cotton, and more. Monsanto goes after organic farmers when genetically altered pollen from Monsanto's genetically altered patented crops blows in the wind and is found on organic farms.[13] For more information on this topic, ask warrior womyn Vandana Shiva, PhD. She knows all the details about the Monsanto GMO story.[14] Or read one of her multitude of books on the subject, such as *Biopiracy: The Plunder of Nature and Knowledge*. Or better yet, watch her recently released documentary, *The Seeds of Vandana Shiva*.[15]

Butterflies were dying in the mid-1980s, and biologists couldn't seem to explain why. Butterfly populations have been continuing to die off and are dying now in real time. And why has there been such a huge decrease in the population of the world's pollinators, including the bees? What connections are you seeing?

Further Developments

I had lots of incredible conversations with the IPL scientists in those days while walking to the A&P for lunch. We had conversations in the lab as well. They treated me as an equal and listened carefully to all the ideas I had. They understood the value of listening to the wonder and excitement of young undergrads like me and others who worked in the lab. They were incredible mentors for me, in spite of what I understand now about the whole experience many decades later. The truth is, we

---

[13] https://corporateeurope.org/en/2022/09/researchers-vested-interests-lobbying-undermine-gmo-safety-rules.

[14] https://navdanyainternational.org/webinar-gmos-are-a-failed-technology-the-future-is-gmo-free-highlights/.

[15] https://vandanashivamovie.com/, 2021, accessed July 28, 2023.

learn from all our life experiences. And we have the potential to change course once we come back to the ground of our BEings and work from that place. How have you been changing course recently?

The Development of the Dot Plate Technique

One day during that time frame, my cousin was visiting our family at the home where I grew up in Maryland. He was a PhD scientist at a prominent scientific corporation. I was telling him about the laboratory work I was assisting with at the Insect Pathology Laboratory and how, as a laboratory technician, I prepared and poured agar plates. He then told me about a technique he knew of, an agar plate dot technique.

I immediately recognized the application to the work we were doing in the IPL lab and shared the idea with the other scientists. We were isolating many strains of Bt, and I knew this dot technique, with multiple agar dots on each plate, would be more efficient than using one full agar plate per strain of bacteria. One of the scientists was so excited that he designed, developed, and created a piece of equipment made from metal to inject up to thirty strains of bacteria into a single dot plate. I became a

Foodie Memories (for Some Comic Relief)

From my college years with the scientists at the IPL and as a former bright-eyed college undergrad, I have fond memories of walking to the local A&P for lunch on many occasions. I would get a delicious turkey sub sandwich loaded with tomatoes, lettuce, mayonnaise, and sometimes pickles. Believe it or not, my mouth is watering. Yup, this vegan's mouth is watering at the memory of that sandwich! I'm also remembering the whole wheat pita sandwiches I got at the food cooperative at the University of Maryland in College Park, where I was attending undergraduate school at that time. Those sandwiches often were vegan (well, maybe vegetarian with the mayo!) without my even realizing. Hummus, sprouts, lettuce, tomatoes. Mmmm. More mouthwatering going on right here right now!

Our Soul Purposes Unfold

As we move into the truth of the cells of our somas and into our true humyn natures, we move out of our own way. I now know deeply that I have been put on this planet to be an integrator, to ask questions and help others understand connections and connectivity where many are not looking for and, therefore, not seeing connections. The transfer of the use of the dot plate procedure I brought to these scientists many decades ago was because of a conversation I had with my mother's godchild and my cousin. Go with your Spirit, the Spirit of G-d working through you!

dot plate chef, pouring dot plates from that point on. I injected many different strains (up to thirty different species types) of bacteria on each agar plate.

That multiple-dot agar technique became the basis for a scientific article I coauthored during my college days while working at the IPL. Many scientific articles followed that initial article inspired by my cousin. Deep gratitude, Cuz! I was generously rewarded for sharing my and my cousin's idea with the three PhD scientists at the IPL. In addition to the appearance of my name as the second author on a scientific article on the dot plate idea and technique, which saved the government money, I was awarded a $1,000 cash prize. That was a *lot* of money to me at that time, and I was thrilled! It turns out I was an unintentional author many decades ago. Sometimes things fall into our laps!

Discovering Another Piece of the Story

In February 2022, I googled to see if I could find the reference from the article I thought had been published while I was still an undergraduate at the University of Maryland (around 1980 or 1981). And what did I find? Oh wow. First, I learned that article I coauthored had been published in 1985, three years following my undergraduate days (at the midpoint of my optometry graduate school education). Second, I learned by doing a bit of research on the internet that the article I coauthored published in 1985 has been referenced repeatedly since then by many authors of scientific papers in many scientific journals. I was blown away that the article I coauthored had been referenced dozens of times since the publication in 1985 and then totally blown away again by an acknowledgment at the end of a related 1987 article I discovered (more on that below). I took a two-hour writing break to eat lunch, do some sunning and some more R&R, and pick my jaw up off the floor. I'm back now to report this stunning full-circle moment.

Although I have not yet located the original print 1985 article[16] online or elsewhere (I do have it somewhere in physical form in a file I'm still looking for!), I located a June 1987 article online in the *Applied and Environmental Microbiology Journal* published by the American Society for Microbiology. The acknowledgment at the end of the 1987 article "Selective Process for Efficient Isolation of Soil *Bacillus* spp" by Russell Travers, PhD; Phyllis Martin, PhD; and Charles Reichelderfer, PhD, says, "We thank Elisa B. Haransky for not taking our word on 'known' information and for asking the questions that led to this procedure."

I do not remember ever seeing this article with the acknowledgment above or any of the other articles that followed. I may have seen that second article from 1987 as I was graduating from optometry school and smiled in acknowledgment those many moons ago. In any case, I had no idea until writing this book that so many others have been referencing this article!

---

[16] P. A. W. Martin, E. B. Haransky, R. S. Travers, and C. F. Reichelderfer, "Rapid Biochemical Testing of Large Numbers of *Bacillus thuringiensis* Isolates Using Agar Dots," *Biotechniques* (1985): 3:386–392.

Moving and BEing into the Future and
Connecting More Dots from the Past

I deeply understand the implications of genetically modified organisms (GMOs) because of my science lab experience back in 1980 when I was an older teenager. I understand about toxicity from a felt sense of my own gut discomfort in college. I understand that when we have kinesthetically and proprioceptively experienced something, when we are clear-bodied and clear-minded and allow Spirit Source, or G-d, to work through us, the truth is revealed.

My first job in college in the late 1970s was as a technician in a scientific laboratory in the Agronomy Department at the University of Maryland in College Park, measuring nitrogen and phosphorous levels in soil samples. The idea of this study was to ultimately optimize crop production. Nitrogen and phosphorous are critical components for plant growth.

Fast-forward forty-plus years to connect some more dots. I read an article titled "Improving Agricultural Efficiency with Nanoparticles" in the spring and summer 2022 issue of *Engineering* magazine (published by Carnegie Mellon, my husband's undergraduate alma mater). One goal of the scientists' research is to "(create) nano-enabled materials for targeted delivery to chloroplasts, capable of turning chloroplasts into ubiquitous solar powered molecular factories for personalized biomanufacturing devices." The team members, from multiple universities, have plans to use "nanotechnology and plant biology to modify these organelles, usually dedicated to capturing sunlight to produce energy, to create an engineered mRNA vaccine." Does this sound like gobbledygook to you? Is this technology already in use? How much does the general public understand about these new bioengineering technologies? What are our next steps to move into health, wellness, and vitality by interacting with nature on her terms rather than ours?

How many more dots do we need to connect? The following statement is directly from the abstract of a research article on the National Science Foundation website, titled "Bio: Rapid Biomanufacturing of mRNA Vaccines in Plant Chloroplasts": "This project aims to enable rapid manufacturing of oral vaccines against viruses in plants without the need of specialized equipment or skills."

Will mRNA vaccines soon be delivered through our food? Is there open discussion with all the research scientists involved about this technology in the mainstream media? I have not seen this discussion in the mainstream media. Have you? Does the population at large understand the implications of GMOs in our food system? Where are those long-term scientific studies? All of us in the collective consciousness need to pay attention to the field of nanotechnology and the use of nanoparticles, especially if we've never heard the term *nanoparticles*! I seriously question human scientific intervention into the roots of our G-d-given blueprint, our RNA and DNA. How about you? Have you looked up the definition of *nanoparticles* yet? Do you know this technology has been part of a lot of our lives for decades, if not longer— for example, in the food, pharmaceutical, and cosmetics industries?

Did you know that "in March 2022, scientists confirmed they had found microplastics in human blood for the first time"? (This was reported by the *Pittsburgh Post Gazette* on June 23, 2022, in the article "Sixty Years Ago, Pittsburgh's Rachel Carson Was More Right Than She Knew" by Jack Doyle.) For now, let's leave further discussion of nanoparticles, microplastics, GMOs, Roundup (glyphosate), and Roundup Ready crops for another time.

As I wrapped up editing this nature section in February 2023, a train loaded with toxic chemicals used in the production of plastics derailed in East Palestine, Ohio, USA, sixty miles from our home in southwestern Pennsylvania. Trains derail. Will we focus on train safety and the boxcars that are dangerously stacked two high? Yes, that's an important focus. What are we all going to do as a collective to help one another so that trains don't need to haul toxic chemicals? Where was this train headed? Could it have been heading to the newly opened Royal Dutch Shell Petrochemical Plant, the second largest in North America, to produce nurdles, the small plastic pellets used in the production of all things plastic (including the mRNA injection) in our throw-away plastic culture? How many of these trains are passing through Pittsburgh, Pennsylvania, on a daily basis?

Will we let go of lawn sprays that require toxic chemical applications? These toxic applications go way beyond adding nitrogen and phosphorous to lawns and food crop soils. Will we let go of genetically engineered plants, genetically engineered vaccines, and beyond? Or will we continue to go down these rabbit holes without fully understanding the long-term ramifications on the health and well Being of the web of life? Will we strive to improve our eyesight and insight naturally and trust our instincts? Will we take more time to connect to our somas, to nature, and to G-d?

Abundant Solutions!

Many create, write, and speak about the importance of rich, biodynamic living soil (loaded with living organisms that create the immune system underneath the ground) as the basis of all life. While studying for my master's degree in Spiritual Nutrition in 2017 and 2018, I read the book *Topsoil and Civilization*. The importance of conserving and preserving our topsoil cannot be overemphasized. Our inner ecosystems are our inner soil. Our inner soil inside us depends on the integrity of Earth's soil. Civilizations tumble when they cannot eat pure, unadulterated food grown in living soil. And we are in free fall, if you haven't noticed yet!

What have we learned from the keystone wolf species? What will we learn, and how are we implementing our regenerative future now? There are many ways to step into our own natures more authentically through stepping into and working in harmony with the natural world that surrounds us. The Biomimicry, Biodynamics, Permaculture, Agroforestry, and Food Forests Everywhere movements are exploding worldwide. Are you part of these movements yet?

Western culture is gaining a deep, embodied, felt sense and intuitive understanding of the importance of indigenous cultural practices. And Westerners are beginning to understand and crave connection to their own indigenous roots and indigenous ways of BEing. We are hungry for the wisdom of our ancestors and tribal natures and understanding that in order to move forward in this wild world, we had best honor and appreciate from where we came and work together as *one*, all the while getting out of our own way!

Yes, We Can Do This as a Collective One!

We are all here on this earth plane in these moments for different reasons, with different backgrounds and missions. Though we may not know why we are here, I hope that you

A Prayer

A special prayer of thanks directly from Source to Vandana Shiva, PhD, for her seminal work, writings, and activism for preserving the seeds and soils of the world, teaching organic farming methods, and supporting small farms worldwide. Her work through Navdanya.org is invaluable as a resource for the world!

have gleaned some nuggets of wisdom from these pages and that these last few pages have not shut you down!

Wherever you are on the spectrum of belief or disbelief in this tale I've been telling, there's one appeal I have for sure as this nature section comes to a close. Consider these stories, these threads, these connections, and decide for yourself how and who you will choose to Be and how you will choose to move through these wild and wonderful times.

Remember, you are sovereign. You are a humyn Being, and you have choices. And if damage was done or is actively being done to you or through you due to industrial agribusiness, the pharmaceutical industry, or other toxic inputs, know that there are ways to reverse that damage and keep your body, mind, spirit, and soul immunity healthy. You can stoke your vibrancy and wellness in order to thrive as you rise into all you are meant to be in this physical, mental, emotional, and Source-energy form. I understand that we all make our own choices. Simply remember that even if we've made one decision in the past, when we learn more background information, we can change our minds. It may take courage and a leap of faith. And that's fine! G-d—or Spirit, or Source—is watching over us All Ways in all ways!

BEing in Nature with a Daily Nature Practice

Consider meditating in nature, near nature, or around some natural materials twice a day for twenty minutes each time, visualizing loving-kindness and peace for yourself. Then emanate the energy of balance, bliss, and loving-kindness all around the planet and out into the cosmos and back again!

May we all be blessed with integrity, clear thoughts, and the ability of discernment!

Nature Section Suggestions:

- If you'd love to participate in the rejuvenation of Planet Earth right now, check out Permaculture and Agroforestry models locally and from around the world. It all starts locally, first with our inner ecosystems and inner spirit from the depths of our DNA. And then it all ripples out into the cosmos!
- Create a food forest in your neighborhood.
- Talk to your neighbors about letting go of lawn chemicals. If the neighbors have lawn-care companies, talk to the owners of those businesses.
- Look up Project Drawdown and Rob Hopkins and the Transition Town Movement (based in Permaculture).
- If you're into architecture, healthy buildings, and urban planning, check out ILFI.org and the Well Standard.
- If you are a grassroots person, investigate Rewilding your lifestyle, and check out the worldwide Permaculture movement—though Permaculture in general, in my experience, has not yet caught on to Veganic Permaculture principles.
- There are many vegan groups to explore as you eat more plants one bite at a time!

SPIRIT

- ❖ Community, meditation, and prayer
- ❖ Self-care as health care
- ❖ Reconnecting with your indigenous roots

Chapter 15
BEGINNING

You have to love yourself enough to heal yourself.

—Rabbi Shaman Gabriel Cousens, MD

My CONSCIOUS THOUGHT, MY THINKING mind, is just 5 percent of my total awareness. "So," you say, "the other 95 percent is the subconscious and unconscious? Wow, I guess we are just getting this party started!" It is not possible to separate my life from my practice anymore. Mothering and parenting continue but in a different way with grown children. Life continues, and enlivening my own consciousness happens in the HERE and NOW on a day-by-day and moment-to-moment basis.

Spiritual Vision

Regular Vision

EmbodyVision

Eyesight

Insight

How does it all connect?

Through the study of various components of spiritual nutrition with a *visual twist*, we connect the dots and realize we are all one. One. *One!*

What follows is an alphabet soup of insights into the web of life, an Aleph-Bet (the first two letters of the Hebrew alphabet). Also, other eclectic offerings in between. Ahhhh. Let's dive in! Drink in the pure waters and the flow of life on all levels. From a place of groundedness, believe in the energy flowing through you. Keeping your vibration high. Listen to the quiet voice from within. BE High on Life. Witness yourself from the inside out and outside in, and heal yourself by letting go of illness, strife, and grief. Replace negativity with positivity. Simultaneously at times. And so it IS! Let's connect some more dots in unexpected ways. Imagine that!

Aleph: In the Beginning

Alphabet. The Aleph Bet. The beginning of the alphabet.

A (*Aleph*) **is for** *alignment* **of our spine.** When our spine is in alignment, the muscles can follow the alignment of the vertebral bones and all of the bones of our body. When aligned, the muscles can follow the bones easily, slide, glide, and flow in the natural direction of their movement. The rest of our inner ecosystem then follows symbiotically. And we come into the seamless knowingness of oneness with and within ourselves and with G-d, or Source, or Spirit.

B (*Bet*) **is for** *Beginning.* Beginning anew. Beginning fresh. Beginning again.

New Beginnings are necessary, especially now in these precious moments of personal, spiritual, and cultural transformation worldwide!

Reframing Our Flow of Consciousness

How are you flowing?

Remember to read between the lines and reach out to me to continue studying and practicing any or all of the experiential offerings or concepts presented in this book. What does reading between the lines mean? It means to trust that still small voice that comes in. Some call it intuition; some call it the voice of G-d or angels or other beings. Whatever *it* is, no worries. Trust what you are sensing, feeling, and knowing that is bubbling up from deep within. Act from the knowingness that rises. If not now, then when?

The consciousness journey is life in each moment.

Connecting the Dots through Our Hearts and the Spiritual Nutrition Lifestyle

Let's weave all of these components together in any order you choose!

- Peace with Self
- Developing Intuition and Being Inspired
- Daily Gratitude Practice(s)
- Spirituality of the Plant-Based Lifestyle
- Meditation
- Yoga and Movement
- Going Within
- Easy Does It
- Fun and Lightness
- Being Open to the New
- Questioning and Questioning Again
- Changing Perspectives and Shifting Awareness
- Peace with Community by Giving Back
- Raw, Vegan, Organic Living Foods (That We Grow!)
- Peace with Family
- Serene, Loving Relationships with All (Family, Friends, and Acquaintances)
- Contact with Nature and *Tikkun Olam* (Healing the Earth)
- Trusting Divinity to Work through Us
- Serving the Universe and Cosmos from and through Our Heart
- Connection with G-d in Each Moment
- Moving through Duality into the ONE Awareness, G-d Spirit

Peace with Self

How do we step into and remain in the energy of joy, vitality, and fullness of presence in mind, body, spirit, mental, physical, and emotional BEingness? How do we move in our daily lives with ease and grace? How do we move beyond duality, thinking we are separate from nature, into the understanding that we are one with nature?

Just as our physical dual natures (two eyes, two ears, and two of many parts of us) can be coordinated as one, our consciousness can be one with the One as well. Duality as monocularity, using one eye at a time, individually, without clear communication. Oneness involves the two eyes, two sides of the brain, and our entire bodies in clear communication through and through! Binocularity, or single simultaneous binocular eyesight and vision, is the Oneness of US! Easily blending the duality, the duplicities inside us, into one and oneness. Being at Peace through and through, centered and aligned in body, mind, and spirit, is what I lean into on a moment-to-moment basis, sometimes consciously and now mostly unconsciously.

We all know how to sleep, but resting
with full awareness is something
you must learn how to do.

—Alejandro Chaoul, PhD,
Tibetan Yoga for Health & Well-Being:
The Science and Practice of Healing
Your Body, Energy, and Mind

Meditation, Connecting with Strength

The book *Torah as a Guide to Enlightenment* says that the Ba'al Shem Tov[17] stated in Tsava'at Harivash[18] that "meditation is seven times stronger than Torah study." This is a powerful statement.

Life, much of the time, has become a walking, breathing meditation for me. Being with one's self, emptying, surrendering, and being in balance between the nothing and the something, the *b'limah* and the *mah*. Understanding that we are all ONE. Surrendering to the One and following the Ten Speakings (a.k.a. the Ten Commandments) given to Moses on Mount Sinai. These are some of the most important gifts and lessons of the Torah.

Moving into Meditation

Life is a journey, a journey of knowing Source. Meditation is key for coming back to the knowing of ourselves and disappearing into the nothing.

You say you've never meditated? No worries. You may not realize that meditation is part of life and love. It's never too late to begin! Choose a mantra (a word, phrase, sound, series of tones, song, or poem), and repeat it over and over again. Eventually, in a moment, a day, a week, or years, your mind will be clear, and you'll be sitting and learning from Source directly, not only about yourself but also about everyone and everything seen and unseen. Then, eventually, if you stay with the

---

[17] The Ba'al Shem Tov was a learned mystic and healer who lived in the early to mid-1700s. He is said to be the founder of Hasidism, a sect of Orthodox Judaism.

[18] The Tsava'at Harivash was written by the Ba'al Shem Tov. It is a manual teaching about *deveikut*, or communion with G-d.

process long enough, you'll simply be able to BE in your activities of daily living (ADLs). With your eyes open or closed, you will simply BE in the present moment. We are living miracles in this physical form. Yes, YOU. I'm talking to YOU! Just remember that.

The idea is to continue meditating every day for twenty to thirty minutes. Once you feel comfortable meditating by yourself or in a group, it's then time to share the wealth with others by creating and facilitating group meditations. Many of us are creating meditations for a ripple of peace around the world. Some say the collective meditation for worldwide peace is what ended World War II!

Here's a sample about how to prepare for meditation. What follows is from a recent free meditation series I've been offering with the ultimate intention of empowering others to meditate in groups for inner peace and world peace.

Worldwide healing begins within.

—ElisaBe, OD, MA

---

1) Find a quiet spot.
2) Sit in a chair; on your bed; or in Easy Pose, Sukasana (cross-legged sitting, a.k.a. crisscross-applesauce pose), on the floor. Your choice.
3) Listen to your breath.
4) Use a mantra you are familiar with (any of a variety of words, images, or phrases or the name of G-d, or Source), or say to yourself, "Breathe in. I'm breathing in. Breathe out. I'm

breathing out," with each inhale and exhale until your mind is empty. Then let go of the mantra.

5) If your busy mind does not empty, observe the thoughts moving by without judgment. Note: Shifting in awareness can take time.

Easy Does It!

The way we move through space, the way we act and feel and BE. It's all ONE. As you've been journeying through these pages, I hope you've enjoyed the ride while BEing more embodied along the route. If you've no clue what I'm talking about, that's okay. Your cells have been listening, hearing, feeling, and sensing. The receptor organs of your eyes and visual pathway and visual and nervous system will be perfectly aligned and along for the ride. Easily and gently. Easy does it!

And while you're reading, bring your blinking, breathing, and presence to your conscious awareness. Simply by bringing usually subconscious habit patterns to conscious awareness, you are acting in a way to reform old, worn-out habit patterns. Then the more easily flowing new patterns will replace the old patterns and become you on a subconscious level once again.

Getting back to vision, where we began: simply by considering improving your eyesight and insight naturally, these concepts become real to your soma, your body, and the changes begin to occur. As you embrace the thoughts and ideas, meditate, pray, and work toward the ideals you think about and visualize, the change occurs. As we open to all the help we're being given from the powers that be—including angels, star beings, light beings, and Source (G-d, the Holy One,

Hashem)—the shift we have all been waiting for is occurring right in front of us. Right in front of the organs we call eyes. Through our visual pathway all the way down our spinal cord into the center of Mother Earth and through our celestial crown and Father Sky to the cosmos and back again. Then we discover we are channels; we, in our total physical and soul form, are *the* vessels for the Divine. Of BEingness. And then everything changes. We begin to witness ourselves. Deeply. We learn to simply BE!

The church bells down the way were ringing just now, just as I finished that last sentence. From the Aleph to the Zed. From *A* to *Z* and everything in between. It's all here for us. All of it. Between our eyes. In our heads and hearts and souls. WE are all we've been waiting for!

Peace with Community by Giving Back

My belief is that we are all here on Planet Earth in this physical form to serve our highest potential to create the more beautiful world we all know is possible. We're also here for G-d (or Spirit, or Source, or however you characterize the energetics of Beingness) to work through us. And for us to get out of and stay out of our own way!

We are all whole. We are all complete. We are here for a specific purpose. Sometimes we know immediately, and sometimes it takes much of our lifetimes to figure out what we're doing here and how we are to serve. And sometimes we think we know what we're doing here, and then the story changes.

Question. Reflect. Breathe, Blink, and BE present with this moment. This present moment is all that is, was, and ever will be. And this moment is precious. I honor all of you in your wisdom. BE in high vibration, and soak in all of the love that surrounds you!

Changing Perspectives

When we change the way we look at
things, the things we look at change.

—Albert Einstein

As our eyesight and vision change, we shift in our perception and see the world differently. All of the tools offered through these pages are for you to play with and experiment with, if you choose to do so. You can then observe yourself to see if anything shifts in your behavior. Is life flowing more easily in these moments?

Sometimes I'm perceived as an agitator or instigator. Most of it is unintentional on a conscious level. Perhaps that's part of my undiagnosed gift of having an on-the-spectrum nature. It takes me time and a different process than many to figure out how my actions are affecting others. Do our actions affect others? Or are others reacting through their own self-induced lenses of perception? I hope you will offer your blessings and high vibrations and do and BE high vibration as well. What more is there in life in this physical form?

During the industrial era of the past century, the interconnectedness and interrelationships between human beings and our internal and external environments have been compromised. When did this cognitive dissonance and separation really begin? Perhaps with the advent of agriculture ten thousand years ago, when we humyns went from BEing foragers living intimately with the natural plant and animal world to planting crops, domesticating animals, and settling in one area permanently. When we began to form what we call *community* in the form of permanent houses, office buildings, government structures and buildings, town halls and town squares, zoos and parks, and chemically laden lawns modeled on the English royalty.

What will it take for us to move into our next stage, the stage that animal rights, environmental, and peace activist Judy Carman calls *Homo Ahimsa*. *Ahimsa* is living and BEing in a way in which we do no harm to animals, plants, or any life animate or inanimate. It is the concept of true nonviolence, beginning from what we eat and drink each day. In her book *Homo Ahimsa*, Judy Carman speaks of "nonviolence as a calling of divine love ... and vegan living as a spiritual path." In many Far Eastern cultures and religious practices, it has meant living life as a vegetarian.

My ahimsa path over the past eight years has been an outgrowth of my cultural heritage as an American Jewish woman identifying most recently as a modern living Essene. The Essenes had a pure lifestyle of moderation in all they did. Have you thought about the path you're on? Are you interested in moving towards nonviolence?

Spirituality of the Plant-Based Lifestyle, including Soulful Spirituality; Offering Gratitude

The circle of life begins and ends with food. What we know of as food is *light energy* transformed into a tangible substance we can see, feel, smell, touch, and hear, all as an experience. The essence of the people we eat with, a right relationship with food, and knowledge of where the food came from feed our souls. The entire ecosystem surrounding our food is important. Who prepared the soil, collected the seeds for planting, and cared for the crops?

If you prepared the food, how did you go about that? What were you thinking about, and what circumstances surrounded serving and eating the food? What about when the food came out the other end of your digestive tract? What was its form? How did that feel, and did you relate that elimination experience to the food experience mentioned above? Did you or do you ever think about where food goes once it exits your physical body? Does this conversation make you feel uncomfortable? Where is the "away" when solids and liquids leave your body and your home? What is the cradle-to-cradle experience? Or is it a cradle-to-grave experience most of us have been living?

Did you offer gratitude before taking the first bite or sip? And did you ever consider creating humanure to fertilize the forests we've been destroying, with gratitude to Pachamama, or Mother Earth? Did you use that finished humanure to fertilize your front-yard garden you transformed from lawn into food forest? Look up the books *Spiritual Nutrition, Conscious Eating, Biomimicry, Cradle to Cradle, The Humanure Handbook,* and *In the Footsteps of Rachel Carson* and the works of Rabbi Akiva Gersh (see the references) to learn more about the circle of life and our role in the process.

- ◆ Explore the energetic nature of taking foods into your body, foods for your body to nourish your spirit and your soul.
- ◆ Discover the basis of a newly formed, expanded sense of spiritual tradition, where hatching the blossoming of the spirit of the new earth with gratitude and grace starts from going inside and considering what you eat in a day or for one meal, one sip of water, or one bite of food in each moment.
- ◆ Life starts with the spiritual side of eating at our mother's breast or with the bottle or, as in my case, both. The journey continues, and we all have our individual food experience. We continue the journey, balancing our microbiome from the outside in and inside out. Many of us have been around the food block.

♦ Shine your light brightly!

♦ Become part of the Radical Light! Let go of absorbing the pain body of yourself or others. Stoke your immune system and the microbiome of your gut and your reproductive system.

♦ Learn about nurturing the roots, your roots, to flow into a lifestyle that supports a vibrantly alive life of loving-kindness, surrounded by all you love always. It's about being in a regenerative space where you effortlessly give more and receive more than you ever could have imagined. Spread your branches, and bask in the sunshine of spirit. Let's do this together!

♦ Step into collaborations and associations with vibrantly creative and alive groups of people from your community and from all around the world, if you feel called to do so.

♦ What do we place in our mouths, what do we feel with our tongues, what goes down our digestive tubes to our stomachs three times a day, and how do we offer gratitude? How do we pray with that? Are we aware of our breath while eating and drinking?

Raw, Vegan, Organic Living Food

When we embrace the raw living-foods Essene lifestyle, vibrant, alive solutions to these sorts of questions seem obvious. Regenerative solutions to the polluted-earth quandary we find ourselves in these days become obvious as well.

C Is for *Cherubim*, *Chia* Seeds, Local *Cultivation*, and a *Cow* in the Room!

The cherubim, or angels on the *mishkan* (sacred space of the divine), face one another. The space between them reflects divine union, the oneness of G-d within us. As we dwell in our binocularity (SSBV) with ease and are one with ourselves, we flourish in service to creation.

Chia seeds, native to South America, are a magnificent source of protein. Mangoes and oranges, native to tropical climates, are wonderful sources of vitamin C and other nutrients. But what if we do not live in South America or in a tropical climate? Is it okay to source these delicious and nutritious items if we do not live where they are grown? The answer: local food cultivation is desirable and optimal.

When we live with and from the earth in the area in which we are born, away from what some like to call *civilization*, some foods will not be available. When we are devoted to local foods, supplementing from outside the local environment is not a desired option. We do the best we can. If we strive toward living the vegan lifestyle but live in Alaska or a very cold climate year-round, we must BE and *do* what is necessary.

I understand that hystorically (intentional spelling), the Inuit Eskimo cultures have subsisted on meat and all parts of animals. I heard Sacha Stone, in April 2022, speaking with an Inuit man who talked about the relationship of the Eskimos with polar bears and wolves. Prior to the invention of guns, harpoons were used to kill animals. No more animals were killed than necessary, the animals were deeply respected and honored, and all parts of the animals were utilized. Living and surviving in the often-harsh weather conditions in the parts of the world where Eskimos live is not to be judged. Judgment in any form is not healthy and not good for our immune systems. That said, there are cows in the room to address, for many of us around the world now have access to plenty of plants but choose to eat a diet heavy in animal-flesh foods instead. The flesh of these animals is retrieved through terrible violence. Does the violence epidemic we see daily, which takes many forms, have anything to do with what and how we are eating—with mostly a total disregard about how and where our food comes from and how we are mindlessly consuming it?

A Cow in the Room

I learned early in 2022 how my great-grandfather died. As a butcher in Europe, he would go to the nearby areas to gather cows for the slaughterhouse. One day the cow my great-grandfather was walking to the slaughterhouse got angry and dragged him across the ground. This dear man suffered a stroke and heart attack and was bedridden for the rest of his life. According to my cousin Richie's account, he died shortly before my grandmother Esther was born.

In Judaism, we are named after those who have passed into another realm before us. My Hebrew name is after my grandmother Esther. Wow. My grandmother grew up not knowing her father, my great-grandfather. I also never knew my grandmother Esther.

Recently, I find myself obsessed with these stories. I never really connected with history in my school days and was not seemingly interested in the history of our family or much about any history at all. Even so, I've been unable to take my mind off this story. Why have I been obsessed?

I've learned about many cows in the room that much of the population choose to overlook. The way Americans and the Western world at large have been consuming natural resources through the food we eat, the goods we wear, and the use of petrochemicals is truly obscene. That's when and if we pay attention to what is really going on. Agribusiness. The meat, dairy, and egg industries. Clear-cutting forests. Using genetic manipulation and artificial intelligence without understanding the long-term implications. Just to name some of the cows in the room.

Spirit has been speaking to me to raise some of the issues. Care for the cows in the room right in front of us. Stop the rape and pillage. Take responsibility for ourselves, one another, and the planet.

Even if our spiritual traditions require that we eat meat as an imperative, isn't it time for us to examine these cows in the room and adjust our ways? How much meat are we asked to eat? What types of foods? Does the care with which animals are treated play into whether we eat those particular animals or not? What quantity of the animal? Which parts of the animal, and why? To fulfill our spiritual obligations, is it okay to reduce the consumption of meat? Is it a requirement to understand how these animals were raised before we eat their flesh? Let's examine the habits of those living in the blue zones around the world. Let's notice in those blue zones how people thrive in community: by eating a cup of beans or lentils a day and a handful of nuts and by eating meals with family, friends, and community slowly and mindfully. Let's all smile and live joyfully together as One.

D Is for *Disgusted* or *Disgusting*

Now, for those of us who have been participating in this experiment of raping the earth through our industry (social, economic, cultural, educational, medical, and pharmaceutical), which is mostly hidden from plain view, it's time to open our eyes and SEE what the mainstream dream has been all about. It's also time for us as individuals to take responsibility on whatever level we are able to ACT in a way that does not participate in this rape and pillage any longer (she boldly says from her pedestal of privilege as she types away on her petrochemically based plastic-and-extracted-semiprecious-and-precious-metal Apple computer, using megabytes of computer memory whose infrastructure is stored in a warehouse in Reston, Virginia [or who knows where]). I could go on. It's a journey for all of us. So many are still blind to the wild experiment they've been participating in and what this has been all about.

E Is for the *Experience* of Beginning Again

In the beginning, there were stories of many indigenous communities, family gatherings, and religious rituals and services. That's the story of many Jewish families in the United States and around the world. That's how it was in the beginning for my family in shtetls in Poland and Russia, and that's how it is now. My extended families are communicating more and more regularly, even while mostly living far apart geographically.

My family is beginning again by examining some family history that was unknown until now. These were stories of hardship as farmers and as city dwellers in the early part of the last century. Even if my family did know these stories, we may not have fully understood their impact on the present somatic energy we might (or might not) be holding inside the cells of our selves.

We begin again by looking, listening, learning, and acknowledging. And then taking the opportunity to soulfully integrate or burn up and release any of the stress, strain, and negativity that is not needed in our present lifetime. We zero point lineages of negativity picked up through family experiences through the ages. In the case of my family, with Jewish heritage, this includes moving through and beyond our persecution and Holocaust hystory. My ancestors fled from Europe to America. They fled from persecution. How about your relatives through the generations? Where do you come from?

Through the recollection of these stories, we offer thanks, gratitude, and loving-kindness to our relatives in the present, the ancestors whose shoulders upon which we stand, and the progeny who will spring forth in the future. With newfound clarity, we continue our work, creating the new earth and BEing fully present in the enlightened energy of the cosmos.

F Is for *Fun*!

Dance. Sing. Swim. Dive. Surf. Raft in the ocean. Creep, crawl, and bear-walk. Walk, hike, jog, run, hop, skip, and jump. Skateboard. Roller-skate. Ice-skate. Ski. Bowl. Golf. Sail. Do what you love! Be merry by learning how to release your own endorphins (the drugs your brain creates naturally) without external ingested or injected stimulants. Imagine that!

G Is for *Going* Within

Remember to take time many times each day for yourself to pamper and go within. Experience your breathing, your breath. Meditate. Walk in nature. Be still while observing yourself in movement from within.

According to the Israeli Ministry of Health,[19] the population of Israel, as of April 2022, was 5 percent vegan—the largest percentage of vegans per population in any country of the world!

---

[19] https://trulyexperiences.com/blog/veganism-statistics-israel/, accessed July 30, 2023.

Chapter 16

FROM HERSTORY TO SHABBOS, THE SABBATH

H Is for *Herstory*

*O*VER THE PAST DAYS, WEEKS, and years since the year 2019, I've thought it would be a good idea to write a book on my most recent life work, all about my master's thesis on the raw living-foods lifestyle and connecting to our spiritual natures. I wanted to share this piece of my life with the public. Puzzle pieces have been emerging and fitting together one by one. Some are pieces of my life that seemed disjointed or unconnected, but the way the puzzle is coming together now is becoming clearer.

As the world shifts and as my body, mind, heart, and spirit open, my understanding becomes more solidified that everything we experience in life is closely connected and is unfolding with perfect timing. That is, if we can be open enough to see the connections and allow the flow of the unfolding, untethered. Interestingly, I've been writing this book as the story of my life unfolds. That's my personal herstory! I've come full circle. How about you? Where are you focused in these moments?

In pursuit of knowledge, every day
something is acquired. In pursuit of wisdom,
every day something is dropped.

—Lao Tzu

I Is for *Intuition* and *Inspiration*

Trust. Once you trust in Spirit, or G-d, or however you refer to a higher power, you'll be guided, and you'll see the way forward without effort. You do not have to know how or why. For me, this realization was a big relief. Many of us were raised believing that we had to work hard to accomplish anything. As we get out of our own way and allow the flow of the universe to unfold gracefully through us more and more, our lifelong visions and goals will unfold seamlessly before our very eyes. You'll trust that you can follow your intuition with ease and that this intuition is your easy guidance.

BE with yourself. Sit and BE. Go within. Get out of your own way. See what's inside, and allow Spirit to work through you. Move into your best, highest purpose under heaven. Rise to the occasion to be the best you can Be and are in this lifetime, and offer your gifts to the best of your ability. That is what it's all about!

J Is for the *Jewels* Within

As we move into the richness of the BodyMind, we become the empty beginner's mind. We open to the possibility of allowing our clear vessels to receive and transmit clear intentions and purity. We are One with Spirit, ease, and grace, no matter what religious or other tradition we hail from. From our indigenous roots, from all directions (north, south, east, west), from Mother Earth and Father Sky, we are all of THAT!

BE curious!

The time is Now. The time to move into our regenerative future where we give back more than we take from ourselves; our cells; our bodies, minds, and spirits; and our Mother, Mama Gaia. We've been inappropriately sucking energy from, taking from, and raping ourselves and others for way too long. Perhaps for more than five thousand to ten thousand years. And we've been calling ourselves *civilized*!

Now is the time to look deeply within, clean up our inner landscape, and go from there. The clarity and purity of our balanced microbiomes, the landscape of our guts, and the landscape of our entire inner ecosystems will emerge without our even knowing how to go about it all. As we trust the process of Spirit working through us, we rise to find that we are all that we've been waiting for.

K Is for *Karmic* Cleansing and Clearing

We are clearing our vessels so we will optimally hold the light and Be the Light unto the nations and the cosmos. We are clearing our inner ecosystems so our entire selves, including our brains, can think straight, with clarity, and vibrate with the Schumann Resonance (part of Earth's electromagnetic field, whose signals become our entire beings!).

Hear me. "Listen," says the Lord (or Spirit). That Lord is within, and we are vessels of that. What more do we need to understand? Spiritual, religious earth elders live with the realization that we are all One. Are you an earth elder yet? We are all elders of some sort on some level of consciousness!

As theoretical physicist David Bohm and spiritual author Jean Houston tell us, BE the Becoming embodiment of the universe. We are frozen light. Once we unleash this light, we begin to see miracles everywhere, and we become radiant beacons to others. We can chop wood and carry water at the same time as we shine our bright, joyous, luminous lights. A beacon, a calling, a recognition.

L Is for *Lightness*

Feel into the lightness of YOU! Take some time to come into yourself and into your present-moment awareness by noticing the energy of your hands.

We Are Energetic BEings

Rubbing your hands together, notice if you feel any heat. Place your cupped hands in front of your midtorso, with palms facing each other at the level of your *dan tien*, or lower belly, in the area of your solar plexus, pretending you are holding a ball the size of a basketball.

Now imagine a softer ball of energy the same size in between your cupped hands, and play with that ball, gently compressing and releasing the ball. Practice this. Notice the ball contracting and expanding, and notice the energy of the space between your hands. Feel the energy in yourself. Feel yourself as a ball of energy. Know that you can call up your own energy at any time of the day. Your energy, your spirit within you, is there for you all ways.

M Is for *Meditation*

The following is a description from musician Miten on *namaskar*, the prayer pose, which uses the hands in yoga:

We hold hands in gratitude with the awareness that we are all One … and we have a secret smile that cannot be hidden. It's just

A Self-Nurturing Moment

As we live into these tumultuous and magnificent times, I find it especially important to care deeply for myself to serve others at my highest potential. I continue to find more and more ways to delve even further into my indigenous roots to more fully explore and implement the tools, techniques, and "technologies of the ancients," as Gregg Braden says. Meditation and prayer are the most powerful examples of these tools, techniques, and technologies that I find helpful and nurturing. I personally meditate and pray to balance my inner terrain, live the life I love, and share that love with all others on the planet and beyond, energetically and energenetically!

What practices do you find most centering and rejuvenating?

there. Times are tough sometimes, but we always have access to our inner smile. Bring the smile with you when you chant the mantra (or mantras) … How beautiful do I see G-d in you. Let's take a deep breath together and breathe out. Deep breath.

Miten shared this beautiful description on May 21, 2020, during a worldwide global meditation. For more on Miten and Deva Premal's free meditation tunes, go to their website, https://devapremalmiten.com/.

N Is for *Newness*

Beginning Anew

What is next? The exciting
next re-integration.
The letting go of fear through the kidneys
Anger through the liver
The Ego through the skin
Letting go through our skeletons that
contain memories from the generations, and
memories of all that is, was and ever will be.
Letting go of all of these things,
And then Beginning Anew

Shifting Awareness through Experiencing

Juice fasting (some call it *feasting* to distinguish it from dry fasting or water fasting), especially with a spiritual component, can be an epic way to shift our perceptions and future behavior toward ourselves, our families, our communities, and the world.

In early April 2022, I participated in a seven-day Spiritual Juice and Broth Feasting Retreat Journey with Rabbi Dr. Gabriel Cousens (GC in conversation below); his wife, Shanti; his incredible support team; and many others, including RD below. RD has been participating in long-term fasting since 2002. He spoke beautifully in reaction to a precious moment at the end of our seven-day journey together:

> RD: Breathing a New Spiritual Air ... waiting for it to come in if we can just allow it.
> GC: That's exactly the concept: we need some fresh air.
> RD: Spiritual Essence. It's even subtler than prana ... the degree to which we're capable of being (present) without resistance.

Fasting, meditating, and taking time for ourselves with ourselves allow us to receive the gift of grace. As we go deep within, we experience the Ruach Hakodesh, the divine force of G-d in Judaism. May we all be blessed with clarity and the ability to move inside in order to share our gifts with others on the outside.

O Is for *Opening*

One of the activities during the Spiritual Juice and Broth Feast was an experience of mystical death and rebirth, including a wonderful zero point experience. This mystical death-and-rebirth experience was a half-hour visualization session facilitated by Shaman Rabbi Dr. Gabriel

Cousens and a group of others. It stirred an awakening. What are our Meaning and Purpose? It was a wonderful way to explore our inner depths emerging after burning it all up. The newness emerges from the ashes. Through the ashes.

Following this process, I know I have been integrating much of the mystical death and rebirth, elements of it, into all my offerings. My offerings include visualization sessions, workshops, meditations, yoga, and more. These offerings are rooted in the connections of the visual pathway to the rest of our bodies. We gain awareness of ourselves and of our connections to the other as a reflection of our deep inner knowingness.

What is the difference between the subconscious and the unconscious? Dreams come from the subconscious and the unconscious. Dr. Gabriel Cousens has said, "With meditation, you're alert and conscious; it's a different state. You're drawing on material you're meant to work on." This statement explains to me why sometimes so many thoughts come in and out when I first sit down to meditate. My mind needs time to process. And when so many things are happening all at once, we haven't the time.

As artist Georgia O'Keefe once said (paraphrased), to see a flower takes time. Just as having a friend takes time. Take the time now, my soul family and friends, to get to know yourself!

During a fasting retreat, Dr. Gabriel Cousens also observed, "With meditation you're changing the physiology, and with meditation, the brain is growing in the area of memory. Meditation stimulates the neurons to grow." Cousens notes that in yoga, there's a specific Yoga Nidra (a form of guided meditation) in which you go into a more controlled dream state that happens spontaneously. He says we go deeper in meditation than in sleep states.

P Is for *Paradigm* Shifting

How about telling the whole story and understanding the relationships between all the puzzle pieces? Keeping it real!

Just as there are different levels and layers of consciousness and embodiment, there are different ways of telling stories and of experiencing life on the mental, physical, emotional, and spiritual planes. I have taken you through different experiences and phases of my life (and others' lives and experiences) to illustrate ways I and others have improved, and continue to improve, our eyesight and insights naturally by accessing different levels and layers of consciousness naturally and by accessing the drugs in our own brains, rather than using external stimuli or stimulants (pharmaceuticals). You can learn to do this too, if that's what you're interested in doing!

I've learned to enliven my consciousness and facilitate the same in others who choose to be part of the process. I hope that on many levels, this has been, and will continue to be, an experiential learning and awakening journey for you as well. Some of the information may not make sense to you right now or might make you feel uncomfortable. Part of me wanted this entire book to be extremely high vibration, without any information that would be perceived as controversial or uncomfortable.

Then I realized that the times we are living in right now require that we tell the whole story. The deep spiritual journey has ups and downs. The trick is to ride the waves gracefully and make quick recoveries. I realized the importance of telling the entire story and the importance of taking the next step—connecting the dots even when it doesn't seem the dots are connected in any way. It might seem that the dots are their own islands, even though they are right next to one another with their connectors: the desire to keep our body vessels clean and clear through our thoughts and the food we eat, colonies of cells, mycelial threads, the implications of injections of genetic materials into body systems, air, fluids, soil, land, and more.

Do you now see any of the mycelial connections among vision, movement, the plant-based and vegan lifestyles, Permaculture, taking self-responsibility, the story of the early development of the technique used to isolate Bt, biological insecticides, and the normalization of GMOs in our culture? (More details on GMOs and nanoparticles are in the nature section.) Do you understand why I've been floored by learning about the story of my great-grandfather's profession just now? What dots are you connecting?

Q Is for *Questioning*

Continuously ask questions without needing to know the answers.

It is important to ask questions. Asking questions is important for our continued development. And to know that the answers others tell you might not be the truth. And to understand the importance of going inside through meditation and your breath, or however you best resonate with yourself, to come to your own conclusions over time. And to *trust* yourself.

I am not officially a research scientist, though I have been a clinician researcher for decades. Every humyn being has the capacity to observe and interpret their surroundings and make wise decisions if they choose to continue to enliven their consciousness with each moment. I know I am a thoughtful person who can integrate information and ask important questions others may not be able to ask for a variety of reasons. I learned long ago that when I have a question about what seems confusing, I'm not the only one with the question. So I've become brave. I ask questions. A lot of questions. Without having to *know* the answers in a timely fashion. I encourage you to do the same.

Intuition is the science of energetics.

Normalizing unhealthy ways of being, acting as if they're okay, and not speaking up and out is *not* okay. What am I referring to specifically? I'm talking about allowing inappropriate social interactions; not setting ethical and easily understandable social boundaries; being okay with air, water, and inner ecosystem pollution; investing time, energy, effort, and money into the extractive industries; looking the other way when it comes to the plant and animal and agriculture agribusiness network (which is hidden from most); and thinking that your interpretation of what's going on in the world is the only correct way of approaching things. What are you invested in? I'll stop here. You get the picture. Full transparency, with eagle eyes for reading between the lines, is the new game!

Now is the time to ask questions. Lots and lots of questions. And to keep asking until answers that are new, vibrant, healthy, and fun emerge. You have the potential to do this and BE this. NOW, in these precious moments.

R Is for *Rising* to the Occasion!

The chiasm. The crossing. The decussation. There are times in all of our lives when decisions are made. Either we make the decisions on a conscious level, or the decisions are made for us. Or does G-d—or Spirit,

Hashem, or Source, or however you refer to the Root of It All—make the decisions for us in ways we do not perceive on a conscious level?

I've spent many pages talking about enlivening our consciousness. Do we enliven our consciousness, or are we led on all levels of BEing through a force unknown to us? I believe we are led. And when we get out of our own way, the path becomes crystal clear. Things move gracefully into place! Sometimes they fall into place without our knowing how that movement could possibly have happened—right down to our physical, mental, emotional, and spiritual selves. And our receiving and transmitting potential is clear, bright, and effective.

Whatever the case may be, when we keep our body vessels as clear as possible, our vessels, our bodies, are clearer to receive and transmit love, gratitude, bliss, adoration, clarity, resilience, and kindness.

This moment in time is a great decussation and decision-making moment. Whether or not we perceive it on a conscious level, it is happening all around us and from the inside out. As we learn from the architecture of our physical structures, our optic nerves decussate, or cross, at the optic chiasm in the center of our brains, at the beautiful sella turcica winged-butterfly bone. And there is redundancy in our bodies. Each of our visual fields is represented in each of our eyes. Two ways, two choices. If one channel does not work, there is another at the ready. So no need for worry. Our bodies, our Beings, have us covered. And so it is!

Each of our visual fields in each eye overlaps with the other eye, the other visual field. Double visual representation in our central visual field is the normal way of seeing. Yet suppression exists on a physical level. Some degree of suppression, or a turning off of the vision in one eye or the other, is normal at times. Some suppression that becomes habituated is not normal. Sometimes abnormal suppression gets habituated. That's why optometric vision and movement training and therapy,

EmbodyVision awareness, and an underlying dose of real food and clear soma are wonderful ways to awaken to ourselves, the cells of ourselves!

It's time to rise to the occasion through action. How are you rising? How are you acting?

S Is for *Shabbos,* the Sabbath

Shabbat is a defining day of consciousness.

—*Torah as a Guide to Enlightenment*

There are times to rest. Whether or not a day of rest is built into your spiritual practice, a day of rest each week is a wonderful idea to consider in order to rebuild, rejuvenate, and reset your entire self and to prepare for the week ahead. In Judaism, the Sabbath, or day of rest, is from Friday evening at sunset though Saturday evening at sunset.

In 2015, I met Dr. Gabriel Cousens at his Tree of Life (TOL) Rejuvenation Center in Patagonia, Arizona. I thought I'd be staying there for a few days for my favorite Jewish holiday, Tu B'Shevat. I wound up enrolling in a cleansing and retreat Spiritual Nutrition program and staying there for an entire three weeks! (Note: The TOL was thriving for twenty-five years before Gabriel and his wife, Shanti, moved to Israel in 2020.) Since then, I've been enraptured with the deeper meanings and implications of not only conventional Judaism as it is practiced today but also deep spiritual connection to Source. How do we connect through the rituals and routines of Source practice? How do you connect to G-d and your own G-d-like nature on a moment-to-moment basis?

Chapter 17

FROM TORAH AND THE TRUTH TO NEW BEGINNINGS

T Is for *Torah* and *Truth*

THERE IS REPETITION IN THE Torah, sacred Jewish scripture. Some stories are repeated in the same or different ways throughout the text. There are many ways to interpret these stories and many ways to interpret the levels and layers of our lives. We'll briefly explore this concept through the Torah, the Five Books of Moses.

The Levels and Layers of Torah Interpretation

There are various levels and layers of how people look at and interpret the Torah. The acronym *PaRDeS* describes these four levels. The *P* stands for *p'shat*, or the literal level of interpretation. The *R* stands for *remez*, or the symbolic level of interpretation. The *D* is for *drash*, or the interpretive level, and *S* is for *sod* (hidden), or the metaphysical and spiritual interpretation.

Using this Torah interpretation system as a metaphor, we have moved between multiple ways of enlivening our consciousness in these pages. We have moved in and out of different approaches to presenting information—ways of BEing, seeing, sensing, feeling, moving, acting, and eating. We have read some facts and learned on a literal level. We can hear stories and apply the stories to our own lives. We can experience our lives in each moment with mindfulness and awareness and be embodied in each moment. Or not. We've laid the foundation for some beginning practices to assist us in increasing our awareness and thereby enliven our consciousness.

In the Jewish tradition, we read a different portion from the Torah each week. Each Torah portion is called a *parsha*. There are different English translations of the Torah, with each one differing slightly. Most read from the Chumash (Torah in Hebrew with English translation) book they most resonate with at any given point in time. The Torah translations my husband and I read vary and include the Reform, Conservative, Reconstructionist, and Orthodox, as well as Chabad, movements. Each of the Jewish movements has various translations. There are many Christian translations as well.

In many parts of the Torah, the fourth speaking, or what some call *commandment* (of the ten speakings or commandments), is about observing the Sabbath. Exodus 20:8–11 talks about remembering the Sabbath day and keeping it holy by not doing any work. Rest. The message is to take a rest from the ordinary other six days of our lives.

My reconnection to Source energy through my birth tradition is now getting stronger and stronger. The Torah, a.k.a. the Five Books of Moses, is a primary source book for the Jewish tradition. The Torah is often referred to as a Tree of Life!

My husband, Stan, clarified for me that there are many books that Jewish scholars and others study. He told me, "Those of the Christian faith would say Proverbs and Ecclesiastes [quoted below] are from the Old Testament or Jewish Bible. In Judaism, the Torah refers strictly to the Five Books of Moses. Proverbs and Ecclesiastes are from the section of the Jewish Bible called Writings. It's the third section of the Tanach, which is an acronym and includes Torah, Nevi'm [Prophets], and Ketuvim [Writings]."

There are many beautiful gems of wisdom in the Jewish tradition. Here are a few examples:

> It is a tree of life to those who hold fast to it, and
> those who support it are fulfilled and happy.
>
> —Proverbs 3:18

> For I give you good instruction. Do not
> forsake my teaching. For I have given you good
> instruction, do not forsake My Torah.
>
> —Proverbs 4:2

> Her ways are pleasant ways and
> all her paths are peaceful.
>
> —Proverbs 3:17

> Cause us to return to you, Adonay, and we
> shall return; renew our days as of old.
>
> —Lamentations 5:21

I began my Torah reading journey in earnest when I met Rabbi Gabriel Cousens in 2015. I was intrigued by the weekly parsha interpretations in his book *Torah as a Guide to Enlightenment*. His writing resonated with me beyond measure. I felt the depth somatically to my core each time I read a single sentence. I was raised a secular cultural Jew. My parents, with my mother's influence (as my mom cooked and served meals), had a kosher-style household. My mom did not mix milk and meat together at any meal. My formal Jewish education consisted of weekly Sunday school visits as an older grade schooler and teen and a confirmation ceremony from a Yiddish-Hebrew

School. No Bat Mitzvah. I learned enough Yiddish at school that my parents, who were using Yiddish as their secret language, stopped speaking Yiddish. What a pity!

U Is for *Undulation*

As humyns, we undulate or move between different stages and states of BEing throughout our lives. This is normal!

On the deepest level, the parshas (Torah or Bible portions) talk about our inner temples (our own personal inner mishkans, or sanctuaries) and how we conduct our lives. Honoring the Sabbath once a week from Friday evening to Saturday evening is instruction from Hashem, G-d. As we delve into this idea, we begin to understand the importance of maintaining Shabbos (the Sabbath) consciousness over the course of the entire week and over the course of all our days in this physical form. The idea of building an inner sanctuary, or mishkan, within ourselves for all moments of our lives resonates deeply within me (see parsha Terumah). This way, we have a quiet mind and a quiet body, and we stay out of our own way, so Source can work through us seamlessly.

V Is for *Vision* and *Veganism*

As we eat a purer diet, the vessel of our body clears (see the nutrition section). As we clear our body temple, Source, or G-d, pours through us. Our eyesight, vision, and insight all clear as well. Alive consciousness is the energy of life pouring through us! And we can breathe and move more easily. We are within ourselves. We can hear clearly. And listen. *Shema Yisrael Adonai Eloheinu, Adonai Echod* (Hear, O Israel: the Lord is our G-d, the Lord is One)! We are who we are meant to BE, and *we* are the One we've been waiting for in physical form on this planet!

Natural eyesight improvement is rooted in the concept of overall increased human performance and in being who we truly are as full human beings in relationship to ourselves, those we surround ourselves with, and all sentient beings. Mother Earth, Father Sky, and all of cosmic being-ness support our eyesight and our vision as we allow the process to BEing.

Living into Natural Eyesight Improvement as a Way of Life!

Winding back to natural eyesight improvement, we begin to understand that our eyesight and insight improve as we BElieve and live into the idea of it. And there are supportive real-life techniques and ways of Being to lean into to live and BE this way on a moment-to-moment basis.

Breathing freely in each moment is a critical piece of the plan. We move through dissonance, dis-ease, disgust, and simply being. And we come out on the other side by Being something different from what we were. We change our minds, our bodies, and our BEings in our conscious, subconscious, awake, and dreaming states. Then we move into *doing* and BEing differently than we are used to. We shift. We integrate our new knowingness differently. We learn, practice, and habituate the integration of our new and vibrant total-action systems. How?

Zero point all of it through:

- ho'oponopono: "I'm sorry. Please forgive me. Thank you. I love you."
- prayer in whatever spiritual tradition you resonate with.
- meditation, repeating the name of the ONE—whichever version you most relate to—many times a day until your life becomes one long meditative state of BEingness.

The interweaving of all that is, was, and ever will be is so very important. We are all One. Our work is all one. We realize this as we take the opportunity to cross-pollinate with others in other walks of life.

W Is for *Waves* of Enlivening Consciousness

April 29, 2022

Last night was the thirteenth evening of the Omer. Counting the Omer. The Omer begins the second day of the Jewish holiday of Pesach, or Passover, and ends at the Jewish holiday of Shavuos, or Shavuot (two different transliterations). Check out the incredible Omer Oracle Cards created by Nomy Lamm and Taya Mâ Shere.

For this thirteenth day of the Omer, the card reads, "*Yesod she'b'gevurah* (∞) aligned activation of strong holding. Everything. Pull back the veil on reality. Every thing is connected to every other thing. Perceive the architect, infinite particles aligned in exquisite creation."

May 18–19, 2022

And now today it's Lag B'Omer, the thirty-third day of the Omer. Today is herstoric. Just as we burn fires for Lag B'Omer to burn up anything that is no longer needed, my fire is burning within with excitement. I'm submitting a close-to-final-draft manuscript of this book to my editor today! Yippee!

As we count the days of the Omer, we count some of the days of our lives. We become more reflective than usual perhaps. Just perhaps we consider the possibility of Spirit working through us. And then we realize it is no longer necessary to consider. We follow our own guidance, which, it turns out, is the divine plan, the guidance of the universe. We move in and out of the ultimate joyous, beautiful, bright dance between bright light, shades of gray, and all the shades of the color wheel. And we realize the deep blackness and darkness is not the antithesis of but the linchpin necessary for the emergence of all the joy, love, and true essence of who we are.

X Is for *Decussation*, the Crossing into Newness

Today we have truly crossed into new ways of BEing
as humans on this planet. It's a new day with so much
potential to live into our newness. This is so very exciting
for those of us who choose to ride the waves of innovation
and allowing G-d, Spirit, Source to work through us.

—Caroline Myss on Facebook, February 23, 2022

I use the word *Source* for simplicity to refer to what some call G-d, Spirit, and a variety of other terms. I have offered some exercises, tools, techniques, and tips to help you navigate these moments. I've personally been practicing, modeling, and teaching these tools for my entire adult lifetime and perhaps for lifetimes before this manifestation. Keeping the Sabbath from Friday evening to Saturday evening has become a new habit of mine and an incredibly regenerative habit! For the first time in my life, I'm counting the forty-nine days of the Omer as well. In this physical form, there is so much possibility in every moment. What a joy to be ALIVE!

Y Is for *Yearning*

I trust that some or all of what is written here resonates deeply with your soul and that you choose to integrate one or many ideas into your daily routine to increase your movement vocabulary and practice, improve your eyesight naturally, sprout and eat more healthfully, dive deeply with gentle steps into the natural world many times a day when possible, and deepen your insight into what you are doing here on this planet in these *wild* times! I trust you'll hug more trees more often with the front of your body and connect the back of your body to trees as well! I hope it is informative to read what I've written about opening to our personal stories and acting in our physical form based on Source flowing through us, rather than working hard through effort.

As I was completing this book, I asked Source to help me complete this process with more ease and grace and to please allow me to FLOW with the process even more. After all, if I were efforting as I wrote the book, I would not be modeling the ease, grace, and gratitude I teach and profess to model in my life to live to my highest potential and offer others the best teachings. The connectors came through me even more directly after I asked Source directly. It was then that the story of my great-grandfather the butcher came through. It was then that the story of my time at the Insect Pathology Laboratory (see the nature section) came through and into the present moments.

Agar Dots

The agar dot technique I shared with three PhD scientists around 1980 was a critical missing puzzle piece. The efficiency of using this dot technique was just one aspect of the technique. I've been captivated by reading all the articles that sprang forth following the publication of that article in 1985. The details of the dot-plating story are in the nature section and referenced in the article "Rapid Biochemical Testing of Large Numbers of *Bacillus thuringiensis* Isolates Using Agar Dots."[20]

---

[20] P. A. W. Martin, E. B. Haransky, R. S. Travers, and C. F. Reichelderfer, "Rapid Biochemical Testing of Large Numbers of *Bacillus thuringiensis* Isolates Using Agar Dots," *Biotechniques* (1985): 3:386–392.

The full and deep connections between the agar dots and the mycelial threads of our lives as we move forward through these incredible times are subjects for further exploration. For me, as I continue to share, I do not plan to do so in book form. This form of communication is not the easiest for me, though the angels are telling me (Michal needs deep gratitude and credit here) that writing could be my best form of communication *if I could just get out of my own way*!

To continue this conversation about GMOs (ahhh, now being called *bioengineered* rather than *genetically modified* organisms as of this editing moment in February 2023) and how these dots connect to what's up in the cultures around the world at large, please reach out to me directly through my website, EnliveningConsciousness.com, and we'll go from there!

Spiritual Nutrition and Boosting Our Immunity

As a close-to-final note, let's explore a bit or, rather, review what is best to build our immune systems to repair damage inside the cells from all the environmental physical, mental, emotional, and spiritual insults to our systems.

Building our immunity on all levels from the inside out and outside in is the most important single thing all of us can work on collectively and for seekers of any kind to agree on!

Boosting our immunity on all levels—physical, mental, emotional, and spiritual—and keeping our physical bodies in tip-top shape through impeccable immune systems are our best strategies for wonderful wellness in these post-COVID, still explosive, and who-knows-what's-next times. Keeping my immune system in tip-top shape has become my newest mantra for myself and the suggested mantra for those I serve these days. Keeping my and our vessels clear to be the purest channels for the Divine to work through is how I know I can best protect myself and others and serve in this lifetime in this humyn form.

All of the tools and techniques shared here are the ways I have come to understand how we can, subtly with ease or with a BIG BANG and great effort, shift our awareness and consciousness.

Z Is for *Zohar* and *Zebra*

That about sums it up. Use your imagination to figure out why. Without expectation of how your bliss will manifest. Well, maybe look up *Zohar*, think about the black and white stripes on the zebra (is all we see in this physical plane really just black and white?), and connect the dots to learn about the moral of the story!

VOICING OUR VISION

The rise of the divine feminine in all of us
Vision is Rhythm, the pulse of the light
The rise of the divine light deep in our collective consciousnesses
All right
The rhythm of vibration with the full moon
Here we are on one GIANT balloon
Ready to POP
Into Joy, Wellness, and Love
In all ways!

Trust and understand that you are a vessel of Source, or G-d, or Spirit, and that as you keep your body temple clear and do the work, you will learn from Your Self what you are here for in these NOW moments and how you can best serve humanity at this critical juncture. We are all unique expressions of G-d. We are all here for a specific purpose. So ready, set, here we GO! Over time, we continue to go deeper and deeper. What a joy this all is! Well, most of the time. As I stay open to Source and enjoy Spirit coming through me, the dots of my life are revealing their connections. Even when there are multiple agar dots on a single plate, there are energetic connections through the air and in the holographic quantum field that cannot be measured by conventional means.

Raising Our Vibrations through Cocreation in Community

Raising our vibrations is the key to enlivening our consciousness. Are you in? Do you have some more ideas about how to do so? A bit more than when you opened the first page of this work? Remember to Breathe, Blink, and BE present! We've got this. We're cocreating in each moment. These moments are such an incredible blessing. Thanks so very much for sharing this millisecond with me. Visualize loving-kindness, gratitude, and grace, and let's BE all of it, raising our vibrations together. Forever! We are energetic, Spiritual BEings who have infinite potential. Please continue to remember who you are, who you are meant to be, and why you are here in these moments. Wherever you are, that's just where you're meant to be. Bask in the in-between. Begin. BE!

Deep gratitude to you for Being by my side on this journey. I love you all so much!

Full-Circle Moments

A Concrete Story

July 31, 2022

The full-circle moments in our lives become our lives as we allow life to flow through us. Reflecting on SPiRiT in each moment. Right now, my keyboard is in a completely different dimension than my computer and my computer screen. That ancient computer image is no longer the way. It's time to detach ourselves from the notion that we are less than machines. We are the ultimate technology. As we rise into our sovereignty and reclaim our humaneness and humynness, our understanding of ourselves without ego grows with the knowingness that we are images of G-d. In the image of G-d, we remember that humyn inventions are the figments of our brilliant imaginations. Concrete.

As I gaze out the window this beautiful summer day, I see the syntonics of a powder-blue and vibrant yet subtle pink sunrise. My eyes soak in the beauty as I type. I remember yesterday. So very profound to reconnect yesterday with Darrell and get to know his partner of seven years, Jessy. We walked around my family's suburban home, a thirty-five-year-old Permaculture landscape. Jessy is sharing seeds. To do an experiment with wheat, she says. Permaculture lives. I'll be planting those three varieties of heirloom wheat seeds in our yard in September. And I'll be sprouting some of the seeds on my countertop before then and serving these sprouts sprinkled on salads. Building our collective immunity in community. With and through Nature, Spirit, and Source.

Oh, I see. I'm seeing how it's all coming together. The days of our lives begin to connect. The flow of the here and now and yesterday and tomorrow.

The birds are singing. My keyboard is on my window seat. I'm typing. My computer is behind me, somewhere else in the room, and I'm feeling the breeze. I'm noticing the sunrise. The sun is rising. We are all arising. To Serve.

It is a new day.

The next chapter begins.

New Beginnings!

Spirit Section Key Points

As a route to increasing your self-awareness and the awareness of all that surrounds you and your relationship to all that is, was, and ever will be, consider the following:

- Healthy routines are of utmost importance. Establish some health-supportive routines each day. (I hate to admit this one, but it's true, I tell you!)
- Make a list, with time stamps if necessary, about what you'll be doing tomorrow before going to sleep each night or prior to meditation before sleep!
- Observe the Sabbath, one day a week to begin with, in your own way, beginning with what resonates and going from there.
- Pick ONE practice, such as meditation, prayer, taking a walk, or any behavioral shift of your choice. One practice daily is enough to begin. It's enough if that is what works for you.
- Breathe, Blink, and BE Present!

- You can deepen your insight through improving your eyesight one moment at a time.

- These are useful techniques to practice for maintaining your resilience into elderhood!

- Developmental movement sequencing, along with breathing consciously, is a wonderful daily practice.

- The whole-food, plant-based (WFPB), and sometimes raw, living-foods vegan lifestyle, along with intermittent fasting, is an incredible and important exploration I hope you'll fall in love with!

- Connecting with nature daily out of doors—through forest bathing, grounding in bare feet, or whatever suits you—is an incredibly important ingredient for vibrant health and wellness on an ongoing basis!

- The tips and tools for natural eyesight improvement and all the suggestions mentioned in this text will change your life as you integrate them into your way of BEing.

- Ho'oponopono and other zero point techniques are incredible transformative tools for clearing and cleansing. "I love you. I'm sorry. Please forgive me. Thank you. I love you!"

- Travel at your own pace, your own rate. Follow your own breath. Listen to your Soul Song!

Peace with Community through Tikkun Olam and Giving Back to Community by Sharing All Our Gifts and Inner Explorations with the World!

A Few Words of Gratitude for Spirit, Source, G-d, and the Natural World

- Thank you for helping me to teach others all I have been gifted to learn.

- Thank you, Spirit, for bringing me to this beautiful moment and for providing me with the understanding of amazing food. Thank you, soil, for your stored vitamins and minerals and your natural biodynamic immune system you share with the plants that spring forth from you. Thank you, soil of the earth, for not giving up on us as we redo ourselves through you.

- Thank you, rain, for lubricating the earth and transferring her nutrients up the stems of plants to reach inside of them through their xylem and phloem. Thank you for reaching my spirit through these waters and for the loosening of the stickiness of my lymph and cells to create flow.

- Thank you, sun, for shining your bright light for the trees to grow, for warming my soul, and for lighting me up.

- Thank you, moon and stars, for lighting up the night sky and creating the monthly and ethereal patterns of the tides and the celestial seasons.

- Thank you, trees, for collecting the wonderful light energy and for transferring that bright light to me through the captured biophoton energy of the leaves and fruits of the trees. Thank you, trees, for creating the oxygen for all land life to breathe in the essence of all life.

- Thank you, earth, for transferring the inner balance of your inner ecosystem to my inner landscape to create my healthy biodynamic microbiome.
- Thank you, nature, for sharing the inner balance of life that you are so naturally as the sun, the moon, the cosmos, and the interaction with Mother Earth and all her inhabitants. And so it is.

The Layers of Acknowledgments Run Deep and More Herstory

I have learned so much through the vision and dedication of all of those I've had the honor to work with, from mothers with babies in their wombs to elders beyond one hundred years. To them, I owe a large part of my purpose here in this physical form. Through all of you, I have been expressing and facilitating natural eyesight improvement and deep visual transformation from the inside out with individuals and groups for more than three decades.

Bruce Lipton, in his book *The Biology of Belief,* describes how we as humans can shift the expression of our DNA and RNA. Deepak Chopra; Joe Dispenza, Michael Beckwith, Tim Whild, Gregg Braden, Christiane Northrop, Zach Bush, Lori Ladd, the multitude of people who hosted the Event, Jason Shurka and UNIFY, and many more individuals and groups are facilitating this understanding during our mass awakening. There is so much room for remembering what our original purpose for being here on the planet is.

With this realization comes the understanding that we are working in synchrony with one another and with the collective consciousness. And each of our actions creates an equal and opposite reaction. We are now in the era of energy medicine practice in each of these precious moments. Look to Donna Eden, Marianne Williamson, Barbara Ann Br.ennan, Christiane Northrup, Richard Gerber, and other energy medicine practitioners and authors for more detailed descriptions. In the meantime, enjoy this introduction to living and Being in this world with joy, wonder, and the attitude of deep gratitude moment to moment.

More Acknowledgments and Herstory!

So many have influenced my understanding of eyesight and vision and the entire visual and movement action system rooted in nutrition, nature, and spirit that it's hard to know how to continue with the thanks. I want to thank the multitudes of optometric luminaries, including some who have passed from this physical form and many who are very much alive.

Stepping into the Developmental Optometry Paradigm

My Optometry School Admissions Interview

My interview for entrance to optometry school was with Dr. Michael Gallaway. Little did I know when I was swaying back and forth in my chair as I described my background in both ballet and modern dance that Dr. Gallaway was listening with a deep understanding of the relationship between eyesight, vision, and movement. As a staff member in the pediatrics and vision therapy department of the Eye Institute of the Pennsylvania College of Optometry (PCO) at that time, he understood exactly what I was talking about. He could read my movement!

I do not remember if I learned about the field of optometric vision therapy during that interview or later in my optometric education, but I sure do remember that interview. Over the decades, Dr. Gallaway has practiced optometric vision therapy (OVT) and conducted numerous studies affirming the benefits of OVT. I enjoyed learning from him during my rotation through the pediatrics department at PCO.[21]

---

[21] https://gbvisiontherapy.com/our-staff/meet-dr-gallaway/.

As an Optometry Student

As a fourth-year optometry student extern, I was blessed with learning from Dr. Stu Clark, Dr. Bruce May, and their vision therapist, Lauren May; Robert Copeland and Glenn Corbin; Arthur Seiderman; Dr. Poquis at the Naval Medical Center in Bethesda, Maryland; and Dr. Dale Lockhart during a rotation at the Cherry Street Veterans Administration in Philadelphia. These practitioners and the Kraskin Invitational Skeffington Symposium (KISS) conference were part of my original exposure to the field of integrative vision care, including the diagnosis and treatment of eye disease and improvement of vision naturally. Deep gratitude to all of you!

My Optometric Colleagues

Many of my dear optometric colleagues in the last century in the field of developmental optometry had optometry in their families. Their parents, grandparents, or siblings were in the field of optometry. These incredible close connections with family made my interactions with these individuals feel like family interactions as well. I was "adopted" into the optometry family as a brand-new optometrist, and it was a wonderful way to begin my career. I was part of the Institute of Behavioral Optometry (IBO), in monthly meetings in the office of Dr. Robert Kraskin and Dr. Jeffrey Kraskin, along with Robert's wife, Marion Kraskin, who ran their office in Washington, DC. In this experiential study setting, I learned to integrate my clinical practice with the work of Gerry Getman, John Streff, Richard Appel, and others who studied at the Yale Clinic in Child Development. I learned from Jeff Kraskin, Walter Kaplan, Amiel Francke, Paul Harris, Nancy Lewis, Paul Lewis, Marsha Benshir, and so many others.

Doctors Robert and Jeff Kraskin, Robert Jacobs, Wendy Garson, and Harry Wachs were the primary originals who took me under their wing. As a young optometrist, I had the honor of practicing both at the George Washington University Reading Center (GWURC) with Harry Wachs and in the office of Dr. Wendy Garson and the late Dr. Robert Jacobs in McClean, Virginia. My first private practice experience as a young optometrist was in McClean from 1987 through fall of 1990, when I got married and whisked away to Pittsburgh, Pennsylvania, by Stan Beck. Once in Pittsburgh, I enjoyed learning with the Behavioral Vision Project, a group of optometrists carrying on the work of the late Bruce Wolff and others. It was an honor to practice in the offices of Roberta Horowitz and Zarky Rudavsky.

And there are many who are not practicing optometrists but who influenced me greatly. Some are professionally trained; some are not. Some are students, some have been patients over the years, and some are friends. Studying science by implementing scientific techniques in a Newtonian fashion, as we've applied science to clinical settings for the past few hundred years, has now morphed into a different form of science — the science of energy. The late Bates was an ophthalmologist by training. I believe he was an early integrative energy practitioner. He was hazed in his profession, and his medical license was taken away. His brilliant work in natural eyesight improvement, which became the Bates Method,[22] was well ahead of its time—as it continues to be today within the formal eye care professions.

Paradigm Shifting: Time to Realign with Our Mother Earth

Has the time finally arrived when the natural eyesight-improvement lifestyle will be normalized instead of shunned? Has the time come

---

[22] William Horatio Bates, *The Bates Method for Good Sight without Glasses* (London: Faber & Faber, 1944).

when professionally trained eye care professionals can admit publicly that the indiscriminate use of lenses, prisms, pharmaceuticals, and surgeries without regard for long-term stress effects on our bodies and the collective community at large must be considered? Has the time come for us to do something about this situation as a worldwide living, breathing community?

Thank you, Darrell Boyd Harmon, Patricia Lemer, Peter Grunwald, Claudia Muehlenwag, Dr. Rabbi Shaman Indian Dancer Gabriel Cousens, Bruce Lipton, Gregg Braden, Shlomo Shoham and all those who are part of the Sustainable Global Leadership Academy, Patricia DeMarco, Brian the Healer, Christiane Northrup, Lori Ladd, Tim Whild, Brené Brown, Eleanor Criswell Hanna, Ramona Myles, Ama Mothershed, the entire Balkissoon family (especially Emma Lucia Priscilla Balkissoon, whose three names together mean "Ancient Universal Light"), Devorah L., and many others.

So much gratitude is flowing through my heart and soul from my deeply held experiences with BodyMindCentering; Bonnie Bainbridge Cohen; BodyMindMovement with Mark Taylor; and all the gentle, strong, wise, and amazing souls I met during those years on the road to the Somatic Movement Therapy (SMT) and Somatic Movement Education (SME) certification. EmbodiYoga with Lisa Clark is another continuing influence. Lisa is an incredible and dear teacher and mentor to me and many others moving gracefully and mindfully along the path of emergence into the newness of discovering our deep and hidden selves.

My beloved is the cosmos. My
beloved is the universe.

—Lisa Clark

More movers who have influenced me more than they know include David Appel; Don Zuckerman; Ellen Barlow; Sheila Caffrey; Moshe Feldenkrais; F. M. Alexander; Thomas Hanna; the Association of Hanna Somatic Educators (AHSE) folks, including Eleanor Criswell Hanna; my ballet, modern dance, and flamenco teachers as a youth, Hortensia Fonseca, Roy Gean, Mary Day, and Alvin Mayes; and more.

A Summary of More Influences along the Way

- Most of all, our parents, grandparents, and relatives and the real DNA from the elders we knew and did not know in our rich cultural upbringing.
- Dance, yoga, and other students and teachers of the somatic arts movement communities.
- The Permaculture community, especially in Pittsburgh, Pennsylvania; the participants in Sustainable Monroeville; the founding individuals and organizations of Reimagine the Turtle Creek Watershed and Airshed Communities+, ReimagineTCWAC; Reimagine Fayette County and other Reimagine and Transition Town Communities; the participants (the movers and shakers) in the Schwartz Living Market process; and the Schwartz Living Market Living Building Challenge process on a historic main street on Pittsburgh's South Side, which came close to being Living Building Challenge (LBC) certified with the Materials petal. There will be a volume on that chapter of my life in the process of emergence of this new earth one day! Stay tuned as the story unfolds.
- The amazing community of Vegan Spirituality and Vegan Spirituality-Southwest PA. Vegan Spirituality is a project of In Defense of Animals (IDA). A huge shout-out to founder Lisa

Levinson, one of my most recent mentors, Judy Carman, and to all the participants in Vegan Spirituality and the participants in Vegan Spirituality and Vegan Spirituality-Southwest PA communities. A shout-out to Ellie, Sean, Chris, Aviva, Carolyn, and Nick of the Pittsburgh Vegan Society (PVS); Sally Lipsky and Linda and Jim Jones of Plant-Based Pittsburgh; and Jeff Cohan, formerly of Jewish Veg. And to Will Tuttle and Lisa Wong. Thanks, Jim McCue, Olga Kull, Michal, Shanti Gabriel Gold, and, of course, Source.

- The many spiritual leaders, congregations, and congregational friends I've crossed paths with through the decades.

- The millionaire roundtable ladies, Jade Groff, Alina Bartnett, and others I met through Sage Lavine courses.

- Editor Robin Quinn for staying the course; and editors Hannah Martineau and Lisa, Ann Minoza and Tracy, Heather Carter, Evan Yeary, and the others at Balboa Press.

- Thanks so much indexer extraordinaire Cindy Coan. Thanks Marsha and Randy Boswell for the Spanish spelling and grammar edits.

- Optometric colleagues, professors, and elders way beyond those mentioned here. Special thanks to optometrist Miroslava Zeleznik-Landis for friendship and wisdom, beginning in our school days.

REFERENCES AND ADDITIONAL RESOURCES

Alexander, F. M. *Constructive Conscious Control of the Individual.* London: Methuen, 1923.

Alexander, F. M. *The Use of Self.* New York: Dutton, 1932.

American Optometric Association. Convergence Insufficiency. Accessed October 19, 2023. https://www.aoa.org/healthy-eyes/ eye-and-vision-conditions/convergence-insufficiency.

Andrich, Patti. *Indicators of Primitive and Postural Reflexes Assessment (IPPRA).* Optometric Extension Program Foundation, 2022.

Aposhyan, Susan. *Heart Open, Body Awake: Four Steps to Embodied Spirituality.* Shambala Publications, 2021.

Ayres, Jean. *Sensory Integration and the Child.* Los Angeles, CA: Western Psychological Services, 1987.

Barnard, Neal. Physicians Committee for Responsible Medicine. Accessed July 13, 2023. https://www.pcrm.org/health-topics/ diabetes.

Barnard, Neal. Physicians Committee for Responsible Medicine. 21-Day Vegan Kickstart. Accessed July 13, 2023. https://www.pcrm. org/vegankickstart.

Barnard, Neal, with Bryanna Clark Grogan. *Dr. Neal Barnard's Program for Reversing Diabetes: The Scientifically Proven System for Reversing Diabetes without Drugs.* New York: Rodale Books, 2007.

Barry, Susan R. *Fixing My Gaze: A Scientist's Journey into Seeing in Three Dimensions.* New York, NY: Basic Books, 2009.

Barry, Sue. StereoSue.com. Accessed August 23, 2023. https://stereosue. com/wp-content/uploads/2020/05/Brocks-Lecture-Notes-on-Strabismus.pdf.

Bates, William H. *The Bates Method for Better Eyesight without Glasses*. New York, NY: Henry Holt and Company, 1971.

Benson, Herbert. *The Relaxation Response*. New York: Avon Books, 1975.

Benyus, Janine M. *Biomimicry*. New York: Morrow, 1998.

Bernard, André, Wolfgang Steinmüller, and Ursula Stricker. *Ideokinesis: A Creative Approach to Human Movement and Body Alignment*. Berkeley, CA: North Atlantic Books, 2006.

Berne, Sam. *Creating Your Personal Vision: A Mind-Body Guide for Better Eyesight*. Santa Fe, NM: ColorStone Press, 1994.

Berthoz, Alain. *The Brain's Sense of Movement*. Translated by Giselle Weiss. Cambridge, MA: Harvard University Press, 2000.

Blair, Katrina. *The Wild Wisdom of Weeds: 13 Essential Plants for Human Survival*. White River Junction, VT: Chelsea Green Publishing, 2014.

Borsting, Eric. G. Lynn Mitchell, Marjean Taylor Kulp, Mitchell Scheiman, Deborah M. Amster, Susan Cotter, Rachael A Coulter, Gregory Fecho, Michael F. Gallaway, David Granet, Richard Hertle, Jacqueline Rodena,Tomohiko Yamada, and the CITT Study Group. "Improvement in Academic Behaviors Following Successful Treatment of Convergence Insufficiency." *Optom Vis Sci* 89, no. 1 (January 2012): 12–18. https://www.ncbi.nlm.nih.gov/pmc/articles/PMC3261761/ (2012).

Boutenko, Victoria. *Green for Life: The Updated Classic on Green Smoothie Nutrition*. Berkeley, CA: North Atlantic Books, 2010.

Bush, Zach. Zach Bush, MD. Accessed July 27, 2023. https://zachbushmd.com.

Campbell, Nelson. PlantPure Nation. Documentary. Accessed July 17, 2023. https://www.plantpurenation.com/pages/watch-the-film.

Campbell, Nelson. PlantPure Nation. Accessed March 11, 2023. https://www.plantpurenation.com/.

Campbell, Rebecca. *Letters to a Starseed: Messages and Activations for Remembering Who You Are and Why You Came Here.* Carlsbad, CA: Hay House, 2021.

Campbell, T. Colin. *The China Study: Revised and Expanded Edition: The Most Comprehensive Study of Nutrition Ever Conducted and the Startling Implications for Diet, Weight Loss, and Long-Term Health.* Dallas, TX: Benbella Books, 2016.

Carman, Judy McCoy. *Homo Ahimsa: Who We Really Are and How We're Going to Save the World.* Lawrence, KS: Circle of Compassion Publishing, 2020.

Carr, Kris. *Crazy Sexy Juice: 100+ Simple Juice, Smoothie & Nut Milk Recipes to Supercharge Your Health.* Carlsbad, CA: Hay House, 2016. https://KrisCarr.com.

Carter, Vernon Gill, and Tom Dale. *Topsoil and Civilization.* Revised ed. University of Oklahoma Press, 1974.

Chef AJ. Accessed July 10, 2023. https://ChefAJ.com.

Chodron, Pema. *Welcoming the Unwelcome: Wholehearted Living in a Brokenhearted World.* Boulder, CO: Shambala, 2019.

Clark, Lisa. Lisa Clark Body-Mind Centering and Yoga. Accessed on July 13, 2023. https://www.lisaclarkyoga.com/.

Clement, Anna Marie, with Kelly Serbonich and Chad Sarno. *Healthful Cuisine.* Healthful Communications, 2013.

Clement, Brian. *Lifeforce: Superior Health and Longevity.* Summertown, TN: Book Publishing, 2007.

Clement, Brian, with Theresa Foy DiGeronimo. *Living Foods for Optimum Health: Your Complete Guide to the Healing Power of Foods.* New York: Three Rivers Press, 1998.

Cohen, Bonnie Bainbridge. *Basic Neurocellular Patterns: Exploring Developmental Movement*. El Sobrante, CA: Burchfield Rose Publishers, 2018.

Cohen, Bonnie Bainbridge. Body-Mind Centering. "The Role of the Organs in Movement." Accessed July 13, 2023. https://www.bodymindcentering.com/the-role-of-the-organs-in-movement/.

Cohen, Bonnie Bainbridge. *Sensing, Feeling, and Action: The Experiential Anatomy of Body-Mond Centering*. 3rd ed. Northampton, MA: Contact Editions, 2012.

Colbin, Annemarie. *The Book of Whole Meals: A Seasonal Guide to Assembling Balanced Vegetarian Breakfasts, Lunches & Dinners*. New York: Ballantine Books, 1983.

Cook, Ken. Environmental Working Group. Accessed July 27, 2023. https://EWG.org.

Corporate Europe Observatory. Accessed July 27, 2023. https://corporateeurope.org/en/2022/09/researchers-vested-interests-lobbying-undermine-gmo-safety-rules.

Cousens, Gabriel. *Conscious Eating*. Berkeley, CA: North Atlantic Books, 2000.

Cousens, Gabriel. *Creating Peace by Being Peace: The Essene Sevenfold Path*. Berkeley, CA: North Atlantic Books, 2008.

Cousens, Gabriel. *Rainbow Green Live-Food Cuisine*. Berkeley, CA: North Atlantic Books, 2003.

Cousens, Gabriel. *Spiritual Nutrition: Six Foundations for Spiritual Life and the Awakening of Kundalini*. Berkeley, CA: North Atlantic Books, 2005.

Cousens, Gabriel. *There Is a Cure for Diabetes: The 21-Day+ Holistic Recovery Program*. Berkeley, CA: North Atlantic Books, 2013.

Cousens, Gabriel. *Torah as a Guide to Enlightenment*. Berkeley, CA: North Atlantic Books, 2011.

Cousens, Gabriel. Zero Point Course Offering. Accessed July 13, 2023. https://www.drcousens.com/zeropoint.

Criswell, Eleanor. *Biofeedback and Somatics: Toward Personal Evolution.* Novato, CA: Freeperson Press, 1995.

Davis, Brenda, and Tom Barnard. *Defeating Diabetes: A No-Nonsense Approach to Type 2 Diabetes and the Diabesity Epidemic.* Summertown, TN: Healthy Living Publications, 2003.

Davis, Brenda, and Vesanto Melina. *The Kick Diabetes Cookbook: An Action Plan and Recipes for Defeating Diabetes.* Summertown, TN: Book Publishing Co., 2018.

Davis, Brenda, and Vesanto Melina, with Ryan Berry. *Becoming Raw: The Essential Guide to Raw Vegan Diets.* Summertown, TN: Book Publishing Co., 2010.

Davis, Menachem. *The Schottenstein Edition Interlinear Chumash: The Torah, Haftaros, and Five Megillos with an Interlinear Translation and a Commentary Anthologized from the Rabbinic Writings; Shemos/Exodus.* Edited by Nosson Scherman and Meir Zlotowitz. Me'sorah Publications, November 2019.

Dawkins, Hazel Richmond, Ellis Edelman, and Constantine Forkiotis. *The Suddenly Successful Student: A Guide to Overcoming Learning and Behavior Problems, How Behavioral Optometry Helps.* USA: Writing Team, 1990.

DeMarco, Patricia. *In the Footsteps of Rachel Carson.* Urban Press, 2022.

Dietary Guidelines for Americans, 2020–2025. USDA. DietaryGuidelines.gov. Department of Health and Human Services. Accessed July 10, 2023. https://www.dietaryguidelines.gov/sites/default/files/2021-03/Dietary_Guidelines_for_Americans-2020-2025.pdf.

Eisenstein, Charles. *The More Beautiful World Our Hearts Know Is Possible.* Berkeley CA: Atlantic Books, 2013.

Eisenstein, Charles. CharlesEisenstein.substack.com. "The Next Story." Accessed July 27, 2023. https://charleseisenstein.substack.com/p/what-is-the-next-story.

Elliott, Clark. *The Ghost in My Brain: How a Concussion Stole My Life and How the New Science of Brain Plasticity Helped Me Get It Back.* New York: Penguin Books, 2015.

Elon, Ari, Naomi Mara Hyman, and Arthur Waskow, eds. *Trees, Earth, and Torah: A Tu B'Shvat Anthology.* Philadelphia, PA: Jewish Publication Society, 1999.

Esselstyn, Rip. *Plant-Strong: Discover the World's Healthiest Diet—with 150 Engine 2 Recipes.* New York: Grand Central Publishing, 2019.

Feldenkrais, Moshe. *The Elusive Obvious or Basic Feldenkrais.* Cupertino, CA: Meta Publications, 1981.

Flores, H. C. *Food Not Lawns: How to Turn Your Yard into a Garden and Your Neighborhood into a Community.* White River Junction, VT: Chelsea Green, 2007.

Flynn, David, and Stephen Flynn. *The Happy Pear.* UK: Penguin, 2016.

Forrest, Elliot B. *Stress and Vision.* Santa Ana, CA: Optometric Extension Program Foundation, 1988.

Frey, Darrell E. *Bioshelter Market Garden: A Permaculture Farm.* Gabriola Island, BC: New Society Publishers, 2011.

Frey, Darrell, and Michelle Czolba. *The Food Forest Handbook: Design and Manage a Home-Scale Perennial Polyculture Garden.* Gabriola, BC: New Society Publishers, 2017.

Fukuoka, Masanobu. *The One Straw Revolution.* New York: New York Review of Books, 1978.

Furth, Hans G., and Harry Wachs. *Thinking Goes to School: Piaget's Theory in Practice.* New York: Oxford University Press, 1975.

Gallaway, Michael, Mitchell Scheiman, G. Lynn Mitchell. "Vision Therapy for Post-Concussion Vision Disorders."

Optometry and Vision Science 94, no. 1 (January 2017): 68–73. https://journals.lww.com/optvissci/Abstract/2017/01000/Vision_Therapy_for_Post_Concussion_Vision.11.aspx.

Gallop, Steven J. *Looking Differently at Nearsightedness and Myopia: The Visual Process and the Myth of 20/20.* Outside the Boox, 2022.

Gelb, Michael. *Body Learning: An Introduction to the Alexander Technique.* New York: Henry Holt and Company, 1981.

Gerber, Richard. *Vibrational Medicine: New Choices for Healing Ourselves.* Santa Fe, NM: Bear and Company, 1988.

Gesell, Arnold, Frances L. Ilg, and Glenna Bullis, with Vivienne Ilg and G. N. Getman. *Vision: Its Development in Infant and Child.* Santa Ana, CA: Optometric Extension Program Foundation, 1998.

Getman, G. N. *Smart in Everything Except School.* Santa Ana, CA: Vision Extension, 1992.

Goddard, Sally. *Reflexes, Learning, and Behavior: A Window into the Child's Mind.* Eugene, Oregon: Fern Ridge Press, 2005.

Goldner, Brooke. *Goodbye Lupus: How a Medical Doctor Healed Herself Naturally with Supermarket Foods.* Express Results, 2015.

Goodrich, Janet. *How to Improve Your Child's Eyesight Naturally: A Thoughtful Parent's Guide.* Rochester, Vermont: Healing Arts Press, 2004.

Gottlieb, Ray. *Attention and Memory Training: Stress Point Learning on the Trampoline (Based on the Work of Robert Pepper).* Optometric Extension Program Foundation, 2005. Accessed July 13, 2023. https://raygottlieb.com/wp-content/uploads/2020/11/AM-bk-reduced.pdf.

Greger, Michael. *How Not to Diet: The Groundbreaking Science of Healthy, Permanent Weight Loss.* Bluebird, 2021.

Greger, Michael. *How to Survive a Pandemic.* Flatiron Books, 2020.

Greger, Michael. NutritionFacts.org. "Can Diabetic Retinopathy Be Reversed?" Accessed July 16, 2023. https://nutritionfacts.org/video/can-diabetic-retinopathy-be-reversed.

Greger, Michael, and Gene Stone. *How Not to Die: Discover the Foods Scientifically Proven to Prevent and Reverse Disease*. London, England: Pan Books, 2018.

Greger, Michael. "The Latest in Nutrition Related Research." NutritionFacts.org. Accessed March 11, 2023. https://nutritionfacts.org/.

Grossman, Marc, and Glen Swartwout. *Natural Eyecare, an Encyclopedia: Complementary Treatments for Improving and Saving Your Eyes*. Los Angeles, CA: Keats Publishing, 1999.

Grossman, Marc, and Vinton McCabe. *Greater Vision: A Comprehensive Program for Physical, Emotional, and Spiritual Clarity*. Los Angeles, CA: Keats Publishing, 2001.

Grunwald, Peter. *EyeBody: The Art of Integrating Eye, Brain, and Body, Living Life Naturally without Glasses*. 3rd ed. Auckland, New Zealand: Condevis Publishing, 2017.

Grunwald, Peter. *Eyebody: Soulful Seeing—Conscious Living: The Art of Integrating Soul Qualities through Your Eyes, Brain, and Body*. Auckland, New Zealand: Condevis Publishing, 2022.

Hanna, Thomas. *The Body of Life: Creating New Pathways for Sensory Awareness and Fluid Movement*. Rochester, VT: Healing Arts Press, 1993.

Hanna, Thomas. *Somatics: Reawakening the Mind's Control of Movement, Flexibility, and Health*. Cambridge, MA: Da Capo Press, 2004.

Happy Pear. Ireland. Accessed July 10, 2023. https://thehappypear.ie.

Harmon, D. B. *Notes on a Dynamic Theory of Vision*. 3rd rev. Austin, TX: Harmon, DB, 1958.

HeartMath Institute: A Nonprofit Organization. Accessed July 17, 2023. HeartMath.org.

Hellerstein, Lynn F. *See It. Say It. Do It! A Parent's & Teacher's Action Guide to Creating Successful Students & Confident Kids.* Centennial, CO: HiClear Publishing, 2010.

Hewitt, Ben. *The Town That Food Saved: How One Community Found Vitality in Local Food.* New York: Rodale, 2010.

"History of *Bt*." University of California at Santa Barbara. Accessed July 13, 2023. http://www.bt.ucsd.edu/bt_history.html.

Hopkins, Rob. *The Transition Handbook: From Oil Dependency to Local Resilience.* Green Books, 2014.

Hubbard, Barbara Marx. *Conscious Evolution: Awakening the Power of Our Social Potential.* Novato, CA: New World Library, 1998.

Huxley, Aldous. *The Art of Seeing.* Berkeley, CA: Creative Arts Book Company, 1982.

Jane Unchained. Accessed March 11, 2023. https://unchainedtv.com/.

Jaroudi, Brittany. Accessed December 21, 2021. https://thejaroudifamily.com.

Jenkins, Joe. *The Humanure Handbook: A Guide to Composting Human Manure.* Joseph Jenkins, 2005.

Jensen, Bernard. *Iridology Simplified: An Introduction to the Science of Iridology and Its Relation to Nutrition.* 5th ed. Bernard Jensen, 1980.

Jones, Beverly, with Karen Wolff Klaine. *Visual Behavior.* Cincinnati, OH: Lockwood Press, 1995.

Jones, Frank Pierce. *Body Awareness in Action: A Study of the Alexander Technique.* New York: Schocken Books, 1979.

Kabat-Zinn, Jon. *Wherever You Go, There You Are: Mindfulness Meditation for Everyday Life.* London: Piatkus, 2016.

Kaplan, Roberto. *Seeing without Glasses: A Step-by-Step Approach to Improving Eyesight Naturally*. 3rd ed. Hillsboro, OR: Beyond Words Publishing, 2003.

Kavner, Richard. *Your Child's Vision: A Parent's Guide to Seeing, Growing, and Developing*. New York: Simon and Schuster, 1985.

Kong, Joanne. *If You've Ever Loved an Animal, Go Vegan: Thoughts on Compassionate Awareness*. Creative Commons Attribution-NonCommercial-Share Alike 4.0 International License. https://creativecommons.org/licenses/by-nc-sa/4.0/.

Kong, Joanne, ed. *Vegan Voices: Essays by Inspiring Changemakers*. Brooklyn, NY: Lantern Books, 2021.

Kook, Abraham Isaac. *Rav Kook's Introduction to Shabbat Ha'aretz*. Translated with an introduction by Julian Sinclair. New York: Hazon, 2013.

Kraskin, Robert A. *Lens Power in Action*. Edited by Paul A. Harris and Gregory Kitchener. Santa Ana, CA: Optometric Extension Program Foundation, 2003.

Kraskin, Robert A. *You Can Improve Your Vision*. Santa Ana, CA: Optometric Extension Program Foundation, 2011.

Kulvinskas, Viktoras P. *Survival in the 21st Century: Planetary Healers Manual*. Summertown, TN: Book Publishing Company, 2010.

Lamm, Nomy, and Taya Mâ Shere. *Omer Oracle: A Divination Deck for Counting the Omer*. Independently published, 2022. www.OmerOracle.com.

Lane, Ben. Free Library. "Nutrition as a Major Oral Therapy for Glaucoma." Retrieved August 4, 2023. https://www.thefreelibrary.com/Nutrition+as+a+major+oral+therapy+for+glaucoma.-a0271811633.

Lang, T. "Reshaping the Food System for Ecological Public Health." *Journal of Hunger & Environmental Nutrition* 4, no. 3–4 (2009): 315–335. doi:10.1080/19320240903321227.

Lemay, Mimi. *What We Will Become: A Mother, a Son, and a Journey of Transformation*. Mariner Books, 2020.

Lemer, Patricia S. *Envisioning a Bright Future: Interventions That Work for Children and Adults with Autism Spectrum Disorders*. Santa Ana, CA: Optometric Extension Program Foundation, 2008.

Lemer, Patricia S. *Outsmarting Autism: Build Healthy Foundations for Communication, Socialization, and Behavior at All Ages*. Berkeley, CA: North Atlantic Books, 2019.

Liberman, Jacob. *Light: Medicine of the Future*. Santa Fe, NM: Bear and Company, 1991.

Liberman, Jacob. *Take Off Your Glasses and See: A Mind/Body Approach to Expanding Your Eyesight and Insight*. New York: Three Rivers Press, 1995.

Liberman, Jacob, with Erik Liberman. *Wisdom from an Empty Mind*. Jacob Liberman, 2001.

Lieber, David L., ed. *Etz Hayim: Torah and Commentary*. Rabbinical Assembly, Summer 2019.

Lipton, Bruce H. *The Biology of Belief: Unleashing the Power of Consciousness, Matter & Miracles*. Carlsbad, CA: Hay House, 2016.

Martin, P. A. W., E. B. Haransky, R. S. Travers, and C. F. Reichelderfer. "Rapid Biochemical Testing of Large Numbers of *Bacillus thuringiensis* Isolates Using Agar Dots." *Biotechniques* (1985): 3:386–392.

Mason, P., and T. Lang. *Sustainable Diets: How Ecological Nutrition Can Transform Consumption and the Food System*. London, UK: Taylor & Francis, 2017.

May, Kevin. *The New Earth Is Here*. Kevin May, 2018.

May, Kevin. *Unlocking Our Superpowers: A Handbook for Transformation*. Kevin May, 2016.

McDonough, William, and Michael Braungart. *Cradle to Cradle: Remaking the Way We Make Things*. New York: North Point Press, 2002.

McLennan, Jason F. *Zugunruhe: The Inner Migration to Profound Environmental Change.* Bainbridge Island, WA: Ecotone Publishing, 2011.

Mills, Milton. *Dr. Milton Mills—Plant Based Nation.* Accessed July 28, 2023. https://drmiltonmillsplantbasednation.com; https://www.preventionofdisease.org/milton-mills.

Mollison, Bill. *Permaculture: A Designers' Manual.* Tyalgum, Australia: Tagari Publications, 1988.

Moran, Victoria. *Main Street Vegan: Everything You Need to Know to Eat Healthfully and Live Compassionately in the Real World.* New York: Penguin Group, 2012.

Mukundananda, Swami, ed. *Bhagavad Gita: The Song of G-d!* Plano, TX: JKyog, 2013.

National Geographic. "Wolves of Yellowstone." Accessed July 15, 2023. https://education.nationalgeographic.org/resource/wolves-yellowstone/.

Nestor, James. *Breath: The New Science of a Lost Art.* New York: Riverhead Books, 2020.

Northrup, Christiane. *Women's Bodies, Women's Wisdom: Creating Physical and Emotional Health and Healing.* Bantam, 2010.

Olsen, Andrea. *Body and Earth: An Experiential Guide.* Hanover and London: University Press of New England, 2009.

Orfield, Antonia. *Eyes for Learning: Preventing and Curing Vision-Related Learning Problems.* Lanham, Maryland: Rowman & Littlefield Education, 2007.

Ornish, Dean. *Dr. Dean Ornish's Program for Reversing Heart Disease: The Only System Scientifically Proven to Reverse Heart Disease without Drugs or Surgery.* Ivy Books, 1995.

Pierce, Alexandra, and Roger Pierce. *Expressive Movement: Posture and Action in Daily Life, Sports, and the Performing Arts.* New York: Plenum Press, 1989.

Pierre, John. *The Pillars of Health: Your Foundations for Lifelong Wellness.* Carlsbad, CA: Hay House, 2013.

Plaut, W. Gunther, and David Stein, eds. *The Torah: A Modern Commentary.* Revised ed. New York: Union for Reform Judaism, 2005.

Rao, Sailesh. Climate Healers. Accessed August 4, 2023. https:// climatehealers.org.

Redcross West, Stephanie. Vegan Mainstream. Accessed August 13, 2023. https://veganmainstream.com/.

"Reimagine Turtle Creek Watershed & Airshed Communities Plus." Reimagine TCWAC. Accessed March 11, 2023.

Robbins, John. *Diet for a New America: How Your Food Choices Affect Your Health, Your Happiness, and the Future of Life on Earth.* Tiburon, CA: H. J. Kramer, 1987.

Robbins, Ocean, and John Robbins. The Food Revolution Network. Accessed July 13, 2023. http://www.FoodRevolution.org.

Roll, Rich. Rich Roll Podcasts. Accessed July 27, 2023. https://www. richroll.com/all-episodes/.

Rouse, M., E. Borsting, G. L. Mitchell, M. T. Kulp, M. Scheiman, D. Amster, R. Coulter, G. Fecho, and M. Gallaway. "Academic Behaviors in Children with Convergence Insufficiency with and without Parent-Reported ADHD." *Optom Vis Sci* 86, no. 10 (October 2009):1169–77. https://www.ncbi.nlm.nih.gov/pmc/ articles/PMC2888729/.

Sacks, Oliver. *The Man Who Mistook His Wife for a Hat and Other Clinical Tales.* New York, NY: Harper Perennial, 1990.

Sacks, Oliver. *The Mind's Eye.* New York: Alfred A. Knopf, 2010.

Sacks, Oliver. Stereo Sue. "A Neurologist's Notebook." *New Yorker Magazine*, June 11, 2006, 64–73.

Scheiman, M. et al., "A Randomized Clinical Trial of Treatments for Symptomatic Convergence Insufficiency in Children," *Arch*

Ophthalmol 126, no. 10 (October 2008): 1336–49, https://doi. org./10.1001/archopht.126.10.1336.

Scheiman, M., M. T. Kulp, S. A. Cotter, J. G. Lawrenson, L. Wang, and T. Li. "Interventions for Convergence Insufficiency: A Network Meta-analysis." *Cochrane Database Syst Rev.* 12, no. 12 (December 2020): CD006768. https://doi.org/10.1002/14651858.CD006768. pub3.

Scheiman, Mitchell, Christopher Chase, Eric Borsting, Gladys Lynn Mitchell, Marjean T Kulp, Susan A Cotter, CITT-RS Study Group. "Effect of Treatment of Symptomatic Convergence Insufficiency on Reading in Children: A Pilot Study." *Clinical and Experimental Optometry* 25 (March 2018). https://onlinelibrary.wiley.com/doi/full/10.1111/cxo.12682.

Schwartz, Richard H. *Judaism and Vegetarianism.* New York, NY: Lantern Books, 2001.

Selye, Hans. *The Stress of Life.* New York: McGraw Hill, 1978.

Shayhew, Lori. Gifts of Autism. Facebook Group. Accessed July 11, 2023. https://www.facebook.com/groups/thegiftsofautism.

Shiva, Vandana. *Biopiracy: The Plunder of Nature and Knowledge.* North Atlantic Books, 2016.

Shiva, Vandana. Accessed July 27, 2023. https://humansandnature.org/vandana-shiva/.

Shiva, Vandana. Navdanya International. Accessed August 15, 2023. https://navdanyainternational.org/

Shiva, Vandana. *The Seeds of Vandana Shiva.* 2021. https://vandanashivamovie.com/.

Spitler, Harry Riley. *The Syntonic Principle: Its Relation to Health and Ocular Problems.* US: College of Syntonic Optometry, 1990.

Stamets, Paul. *Mycelium Running: How Mushrooms Can Help Save the World.* Berkeley, CA: Ten Speed Press, 2005.

Stokes, Beverly. *Amazing Babies Moving: Essential Movement to Enhance Your Baby's Development in the First Year.* Move Alive Media, 2009.

Taylor, Jill Bolte. *My Stroke of Insight.* New York: Penguin Books, 2009.

Taylor, Jill Bolte. *Whole Brain Living: The Anatomy of Choice and the Four Characters That Drive Our Life.* Hay House, 2021.

Taylor, Mark. *Embody the Skeleton: A Guide to Conscious Movement.* Edinburgh, Scotland: Handspring Publishing, 2019.

Torgerson, Nancy, and Kristi Jensen. *The Essential Playbook: How to Maximize Outcomes in Optometric Vision Therapy.* Optometric Extension Program Foundation, 2022.

Travell, Janet G., and David Simons. *Myofascial Pain and Dysfunction: The Trigger Point Manual: Volume 2, The Lower Extremities.* Philadelphia, PA: Lippincott, Williams & Wilkins, 1993.

Travell, Janet G., and David Simons. *Myofascial Pain and Dysfunction: The Trigger Point Manual: Volume 1, Upper Half of Body.* 2nd ed. Philadelphia, PA: Lippincott, Williams & Wilkins, 1999.

Travers, Russell, Phyllis A. W. Martin, and Charles Reichelderfer. "Selective Process for Efficient Isolation of Soil *Bacillus* spp." *Applied and Environmental Microbiology* 53, no.6 (June 1987): 1263–66.

Truth in Labeling. Accessed July 28, 2023. https://truthinlabeling.org.

Tuttle, Will, ed. *Buddhism and Veganism: Essays Connecting Spiritual Awakening and Animal Liberation.* Danvers, MA: Vegan Publishers, 2018.

Tuttle, Will, ed. *Circles of Compassion: Essays Connecting Issues of Justice.* Danvers, MA: Vegan Publishers, 2014.

Tuttle, Will M. *The World Peace Diet: Eating for Spiritual Health and Social Harmony.* New York: Lantern Books, 2016.

Vaughan-Lee, Llewellyn, ed. *Spiritual Ecology: The Cry of the Earth.* Point Reyes, CA: Golden Sufi Center, 2013.

Velez-Mitchell, Jane. Jane Unchained. Accessed March 11, 2023. https://unchainedtv.com/.

Vitale, Joe. *At Zero: The Quest for Miracles through Ho'oponopono.* Hoboken, New Jersey: John Wiley and Sons, 2014.

Wieder, Serena, and Harry Wachs. *Visual/Spatial Portals to Thinking, Feeling, and Movement: Advancing Competencies and Emotional Development in Children with Learning and Autism Spectrum Disorders.* Mendham New Jersey: Profectum Foundation, 2012.

Wigmore, Ann. *Sprouting Book: How to Grow and Use Sprouts to Maximize Your Health and Vitality.* Avery, 1986.

Willett, W., J. Rockström, B. Loken, M. Springmann, T. Lang, S. Vermeulen, and M. L. Jonell. "Food in the Anthropocene: The EAT—Lancet Commission on Healthy Diets from Sustainable Food Systems." *Lancet Commissions,* 393, no. 10170 (2019): 447–92. doi:10.1016/S0140-6736(18)31788-4.

Zero Point Course Offering. Accessed July 30, 2023. https://www.drcousens.com/zeropoint.

Zoltan, Barbara. *Vision, Perception, and Cognition: A Manual for the Evaluation and Treatment of the Neurologically Impaired Adult.* 3rd ed. New Jersey: Slack, 1996.

Working with ElisaBe

My offerings vary. They range from a one-on-one, in-person eyesight and visual consultation, to first referring a person for a conventional or integrative visual evaluation, to beginning with yoga classes, other somatic movement modalities, spiritual nutrition or straight nutrition counseling, and/or meditation.

The integrative approach (to total and holistic vision care) I've created now includes a broad spectrum of other movement, nutrition, nature, and spiritual modalities. Approaches are integrated when I work with people one-on-one or in groups. These modalities and some of the techniques have been sprinkled through this document. The experiential tips and tools are for you to add into your daily routines if you choose to do so.

See my website, EnliveningConsciousness.com, for natural eyesight improvement and nutrition for eyesight and vision information, resources, classes, and courses and other supplemental information related to the content of this book.

Course Offerings: Details for these journeys are on my website: EnliveningConsciousness.com.

- *Deepening Insight through Improving Eyesight: There's More to Vision Than 20/20*, a three-month course
- *Comfortable Computer Eyesight: Three Steps in Three Weeks*

In these courses, we begin with a one-on-one session to discuss your eyeglass or contact lens prescription, your general and ocular health, and any eye or other surgeries or dis-ease processes you might be experiencing. We want to be sure you are disease-free or being followed by an eye care professional for your eye disease issue(s) prior to working together.

We then move on to touch on some of the information detailed in the vision section and other sections of this book. By the conclusion of the courses, another one-on-one session with me has transpired, and you're well on your way into the wide, wild world with more clarity and purpose!

We also go over tips for working with our eyes and hands and bodies sitting in front of an electronic device (a computer screen, an iPad or iPad mini, a cell phone screen, or a variety of other electronic devices) for much longer than is advisable for a humyn BEing!

SHARE YOUR STORY

Let's cross-pollinate our experiences to create the more beautiful world we all know in our hearts is possible. How? We'll begin with a conversation. What type of story would you like to share? Your vision story? Your consciousness story? A combination of your vision and consciousness stories? Feel free to reach me and share through my website, EnliveningConsciousness.com.

ABOUT THE AUTHOR

Dr. Elisa Beth Haransky-Beck has been a neurodevelopmental, functional, behavioral optometrist specializing in natural eyesight improvement in neurotypical (a.k.a. "normal") people and those who are characterized as neurodivergent (a.k.a. on the ADD to autism spectrum) since 1987. In addition to practicing natural vision enhancement, or improving your eyesight and vision naturally, her expertise lies in the areas of sports vision enhancement, movement integration, and the diagnosis and treatment of traumatic brain injury.

She integrates enhancement of cognitive development into her work. This work is based on her training and involvement in many optometric groups and organizations, including as a fellow in the College of Optometrists in Vision Development (COVD), soon to be renamed Optometrists in Vision Development and Rehabilitation Association (OVDRA); the Optometric Extension Program (OEP); the Neuro-optometric Rehabilitation Association (NORA); the College of Syntonic Optometry (CSO); and the Behavioral Vision Project. Her training included direct mentoring through the Center for Vision and Conceptual Development in Washington, DC (as part of the George Washington University Reading Center [GWURC]) under the direction of the late Harry Wachs, OD, a Piagetian optometrist. She practiced with Wendy Garson and the late Robert Jacobs in the late 1980s, prior to marrying and moving to Pittsburgh, Pennsylvania, in 1990.

She graduated from the Pennsylvania College of Optometry (now a part of Salus University and soon, Drexel University) in Philadelphia with a Bachelor of Science degree in Visual Science and as a Doctor of Optometry. She actively practiced optometry with a specialty in the evaluation and treatment of patients with vision-related learning issues, the ADD to autism spectrum, and traumatic brain injury, such as concussion, into 2018. In her practice, she specialized in vision and movement therapy to facilitate healing in those she worked with.

Elisa's background includes an undergraduate degree in Biology with an emphasis in Ecology from the University of Maryland at College Park (1982). She founded Sustainable Monroeville in 2009 and was the founder of the Schwartz Living Market process—a journey into creating a living building (see the International Living Futures Institute). She participated in the first Permaculture Design certificate course offered by Phipps Conservatory in Pittsburgh, Pennsylvania.

Elisa earned a Master of Arts degree in Spirituality and Live Food Nutrition from the Cousens' School for Holistic Wellness of the California School of Integrative Nutrition in February 2019. Her thesis was on the range of veganism and spirituality lifestyles, from junk food veganism to the raw living-foods lifestyle. She founded Vegan Spirituality-Southwest PA in early 2019. She cofounded ReimagineTCWAC.org in 2019.

Background in Somatics

Elisa's formal somatic education movement training began in Amherst, Massachusetts, with now eighty-two-year-old Bonnie Bainbridge Cohen (founder of BodyMindCentering) in the late 1980s, after she graduated from optometry school. Bonnie (with her assistants, including Lisa Clark and others) facilitated a full week of developmental movement experiencing on the floor of a huge gymnasium. She spent the week moving through prevertebrate, vertebrate, and human movement patterns. During the last five minutes of the last day of the weeklong intensive, the participants stood up. They had spent seven days (prior to standing) in utero and in the first year of our humyn lifetimes!

She became certified as a Somatic Movement Therapist and Educator at the School for BodyMindMovement (BMM) in both Pittsburgh, PA and Oregon, under the skilled instruction of Mark Taylor, the school's founder and director. The BMM certification began with a developmental movement week in the late 1980s in Amherst, Massachusetts, with Bonnie Bainbridge Cohen. She completed a five-hundred-hour EmbodiYoga teacher training with the brilliant Lisa Clark. Elisa's most recent certification (September 2022) is in Hanna somatic yoga.

Currently, Dr. Elisa Beth Haransky-Beck teaches, mentors, and coaches those diving deeply those diving deeply into their healing journeys. Her multidisciplinary, multisensory approach draws from her vast background in many healing traditions. Contact her directly through her website: EnliveningConsciousness.com.

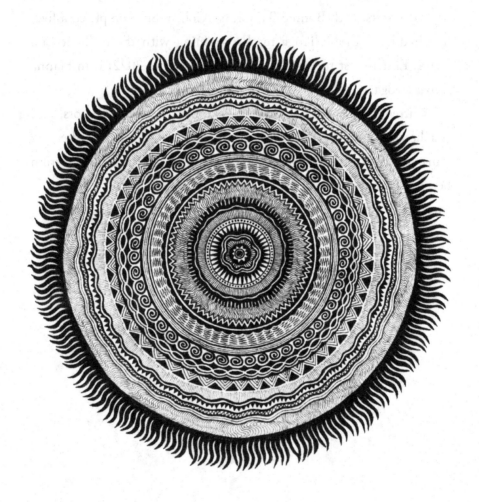

ABOUT THE ARTIST

Self-taught artist Eli Helman, born in 1978, has spent thousands of hours meticulously crafting highly detailed ink drawings. Emphasizing intricately drawn lines and patterns, he explores eclectic subjects through a blend of whimsical and thought-provoking imagery. Inspired by music, humor, travel, nature, science, and history, he hopes viewers will find something new every time they gaze upon his work. All original works are drawn by hand with Micron pens on paper. Some pieces take more than two hundred hours to complete. Since 2010, he has been a full-time artist, traveling around the country, showing his work at art festivals. He lives in western Massachusetts. Learn more at www.elihelman.com.

INDEX

A

academics, strenuous, vision impacted by, 50

accommodation, 109, 127

action, stepping into, 10

actions, effect on others, 265

activities of daily living (ADLs), 38, 39–40, 262

ADD (attention deficit disorder), 60, 121

addiction, 5, 51, 149–150, 151, 178, 230

additives, 149–150

ADHD (attention deficit hyperactivity disorder), 59, 60

advocating for self, 43

agar dots, 245–246, 293–294, 296

aging, 56–57, 222

agribusiness, 158, 160, 270, 283

agriculture, 150–151, 214, 223, 265

Ahimsa, 266

air pollution, 150–151

aleph (beginning), 258

Alexander, F. M., 90, 114

"All Eternal" (poem), 24

Almond mylk/Nut mylk (recipe), 184

almonds, 197–198

Amazon rain forest, 211, 212

animal kingdom, 89

animal products, 156–157, 160, 162

animals

abuse of, 145, 158, 210–211

advocates for, 159

in agriculture, 214

bacteria *versus,* 157

development, 89–90

domestic, 158, 253

killing, 269

refraining from harming, 266

relationship with, 209

removal from system, 223

rights of, 140

sensitivity to, 226

vocabulary referring to, 144–145

anisometropia, 54

anterior segment diseases, 32

anterior segment surgery, 34

antivirals, 202

Aposhyan, Susan, 6

apple carrot juice, 170, 172–173

arriving early, 19

artificial intelligence (AI), 5, 47, 230, 270

Asian restaurants, 188

Association of Hanna Somatic Educators (AHSE), 88

astigmatism, 29, 48, 52–54, 71, 72

Asymmetric Tonic Neck Reflex (ATNR), 133

ATNR (Eye-Hand-Mouth sequence), 106

attention span, short, 43

authentic selves, 4, 6

local food, 181, 269

loved ones, spending more time with, 214

loving-kindness, lifestyle supporting, 268

lunch and dinner recipes, 184–186, 187–194

M

macula (fovea), 26

macular degeneration, 34

male-female spectrum, 66

male-persona-dominated structure, 66

mantra, 224, 261, 262, 263, 295

May, Kevin, 73

meals, liquids away from, 175–176

meaning, experience role in, 201

meat

    cost of, 209

    cutting down on, 227, 271

    eating, 210, 269

    as food group, 152

    genetically modified, 168

    industry, 270

    as main course, 153

    mimicking taste of, 190

    as protein source, 150

meatless Monday, 71, 140

medical mainstream, 64–65, 66

medical systems, trauma embedded through, 116

medicine, modern *versus* diet, 74

meditation

    alert and conscious during, 280

    Beingness and, 290

    detoxification, role in, 202

    going inside through, 282

    moving into, 261–273

    in nature, 252

    nurturing self through, 214

    practicing, 298

    recommendations for, 206, 207

    yoga and, 277–278, 280

meibomian gland dysfunction (MGD), 74–76

mental health issues, diet for those with, 70

microbiome(s)

    balancing, 267, 276

    connecting with, 211

    fully functioning, 147

    healthy, earth role in creating, 302

    inner ecosystems including, 241

    stoking, 268

micromovements, 109

microplastics in human blood, 249

microscopic organism colonies, 240

microwaves, 187

milk, 152, 201, 288

Mills, Milton, 186

mind, shift in, 116

mind, visual system integration with, 100–101

mindfulness, 166, 286–287

Miso Soup (recipe), 193

Miten (musician), 277–278

Mni Wiconi (Lakota saying), 167

Modern Living Essene way of life, 142, 207, 266

Mollison, Bill, 193

mom optometrist, 112, 113

monovision, 54, 55–56

O

oat groats, 176

Oatmeal with Plant-Based Mylk and
    Toppings (recipe), 181

oats, 181

obesity, 146

"Observing Nature" (poem), 236

occipital cortex, 69

occupations and astigmatism, 53

oculoplastic surgery, 34

O'Keefe, Georgia, 280

Omer, 291, 292

Oneness, 260, 291

on-the-spectrum nature, 265

opening, 279–280

ophthalmologists, 31, 32, 33–34

ophthalmoscope, 70

optic chiasm, 284

opticians, 31

optic nerve, 69, 284

optics, 53

optometric developmental testing, 63

Optometric Extension Program
    Foundation (OEPF), 60

optometric vision and movement
    therapist, 112–113

optometric vision therapy (OVT)
    disease, ruling out before, 41
    natural eyesight improvement
        through, 44
    overview of, 33
    self-awakening through, 284–285
    soft neurological signs diagnosing
        and treating in, 67
    specialty in, 32

stress-revealing behaviors
    disappearing with, 43
techniques and lifestyle changes
    including, 72
tools and techniques in, 121
vision, movement, and, 60–62

optometric vision training, 76

optometrists, 32–33, 34, 40, 63–64,
    65–66

optometry, 6, 61, 88

organically grown foods, 154, 235

organically raised plants, 160

organic farms, 244

organic foods, 211, 236

organic industrial agriculture, 223

organic produce, juicing with, 172

organic seeds, sprouting, 177

organic *versus* meat and dairy
    costs, 209

organs, 105–106, 123–124

others, actions mirrored by, 209

outer ecosystem, 149–152

outer nature, 5

outer vision, 151

oven, dehydrator as substitute for, 197

overeating, 178

overnight oats, 199

Overnight Oats (recipe), 180

overworking habit patterns, 51

P

pair structures experiential interlude,
    124–125

palming, 47–48

pandemic, 202, 210

paradigm shifting, 281–282

S

Printed in the United States
by Baker & Taylor Publisher Services